PENGUIN

THE

Alex Kershaw is the author of two widely praised books about the Second World War – *Bedford Boys* and *The Longest Winter* – as well as acclaimed biographies of Robert Capa and Jack London. He has been a journalist and screenwriter and has written for the *Sunday Times*, *Guardian*, *Observer* and *GQ*. He was born in the UK and has lived in the US since 1994. He lives in Vermont.

The Few

July–October 1940

ALEX KERSHAW

PENGUIN BOOKS

PENGUIN BOOKS

Published by the Penguin Group
Penguin Books Ltd, 80 Strand, London WC2R ORL, England
Penguin Group (USA) Inc., 375 Hudson Street, New York, New York 10014, USA
Penguin Group (Canada), 90 Eglinton Avenue East, Suite 700, Toronto, Ontario, Canada M4P 2Y3
(a division of Pearson Penguin Canada Inc.)
Penguin Ireland, 25 St Stephen's Green, Dublin 2, Ireland (a division of Penguin Books Ltd)
Penguin Group (Australia), 250 Camberwell Road, Camberwell, Victoria 3124, Australia
(a division of Pearson Australia Group Pty Ltd)
Penguin Books India Pvt Ltd, 11 Community Centre, Panchsheel Park, New Delhi – 110 017, India
Penguin Group (NZ), 67 Apollo Drive, Rosedale, North Shore 0632, New Zealand
(a division of Pearson New Zealand Ltd)
Penguin Books (South Africa) (Pty) Ltd, 24 Sturdee Avenue, Rosebank, Johannesburg 2196, South Africa

Penguin Books Ltd, Registered Offices: 80 Strand, London WC2R ORL, England

www.penguin.com

First published in the United States of America by Da Capo Press 2006
First published in Great Britain by Michael Joseph 2007
Published in Penguin Books 2008
2

The author gratefully acknowledges permission to use extended quotations from
"Yankee Eagle over London" by Eugene Tobin originally published in *Liberty Magazine*,
March 29, 1941. Copyright © 1941 by Macfadden Publications Inc. Reprinted by
permission of Liberty Library Corporation from *Liberty Magazine*.
Copyright © 2006 by Liberty Library Corporation.

Typeset by Palimpsest Book Production Limited, Grangemouth, Stirlingshire
Printed in England by Clays Ltd, St Ives plc

ISBN: 978-0-141-01850-8

www.greenpenguin.co.uk

Penguin Books is committed to a sustainable future
for our business, our readers and our planet.
The book in your hands is made from paper
certified by the Forest Stewardship Council.

For Felix

Contents

Acknowledgments   ix

Part One   The Fall of France

1 Soldiers of Fortune   3

2 The Ace of Spades   21

3 Prelude   27

Part Two   Duel of Eagles

4 Per Ardua ad Astra   51

5 The Burning Blue   69

6 First Blood   79

7 The Channel   87

8 Tally-Ho!   107

9 That England Might Live   117

Part Three   The Narrowest Margin

10 Huns in the Sun   135

11 Achtung! Spitfeuer!   145

12 The Blitz   161

13 Their Finest Hour   169

Part Four　Last Flights

14　Horrido!　189

15　The Eagles　199

16　Dawn Patrol　219

　　Epilogue—They Shall Not Grow Old　231

The "Few"　235

Battle of Britain　237

Notes　241

Bibliography　289

Index　303

Acknowledgments

Over several years, many people helped enormously with the research for this book. I would like to thank the following relatives, pilots, experts, and institutions for their time and generosity.

Frank Brinkerhoff provided clippings, letters, and other information on Phillip Leckrone. Simon Lillywhite, an expert on Billy Fiske, kindly gave me a tour of RAF Tangmere and the surrounding area, introduced me to several people who knew Billy Fiske, and spent many days in the National Archives in England tracking down flight logs, squadron records, combat reports, and many other invaluable documents that allowed me to pinpoint where and when "the few" were in action. His advice and help were invaluable and the hospitality he and his wife provided went far beyond the call of duty.

On the other side of the Atlantic, researcher Alex Blanton kindly sent me many years of careful research on Fiske and his wife Rose. I also cannot thank him enough.

I should mention two names among many people in Britain who have devoted themselves to preserving the memory of "the few": the indefatigable Bill Bond and Ed Sergison of the Battle of Britain Historical Society, whose magazine, *Scramble*, was also most useful. Philip Caine, the leading authority on the American Eagles squadrons, spent an afternoon with me in the archive at the Air Force Academy in Colorado Springs locating records and files and answering many questions. Bill Edwards and his wife generously hosted me in Colorado Springs and provided great encouragement. His fellow Eagle pilots Steve Pisanos, Bill Geiger, Luke Allen, and Dusty Miller also gave me an insight into what it was like to be an American in the Royal Air Force (RAF) in the early years of the war.

The following people also provided wonderful information about Billy Fiske: Battle of Britain pilot Jack Riddle, Dr. Courtney Willey, Ben Clinch, Melanie Carver, Ken Bailey, Geoffrey Faulkner, and Pat Zabalaga, who sent many letters and diary extracts.

I was extremely fortunate to find Helen Maher, who gave me everything she could find about her brother, Eugene Tobin. I spent wonderful days in Olympia and in England with her and will always remember her wonderful humor, the example she sets through her love of life, and her deep devotion to an incredible American—her brother.

Tobin belonged to 609 Squadron during the Battle of Britain. I would like to thank the following for providing details about Tobin, 609, and other pilots who flew in one of the RAF's greatest squadrons: Geoff Nutkins; Chris Goss; David Darley, son of Squadron Leader Horace Darley; and Mark Crame, a true English gentleman who read the manuscript, provided endless advice and encouragement, sent many photographs, and tracked down many leads. Thanks to a new generation of memorialists and enthusiasts like Mark, "the few" will continue to be remembered long after they have gone.

I was fortunate to have the Donahue family's full support. They provided a treasure trove of material and many hours of enjoyable anecdotes during my visits to Springfield, Massachusetts. Minnesotan Lyle Harrison has done more than anyone to celebrate and commemorate Art Donahue, and I am deeply grateful to him for reading the manuscript, spending days showing me around St. Charles, and putting me in touch with several people who provided wonderful information and memories. The following people were also helpful: Scott and Judy Smith; John "Red" Campbell, Donahue's fellow 258 Squadron pilot; Alfie Butts; Dwayne Reed of the National Air Force Academy Archives; and Jim Donahue. Trevor Gray and Richard Jones both flew with Donahue and were generous with their time. They are just two of "the few" who are still going strong. Harold Krow, Bud Vogel, and Ron and Lloyd Hemming had vivid recollections of Donahue as a boy.

Joe Iamartino of the Thompson Historical Society helped me

unearth the background of the remarkable Andrew Mamedoff, and Steve Poole on the Isle of Man gave me wonderful insight into Mamedoff's last flight. Dave Cassells also provided some insight into Mamedoff's teenage years.

I am indebted to the following institutions for a great deal of research: the RAF museum in Hendon, the National Archives in London, the British Library, the Imperial War Museum, the New York Public Library, Williams College, and the National Air Force Academy. I am also grateful to the following leading experts, who kindly replied to my inquiries and helped point me in the right direction: Tony Holmes, Paul Ludwig, and Chris Goss, who also provided wonderful photographs.

Deborah Sullivan was a great help in compiling the bibliography. My wife, Robin, transcribed countless hours of interviews and found most of the photographs in the book. Lindsay Sterling was as professional as ever in reviewing the earliest stages of the manuscript. John Snowdon kindly accompanied me to Middle Wallop with Helen Maher and took wonderful photographs. I will never forget visiting Runnymede memorial with his parents late one summer afternoon. John's father was an armorer for many years in the RAF and served during 1941 at Middle Wallop.

Again, the wonderful team at Da Capo could not have been more helpful and supportive. It has been a delight to work on a third book with my editor, Robert Pigeon, a good friend and invaluable ally. I am also deeply grateful, as ever, to my agent, Derek Johns, and his colleagues at A. P. Watt, particularly Rob Kraitt—the most tolerable Arsenal fan I have ever met. In Los Angeles, the inimitable and beautiful Lisa Wachter and wonderfully cool-headed Keith Fleer were also helpful beyond words.

I spent the first twenty-eight years of my life in England before moving to America. Time apart has only made the heart grow fonder. I miss my oldest and dearest friends and family more than ever. Finally, I can only hope that my son, Felix, and others from his generation will one day be as grateful as I am to the men and women, past and present, of Britain's Royal Air Force.

HIGH FLIGHT

Oh! I have slipped the surly bonds of earth
And danced the skies on laughter-silvered wings;
Sunward I've climbed, and joined the tumbling mirth
Of sun-split clouds—and done a hundred things
You have not dreamed of—wheeled and soared and swung
High in the sunlit silence. Hov'ring there,
I've chased the shouting wind along, and flung
My eager craft through footless halls of air.
Up, up the long, delirious, burning blue
I've topped the wind-swept heights with easy grace
Where never lark, or even eagle flew—
And, while with silent lifting mind I've trod
The high untrespassed sanctity of space,
Put out my hand and touched the face of God.

John Gillespie Magee, Jr.
Nineteen–year–old American pilot,
killed December 11, 1941

Royal Air Force and Luftwaffe Dispositions

The Few

PART ONE

The Fall of France

This blessed plot, this earth, this realm, this England.

William Shakespeare, *Richard II*

1. Soldiers of Fortune

This is the story of some of our countrymen who did not
wait to be stabbed in the back. Long before the rest of us
realized it, these boys, with that deep wisdom given to the
very young, knew that this too, was our war. They were no
adventurers, killing for gain. They couldn't resist the call of
their blood; liberty and tolerance and love for freedom had
been bred in them.[1]

Quentin Reynolds, radio broadcast

Winston Churchill sat in the back of a black Daimler, dressed
in a dark pinstripe suit, late on the afternoon of May 10,
1940. He was on his way to Buckingham Palace, where he would
be officially invited by the king to lead a new government. After
a decade in the political wilderness, the sixty-five-year-old
statesman's hour had finally arrived: Neville Chamberlain, the
conservative prime minister, had stood down that morning, and
Churchill had been selected by party bosses as the best man to
lead the country in what were bound to be its most trying hours.

That morning, just after dawn, it had been reported that Nazi
Germany had launched massive surprise attacks on Luxembourg,
Holland, and Belgium and had pierced the French border. More
than 1,700 German Luftwaffe bombers had filled the skies above
northern Europe, taking so many citizens by surprise that some
even waved up at the planes, not seeing the black crosses on the
bombers' fuselages.

As thousands of panzer tanks continued to storm across
northern Europe, Churchill accepted the king's invitation to
become prime minister. It was drizzling as he was then driven

back to his residence at the British Admiralty. His bodyguard, Inspector William Thompson, was also seated in the Daimler as it passed through the heart of Whitehall. He congratulated his new boss on becoming prime minister, the culmination of more than forty years in Parliament. "I hope it is not too late," Churchill replied. "I am very much afraid that it is. We can only do our best."[2] To his amazement, Thompson saw that Churchill was on the verge of tears.

Union Station in Los Angeles was busy, full of passengers bidding farewell to families before boarding trains. Among those holding tickets were two nervous young men: twenty-three-year-old Eugene "Red" Tobin, the son of a real estate broker, who had spent most of his wayward youth in Los Angeles, and twenty-seven-year-old Andrew Mamedoff, a White Russian, inveterate gambler, and womanizer. From a distance, Tobin was the more striking with his flaming red hair and lanky frame.

Both were about to embark on what they knew would be the most exciting and dangerous chapter of their lives. The 8:15 p.m. train would eventually take them to Canada, then on, they hoped, to Europe, to fight against the Luftwaffe. In so doing, they would break several strict neutrality laws and become outlaws in their own country.

At the outbreak of war in 1939, a presidential proclamation had made it illegal for any American citizen to join a warring power's military and also to "hire someone to go beyond the territorial limits of the United States—to Canada, for example—to enlist in a foreign country's military." The penalties were severe: Tobin and Mamedoff had been warned that, if caught, they could be fined ten thousand dollars, jailed for several years, and stripped of their citizenship and passports.

Tobin was leaving behind his girlfriend, a tall Irish beauty named Anne Haring. In California, he could have continued to fly every day in skies clear of Messerschmitts diving out of the sun to kill him. So why was he now risking everything? There were several reasons. Like Andy Mamedoff, he was certain that the war in

Europe would come to America sooner or later, and he didn't want to be drafted into the army as a grunt when it did. Above all, he was looking to fly the "sweetest little ship" in the world, the Supermarine Spitfire, designed by Englishman Reginald Mitchell, first flown in 1936, and now capable of over 350 mph, three times faster than any plane Tobin had flown: "I just felt I wanted to fly some of these powerful machines . . ."[3] But only by risking his neck in someone else's war would he ever stand a chance of flying the "hottest" machine he had ever set eyes on. The gamble seemed well worth it.

Like so many young Americans in the age of Lindbergh and Earhart, Tobin was obsessed with flying. Nothing else made him feel quite so alive. It was all he had ever wanted to do with his life. And it had enabled him to escape the shadow of his childhood: his earliest memories, other than of marveling at silver biplanes circling lazily above Hollywood, were of watching his mother as she lost a long battle with tuberculosis. Three years later, as an eight-year-old, he had attended an air show and stared in awe as barnstormers performed aerobatics at Roger's Field, on the outskirts of Los Angeles. "My pappy gave me a dollar and I wandered off toward an airplane, an old Fairchild cabin job," he recalled. "I told the pilot I wanted to go for a ride and he said, 'Is it all right with your parents?' My father's back was turned, but a man near him swung around and looked at me at that moment and the pilot thought he was my pappy. We popped around the airport and I just knew I was born to fly. I failed practically every year at school from ditching classes and going out to airports. Finally, when I was older, I realized my ambition—I learned to fly. I did my first solo over Hollywood and I flew a great deal over the Sierras."[4] Eventually, he had saved enough money from working as a mechanic to buy his own plane. That had led to glamorous employment with MGM as a pilot ferrying the studio's stars and other VIPs around California—"a heck of a job." But it had not satisfied his restless spirit.

It was time to leave. Passengers began to file across Union Station's terra-cotta and inlaid marble floor and through the exit to the platform where the 8:15 p.m. train was waiting. Tobin and Mamedoff were soon boarding the train. For all they knew, they might never see the Mission Revival splendor of Union Station, or indeed Los Angeles, again. They were now bona fide soldiers of fortune, making their way illegally to fight in a war that their government had done its best to prevent any American from joining.

Tobin and Mamedoff had been hired by America's most colorful and notorious mercenary, fifty-nine-year-old Colonel Charles Sweeny, friend of Ernest Hemingway and several Latin American revolutionaries, described by *The New Yorker* that year as a "tall, ruddy, hawk-faced, clipped-voiced man who does not mind his collar button showing."[5] It was Sweeny who had seen to it that discreet notices advertising "opportunities" with certain European air forces had been posted at airfields and had appeared in news-papers around the U.S., and to which Andy Mamedoff and Eugene Tobin had eagerly responded.

As soon as the Nazis had invaded Poland, Sweeny had set about organizing a group of flyers modeled after the legendary Esquadrille Squadron of WWI, a unit of dashing young American pilots who had volunteered to fly with the French Armée de l'Air and tangled above the trenches with the Baron von Richthofen's Flying Circus. But Sweeny's plans faced fierce opposition from the State Depart-ment and from several politicians, most of them from the Midwest, where there were large communities of German immigrants. "Many obstacles soon cropped up," he recalled. "The more apparent ones were the Neutrality Law and the attitude of hostility assumed by a large and influential part of the American press. For months I was hounded like a criminal. I began to have a friendly feeling for Baby Face Nelson [Lester J. Gillis, a notorious gangster who was then being hunted by the FBI]. The more real obstacle was the complete apathy of the American people."[6]

Wanting to escape the attentions of the FBI, Sweeny had gone to Canada in late 1939. But even though Canada was at war with Germany, this move had provided only a temporary refuge. After just a few weeks, the authorities had started asking tough questions, and then Sweeny had been grilled at length by no less than Canadian Attorney General Frank Murphy. Time was running out if Sweeny was to avoid being deported to the U.S. to face charges of breaking neutrality laws.[7] Sweeny had quickly arranged passage to Europe but not before managing to set up a secret network, stretching from Los Angeles and other American cities to Montreal and then via Nova Scotia to France.

As soon as Sweeny had arrived in Europe, the network had been activated. Tobin and Mamedoff had then been contacted at Mines Airfield in Los Angeles by a man involved with Sweeny's illegal venture. Would they be interested in going to Finland? The Finnish air force needed every pilot it could get as it waged a fierce battle against the invading Soviets, who had forged a notorious pact with the Nazis the summer before. They would be paid all expenses to Helsinki and one hundred dollars a month as long as they lasted.[8] "I was certainly the guy to go flying up around the arctic circle," Tobin later recalled. "I'd seen snow about twice in my life. But flying is flying I told myself. Finland can't be so different."

The next day, Tobin had quit his job with MGM and had bought gear for flying in subzero temperatures. Mamedoff had sold his plane. But less than forty-eight hours later, the friends had rued their hasty decisions. "I was back, trying to talk the boss into putting me on the payroll again," explained Tobin. "Andy was trying to figure out how he could [get] another crate. It seemed that something had happened up there in Finland. There wasn't a war anymore."[9] In early April 1940, the Finns had ended a bitter and valiant winter campaign. Tobin and Mamedoff would not be going on their great adventure after all. For three days, now unemployed and without planes, they had hung around Mines Airfield, trying to work out what to do next.

They had been too late to fight for a free Finland. But the forces of repression were on the march elsewhere. "There was another war going on," Tobin recalled. "Perhaps we could get into that one. They say if you go looking for a fight you can always find one."[10] A week later, Tobin and Mamedoff had signed up to join the French Armée de l'Air. Another nameless contact, this time a Frenchman, had then arrived at Mines Airfield and given them each a train ticket to Montreal and "a warm though limp handshake."[11]

The 8:15 p.m. Chicago train began to pull out of Union Station. Later that evening of May 10, 1940, Eugene Tobin opened his diary and jotted: "I don't know what's going to happen, but it's sure as hell going to be an adventure."[12] The journey from Los Angeles to Chicago and then to Montreal would take several days, plenty of time for him and Mamedoff to share their anxieties: If they were caught, would they go straight to jail or would Sweeny be able to get them off the hook? And if they did get to Canada without being arrested, how would they get to Europe? Would they fly or take a boat across the Atlantic, where Hitler's U-boats were busy sinking dozens of ships each month?

The train left California and then headed into the darkness of Nevada. Unlike Tobin, Andy Mamedoff was not leaving loved ones behind. He had no blood ties to the state or, for that matter, to America. He belonged instead to a pitiful diaspora—the million-odd Whites who had been forced to flee Mother Russia when the Bolsheviks had ruthlessly crushed their forces during the Civil War of the early 1920s. Had he and his parents tried to hide in some far-flung corner of Siberia, as Cossacks and others had, they would have been hunted down and killed: Lev Mamedoff, Andy's father, had been a marked man. It was said that in 1908 he had arrested a Georgian Bolshevik called Iosif Dzhugashvili, later known as Joseph Stalin, in the Caucasus when the future Soviet Union dictator had been nothing but a long-haired petty criminal and rabble-rouser.

California's clear skies had lured Mamedoff from his previous exile in Thompson, Connecticut, where he had earned a reputation as a foolhardy show-off who had sped around in a flashy Ford convertible, impressing many local girls. Like Tobin, he had not cared much for school, and had been expelled several times from Tourtellotte Memorial High School, where, according to a classmate, he had been the charismatic leader of "a rowdy crew, not necessarily crude, but always looking for action."[13]

Winston Churchill stood at the dispatch box in the House of Commons. It was early afternoon on May 13, 1940, as the chamber fell silent and he began his first speech as prime minister by briefing the assembled members on developments in Europe. The news was far from encouraging. The Germans were waging a stunningly successful campaign of blitzkrieg—lightning war—coordinating massed tank attacks with strikes from the air, in particular from a new dive bomber, the Junkers 87, which had V-shaped wings and a siren that wailed as it swooped down on the Allies' front-line positions. In just three days, thanks in large part to the Luftwaffe, the Germans had swept through territory that had been contested for four years during the Great War of 1914–18. Britain now faced the greatest threat to her survival in a millennium.

Churchill concluded his first speech with words that would set the tone of his oratory in the crucial weeks to come. "I have nothing to offer but blood, toil, tears and sweat. You ask what is our policy? I will say: It is to wage war, by sea, land and air, with all our might and with all the strength that God has given us, to wage war against a monstrous tyranny, never surpassed in the dark, lamentable catalog of human crime. You ask what is our aim? I can answer in one word. Victory, victory at all costs; victory in spite of all terror; victory however long and hard the road may be."[14]

The train finally pulled into a station near the Canadian border. Officials boarded and began to check the papers of occupants in each carriage.

Tobin and Mamedoff waited anxiously.

An official finally stepped into their compartment.

"Where are you boys going, and why?"

"We're on our way to Montreal to see a cousin who runs a fish hatchery," lied Tobin.

"Are either of you flyers?"

"Don't be silly. Do we look like flyers?"

Another official entered and began to check their luggage. Mamedoff and Tobin tried to appear calm.

The official examined a top layer of clothing but delved no deeper. If he had, he would have discovered goggles and logbooks.

"That's OK," he said. "Have a good time and tickle a trout for us."[15]

Tobin and Mamedoff had been given instructions to go to the Queen's Hotel in Montreal, an impressive seven-floor stone building in the city's center. There they were to ask for letters addressed to them, containing cash and train tickets for the next leg of their trip. They arrived at the hotel late the following afternoon, but there were no letters. They decided in any case to check into the hotel. Sooner or later, they would be contacted.

In his hotel room, Tobin pulled out a piece of stationery from his bedside table and began to write a letter to his father in Los Angeles: "By the time you get this I will be well on my way to France?! Now hang on Pa, it's not as bad as that. I am going to get six months of the best training possible, and by then I'll get out (yes I will). The reason I did not tell you before was because I knew you would be against it, and I didn't want a big argument Pa—honest . . . When I get back I will be a *damn good* pilot, and will have no trouble getting a job, because I will have something to offer whereas now I'm nothing but a nothing . . . I guarantee you Pa I will not take any unnecessary chances . . . all I want is the training—nothing more. I can't get in the lousy U.S. Army [Air Corps] so I'll go to France where I can. This is no 'foolhardy stunt'—you may think it is but it isn't . . . your little boy Gene."[16]

In the lobby, Tobin and Mamedoff asked a clerk if any other Americans had also asked for envelopes and checked into the hotel. The clerk pointed to a man seated a few yards away, looking glum and engrossed in an aviation magazine. It was immediately obvious that he was very small: the man's feet did not even touch the ground.

Tobin's younger sister, Helen Maher, would later vividly recall her brother's first encounter with the shortest man ever to fly in the RAF: twenty-six-year-old Vernon Charles Keough. "Gene thought: 'I wonder whether this is the guy we are supposed to meet?' The more Gene looked at Keough, the more he thought: 'I bet that's him. But he surely can't fly. He's too little.' He kept looking at Keough and Keough kept looking back. And finally Gene said to him, 'You're the meanest looking dude I've seen in a long time.'"[17]

That broke the ice. Keough and the other pilots introduced themselves. "I came up from New York expecting to join the French air force, and instead I become a lobby squatter," said Keough. "My luck sure isn't getting any better."

They went to the bar, and Keough, just four foot ten, bought drinks and then told Tobin and Mamedoff they should call him Shorty. He'd been a professional parachute jumper before becoming a pilot.[18]

A fortnight back, explained Keough, he had borrowed five hundred dollars for a down payment on a new plane. He had then allowed a friend to take it up the very day it had been delivered.

Keough paused. He looked grief-stricken.

"What happened?" asked Tobin.

"The dope goes and cracks it up, landing. About the only thing left is the stick, which he's still got in his hand when he crawls out. So I joined the French air force to get away from it all. And now this!"[19]

Tobin ordered more drinks. He liked the look of Shorty, with his wry smile and eyes that didn't miss a thing, darting about like mice.

Keough had grown up in Brooklyn. By his early twenties, he had been scraping by as a barnstormer. Then he had become one of America's first skydivers, eventually risking his life in more than five hundred jumps. "I was talked into making my first jump," Keough would later recall. "I was twenty-four then. It didn't seem so good at first. I didn't like the idea of leaving a perfectly good airplane up there and jumping for no reason at all. Well, I did it at four shows, because the guy I was working for wanted me to. I was so light, you see! Then I found I liked it."

Keough had often landed in the wrong place and a couple of times so far off course that it had taken several days before his mother learned that he was still alive. As a fellow pilot recalled: "People who came to comfort his mother in Brooklyn were in turn consoled by her calm words: 'He'll come back. He always does.' And he always did."[20] There had been good times: bright and windless summer days and large crowds below. And then there "would be a wet Sunday, after we'd built up a show. Then things wouldn't be so hot and I would have to eat on the cuff and put my airplane in hock."[21]

Over more drinks, Tobin learned that Shorty had also volunteered to fight with the Finns. He didn't mind now what air force he joined so long as it wasn't the Luftwaffe.

The Americans were interrupted by a bellhop who handed them the letters they had been promised by their contacts in the States. They ripped them open, discovered train tickets to Halifax in Nova Scotia, knocked back their drinks, and read the instructions accompanying the tickets: "You will take the night train to Halifax. Upon arrival, remain at the station after the other passengers have departed. Discuss flying in a loud voice so our agent can identify you."[22]

In London, the long day was also drawing to a close. Before turning in for the night, Winston Churchill met in his rooms at the Admiralty with the American ambassador, Joseph Kennedy. According to Kennedy, Churchill was worried that Italy, under the dictator Mussolini, would soon seize the chance to enter the war, thereby introducing the nightmare scenario for Britain of having to fight on two fronts—in France and in the Mediterranean. It seemed likely that France would fall quickly to the Germans, and then the Luftwaffe would throw everything it had at Britain in a bloody prelude to invasion. "He said that regardless of what Germany does to England and France,"

Kennedy cabled President Roosevelt after the meeting, "England will never give up as long as he remains a power in public life, even if England is burned to the ground. Why, he said, the Government would move to Canada and take the fleet and fight on."[23] In the meantime, counseled Kennedy, it was imperative that America not be dragged into the war: "It seems to me that if we had to protect our lives, we would do better fighting in our own back yard."[24]

This was not what Roosevelt wanted to hear, but it was entirely to be expected from Joseph Kennedy, a defeatist for whom the pursuit of profit and power was all-consuming. To remove him from the domestic political scene, where he was touted by some as a possible presidential candidate, President Roosevelt had sent Kennedy and his photogenic family to London in the late thirties. As a blinkered isolationist, Kennedy had provided one-sided reports on the worsening European situation, missives in which Roosevelt now had begun to place little faith, knowing Kennedy was more interested in furthering his political ambitions back in America than in being an effective liaison between the British government and the White House. "I thought my daffodils were yellow until I met Joe Kennedy," was one British reaction to the future American president's father.

The train to Halifax was crowded with Canadian troops. In his diary, Tobin wrote: "Everybody talks about the war. They ask us why Americans haven't come in the war. We say pay us the dough and we sure will. They look astonished—adieu."[25]

Finally, the train pulled into Halifax. It was 1 a.m. A few minutes later, the Americans stood shivering on a platform, discussing flying, as they had been instructed. After a while, a short, swarthy man introduced himself, claiming he was acting on behalf of the French government. They were soon following him along dark and rainy backstreets, ducking into alleys to shake off possible tails, until they climbed the steps leading to an office on the top floor of an abandoned warehouse. Their contact opened an old safe, the kind Tobin had seen in black-and-white westerns, and pulled out three pink cards. "As you cannot travel on an American passport, owing to the terms of your government's neutrality laws, I am giving you these documents," he explained.

The pink cards stated that they were of indeterminate nationality and that they were to be given free passage because they had been recruited to the French Armée de l'Air.

The man then pulled out some bundles of cash.

"This will get you to Paris. You are expected on board the ship at seven o'clock this morning. *Bon voyage, mes enfants! Vive la France!*"

"*Vive la France*," replied Tobin.[26]

By 7 a.m., they were walking along a wharf toward a freighter. A foul smell filled the air. "It wasn't the aroma of French perfume," Tobin recalled. "Just plain old mule. Five hundred of them."[27]

They boarded and found that no one spoke English, except for the captain, who said he could take only two of them: Mamedoff and Keough. Tobin would have to cross the Atlantic on the *Pierre L. D.*, another freighter belonging to the same convoy of forty ships bound for France.

Across the Atlantic that morning, in his quarters at the British Admiralty, Winston Churchill received a telephone call. It was from his French counterpart, Prime Minister Paul Reynaud, known in France as the "fighting cock" because of his strutting manner and aggression.

"We are beaten," Reynaud said. "We have lost the battle. The front is broken . . . they are pouring through in great numbers with tanks and armored cars."

Churchill was shocked. He urged Reynaud to fight on, trying to reassure him that all was not lost. But Reynaud was inconsolable.

"All right," Churchill concluded, "I will come over to Paris to talk to you."[28]

As preparations were made to fly to Paris, escorted by an RAF fighter squadron, another message came from Reynaud: "The way to Paris lies open. Send all the troops and planes you can."[29]

Determined to bolster the French premier, Churchill decided

it was time to appeal directly to President Roosevelt for help: "I trust you realize, Mr. President, that the voice and force of the United States may count for nothing if they are withheld too long. You may have a completely subjugated, Nazified Europe established with astonishing swiftness, and the weight may be more than we can bear. All I ask now is that you should proclaim non-belligerency, which would mean that you could help us with everything short of actually engaging armed forces."[30]

Churchill went on to list specific things that America could provide immediately: forty or fifty destroyers to help in convoy duties, several hundred new aircraft, and anti-aircraft guns and ammunition. Roosevelt's reply, the following day, was far from encouraging. The provision of destroyers would, if it became public knowledge, be seized upon by America's many energized isolationists as a contravention of neutrality laws. Only Congress, Roosevelt pointed out, could authorize such provision, and he was "not certain that it would be wise for the suggestion to be made to the Congress at this moment."[31]

There was even more distressing news when Churchill arrived in Paris that afternoon and met with Reynaud and his generals: the Germans, having broken through in northern France, near Sedan, were now driving a fifty-mile-wide wedge between two French armies.

"Where is the strategic reserve?" asked Churchill.

There was no reply from the French commanders.

"Where is the strategic reserve?" Churchill asked again, this time in French.

A senior French general, General Maurice Gamelin, shook his head wearily.

"There is none."[32]

Churchill was dumbfounded. How could the French have left themselves so vulnerable?

Gamelin spoke directly to Churchill: The French were suffering setback after setback, above all because the Luftwaffe dominated in the air. If the RAF could provide more fighter squadrons, this critical disadvantage might be overcome. Then the waves of panzers could at least be delayed, if not halted, as they stormed toward Paris.

Churchill promised to provide six more squadrons. But when he arrived back in London that evening, he discovered that Air Chief Marshal Sir Hugh "Stuffy" Dowding, head of Fighter Command, had persuaded the War Cabinet not to send any more squadrons to the French.[33] "If the Home Defense Force is drained away in desperate attempts to remedy the situation in France," Dowding had argued, "defeat in France will involve the final, complete and irremediable defeat of this country."[34]

The French would get no more squadrons. The end was near.

There had never been a train quite like it—*Asia*, the mobile command post of the second most powerful man in the Third Reich: Reichsmarschall Hermann Göring, head of the Luftwaffe. On May 20, 1940, a security detail led the Italian ambassador, Dino Alfieri, toward the train. It was well camouflaged, heavily fortified with anti-aircraft guns, and parked near a tunnel, close to the German town of Polch, in the event of a sudden attack by the RAF.

The extravagance of Göring's rolling headquarters seduced Alfieri as soon as he stepped aboard. *Asia* was specially weighted for the smoothest ride. It had bathing facilities, a cinema, an expansive dining car where Germany's finest chefs served only the best wines and haute cuisine, and spare carriages to carry art treasures seized from Europe's finest collections. The man who had formed the Gestapo and organized the first concentration camp, who had then become president of the Reichstag and prime minister of Prussia, had clearly been amply rewarded for almost twenty years of fierce loyalty to Hitler.

Göring smiled as Alfieri greeted him and then beamed as the Italian ambassador presented him with the Collar of Annunziata, the highly coveted personal decoration of the Italian king. Göring had not been so flattered since 1918, when he had been awarded the *Orden Pour le Mérite*—the Blue Max—upon replacing the legendary Baron von Richthofen as commander of the Flying

Circus, *Jagdgeschwader* 1.[35] His voice quavering with emotion, his clear blue eyes sparkling with pleasure, Göring thanked Alfieri in fluent Italian and then squeezed sideways out of the carriage only to return a few minutes later with a phalanx of photographers and the medal at his neck.

Later that day, after Alfieri had been treated to a spectacular luncheon, Göring sat in the shade beneath a clump of trees. Seated opposite him at an oak table were two friends: General Hans Jeschonnek, the forty-three-year-old Luftwaffe chief of staff, and Major Josef "Beppo" Schmid, his head of intelligence.[36] Jeschonnek was a highly capable, ruthless Nazi. Schmid, by contrast, was a hopelessly inept sycophant. He could not fly, and he could not understand English, a serious deficiency given his role in assessing the RAF's capabilities. One of his senior colleagues remembered him bitterly as an "alcoholic . . . with a boxer's face, without wit or culture, who started his career with entirely false, optimistically exaggerated opinions."[37]

Suddenly, an aide rushed over and delivered the news that the French and British were almost surrounded in northern France. All that was required to win the war was a swift coup de grâce. But who should deliver it: The Wehrmacht generals with their columns of panzers, or the Me-109s and Stukas of Hermann Göring's Luftwaffe?

Göring was quick to his feet.

"This is just the job for the Luftwaffe!" he blustered. "Get me through to the Führer at once."

Hitler was soon on the line. Göring was at his most confident and persuasive, warning the Führer that he might lose face if he allowed his generals to take credit for finishing off the French and British. The Luftwaffe had been designed precisely for the task at hand; its medium-range bombers, such as the Dornier Do-17Z, the Heinkel He-111, and the Junkers Ju-87B, known as the Stuka, were ideally suited to paralyzing ground forces with terrifying speed.

"Allow the symbol of the new Reich, of the reborn German military, to finish the job," pleaded Göring. "Pull back Hans von

Guderian and Erwin Rommel's panzers for a few days. Let the Stukas and Emils [Me-109s] get to work immediately. Leave it to me and the Luftwaffe. I guarantee unconditionally that not a British soldier will escape."

Hitler liked what he heard. "Go right ahead," he told Göring.[38]

The commander of what was thought to be the greatest air force in history thanked Adolf Hitler and bade him good day. Grinning, he then handed over the telephone to his chief of staff, Hans Jeschonnek, who would arrange a timetable and organize the details of the attack with Hitler's staff.

Meanwhile, Eugene Tobin and his fellow American volunteers were crossing the Atlantic, unaware of the developments in France. That night of May 20, his fourth at sea, a green-gilled Tobin mustered the energy to fill a page in his diary: "I went to the officers' mess and played some records, both American and French. After listening to the French records, I can understand why they are at war . . . Have ten more days of this, by then supposed to be in Brest (if we're not torpedoed). Miss the folks at home, especially my little honey [Anne Haring]. But what the hell can I do about it out here in the middle of the drink? The French had better have some good plans after all of this or I'll start a war of my own."[39]

A week into the voyage, an escorting British destroyer dropped depth charges. A U-boat had been detected in the area and Tobin's boat was farthest from the center of the convoy, wide open to attack. For several hours, the crew manned action stations until finally the captain announced that the immediate danger had passed. The U-boat was one of fifty-seven then operating in the Atlantic and sinking more than fifty thousand tons of shipping a week, threatening to starve Britain into submission. For Rear Admiral Karl Doenitz's underwater predators, it was the "happy time," when sinking stragglers such as Tobin's boat was an almost daily occurrence.

Tobin was soon thoroughly miserable. In his diary, his list of complaints grew longer by the day: bad food, constant drizzle, a head cold, boredom, anxiety over the U-boat threat, and the sullen French crew. Two weeks into the crossing, however, the weather improved, the convoy splintered, and Tobin finally learned that he was going to disembark the following day, May 31, at St. Nazaire in Brittany.[40] The seas became dead calm; other ships in the convoy took on the appearance of ghosts as a heavy mist shrouded the Bay of Biscay. Somewhere in the murk, only a few miles away, loomed the craggy coast of France.

2. The Ace of Spades

Enough words have been exchanged;
now at last let me see some deeds!

Goethe, *Faust I*

It was around 11 a.m. on June 5, 1940, when twenty-seven-year-old Luftwaffe Captain Werner Mölders flicked the magneto switch on his Messerschmitt Me-109 and heard the Daimler-Benz engine roaring to life. A handsome man of medium height with deep-set eyes, dark slicked-back hair, and thin lips, he then taxied across the grass runway, and a few minutes later was taking off with his fellow pilots of *Jagdgeschwader* 53 (JG 53), or as their unit was known to pilots in the Luftwaffe: the Ace of Spades.

A devout Catholic whose sister was a nun, Mölders was resented by some Nazis for openly talking about his faith and their repression of the Catholic Church. Because of his genius for shooting down enemy planes, however, they could not silence him; Reichsmarschall Hermann Göring had made sure of that. He knew Mölders was deeply respected by his fellow pilots and valued him as a brilliant strategist who had reinvented the rules of fighter combat, significantly increasing the kill rate of the Luftwaffe's aces while making it harder for enemy air forces to shoot them down.

Legend had it that "Vati" (Daddy) Mölders, as he was known to his young pilots, had the best eyesight in the Luftwaffe and could spot an enemy plane several seconds before even his wingmen, all of whom had 20/20 vision. Incredibly, it was also said that every time he slipped into a cockpit he had to beat down his one weakness: a gut-wrenching fear of heights. Enigmatic indeed: Unlike many of his fellow aces, Mölders took little pleasure in watching his victims tumble to the ground, even though his father had been killed by their forebears in the trenches during the First World War.

The patchwork farms of northern France were now visible below. Mölders opened the throttle on his Me-109 and checked that his flight of four planes, made up of two pairs, was flying as he had instructed: around two hundred yards apart, with each pair's wingman protecting the flight's tail. The first recipient of the Knight's Cross for shooting down twenty enemy planes in the war, he was as usual wearing a fur-collared flying jacket, a leftover from his days as the highest scoring Condor Legion pilot in Spain, where he had killed at least fourteen anti-fascists in as many weeks in 1938.

A few minutes later, Mölders was flying ahead of his wingman in clear skies over Compiègne. Below, the enemy was in panic and retreat. The invasion of France had so far gone amazingly well, better than even Hitler had expected. Britain's decimated Royal Air Force was now evacuating France lest it be destroyed, leaving Mölders and his fellow pilots to mop up the remnants of the French air force. Two days before, the Ace of Spades had shot down a grand total of eleven French and British planes, and Mölders had made his twenty-second and twenty-third kills: a Hawk H-75A and what he claimed was a Spitfire.

Mölders spied a plane, a Bloch 152. Swooping down, he opened fire and then watched as the French fighter spun down, belching smoke and flame. He did not have to wait long to make his next kill, diving again and this time riddling a Potez 63 with cannon shell and bullets. As he always stressed to his newest pilots, the trick was to strike from altitude, out of the sun—"bouncing" the unsuspecting enemy—and then pull away as fast as possible. Hit and run. Hit and run. That was what the Messerschmitt had been designed for. In a dive it could not be caught. But in a dogfight, particularly against the RAF's Spitfire, it could be out-turned. And so, unless it was unavoidable, Mölders never allowed himself to be engaged on equal terms.

Running low on fuel, Mölders led his flight back to base. It was late afternoon when he returned to the skies above France with JG 53. The shadows were lengthening on the grass fields, the sun dipping in the west, when he spotted a formation of enemy planes below. They were the best that the French air force could put up in defense of their homeland—Dewoitine D.520s. Then things started to go wrong: Another German squadron attacked the French planes before Mölders could order his men to pounce. It was obvious that the other squadron's pilots were novices from the way they opened fire much too soon, thereby alerting the French to their presence. The enemy formation split in all directions, and then the horizon was suddenly full of planes spitting bright tracers. The crucial element of surprise had been lost. Now the Ace of Spades would be in for a real fight.

Mölders hovered above the fray for a while, choosing his moment. Below, three pilots from the overeager German squadron were chasing a solitary French plane without success. It was time to show the neophytes a thing or two. Mölders dived and soon had the French plane in his sights but not close enough to guarantee the kill. Then it dived away sharply. To Mölders's surprise, the pilot was no dolt, expertly slowing his plane so that Mölders overshot and lost sight of his prey beneath his wing. Mölders scanned the sky, neck swiveling, and then looked into his rear mirror. The Frenchman was now on his tail, firing right at him.

"Damn it!"[1]

Mölders banked away and climbed hard into the sun, knowing its glare would make it difficult for the enemy to follow and fire accurately. His engine whined with stress as he pulled back his control stick with the throttle wide open. To his relief, he managed to throw off the Frenchman. He looked down—two other Messerschmitts were chasing a French plane. Above him, vapor trails stretched across the bright blue like shredded white ribbons. He checked his instruments—the altimeter showed three thousand feet. Then disaster struck. Mölders heard a terrible bang. Sparks showered across his cockpit. His throttle was shot to pieces. The controls were useless. His plane began to drop like a stone, nose first. Sub-Lieutenant René Pommier Layrargues, a determined

French ace, had taken Mölders completely by surprise, hitting him with a long burst of machine-gun fire. Mölders was lucky to still be alive.

"Got to get out."[2]

Mölders grabbed the Me-109's jettison lever then released the canopy and glimpsed it flying away. In one fluid motion, he was out of his harness, free of the seat, free of the plane, and tumbling through the sky.

Pommier Layrargues had meanwhile latched on to another Nazi and squeezed off round after round. Again, he had scored, bullets tearing into his second victim of the day.

Mölders pulled on his rip cord. "Suddenly, I found it in my hand, torn off—a terrible fright went through me," he recalled. "I reached above me but the chute had already opened. I hung quite peacefully beneath my parachute and searched for my opponent but there were only Me's circled round me, only Me's! Quite slowly I drifted toward the ground and that ground was still occupied by the enemy—60 kilometers behind the front, west of Compiègne. I drew my pistol and released the safety, then stuck it into my pants pocket. Beneath me two farmers collected their horses and fled. A brief survey of the terrain revealed a small wood, otherwise meadows everywhere. Suddenly the ground rushed up, I pulled my legs up—touchdown was relatively gentle. I got clear of my chute at once and ran toward the wood. Frenchmen came running from the sides. I got to the edge of the wood—bang! A shot whizzed past my ear. I threw away my fur-lined jacket and ran, gasping for breath, to the other side of the wood."[3]

A group of French artillerymen spotted him, gave chase, seized him, and then began to beat him with their rifle butts. Fortunately for Mölders, a French officer shouted for them to stop. Unlike many other German flyers killed or maimed by the French that spring, he suffered only minor injuries and was soon on his way to a French POW camp.

Later that evening, back at base, the young men of JG 53 were stunned when Mölders failed to appear. The loss of their charismatic leader, so early in the war, hit many like an "electric shock."[4] A few days later, the wreckage of his plane was found and a missing-in-action report filed: "A Bf-109 leaving a trail of smoke was observed in this area at a height of 1000 meters; a parachute was seen shortly before the machine went into a spin and crashed. No enemy aircraft was seen to attack. Apparently hit by ground fire or engine failure."[5]

What about Mölders's nemesis, Monsieur Layrargues? From his captors, Werner Mölders learned that one of his pilots from the Ace of Spades had singled out the plane that had attacked him and had shot it down. Monsieur Layrargues had died not long after Mölders's parachute had opened.

The news of Mölders's disappearance spread fast throughout the Luftwaffe. Many of Mölders's acolytes deeply mourned his loss. Others who admired him were not quite so saddened: pilots such as the burly Karl-Hans Mayer of JG 53 and the urbane Adolf Galland of JG 26, fast closing on Mölders's top score of 23. In the pages of *Signal* and other Nazi propaganda magazines, the question was soon being asked: Who among them would now become the war's greatest ace?

3. Prelude

"Look out—here's another!"

"Watch that bastard—smack underneath you, man, under you."

"He's burning—I got him, I got him chaps!"

"Bloody hell, I've been hit."

"Jesus, where are they all coming from?"

"For God's sake, somebody! . . ."[1]

Larry Forrester, *Fly for Your Life*

The nightmare crossing was almost over. On May 30, 1940, Eugene Tobin stood on deck, watching as the Brittany coastline came into full view. As the last of the morning mist burnt off, he entered the port of St. Nazaire, which was larger than he had expected and crowded with ships painted a drab camouflage gray. Wobbling slightly on sea legs, he was soon wandering the narrow streets leading from the docks to St. Nazaire's main square. "Man alive," he noted in his diary, "what a town this is! Everybody wears 1890 clothes, rides bicycles—even old men and women. There's not a woman under 180 pounds. I bet when they're born they have to lift them out with cranes."[2]

Tobin soon contacted a local official who offered to help him get the correct travel papers so he could take a train to Paris. Unfortunately, it was already late on a Friday, so he would have to wait until Monday before the travel bureau reopened. Reluctantly, Tobin returned to his ship to wait out the weekend.

Time was fast running out if Tobin was to help save France. Since Tobin had left Halifax, everything had gone Hitler's way. On May 20, the German panzer columns had reached Abbeville on the Channel coast, completing an encirclement of more than a million British, French, and Belgian troops. French resistance had mostly been pathetic, causing the commander of the British Expeditionary Force, Lord Gort, to snort contemptuously that: "It is no uncommon occurrence to agree with the French to retire at, say, 9 p.m., and find that the French troops had in fact started to pull back at 4 p.m."[3]

By May 26, around 250,000 British troops, the rump of what remained of the British Expeditionary Force (BEF), were surrounded in the French port of Dunkirk and being mercilessly attacked by Göring's Stuka dive-bombers. From the air it seemed that the nearby beaches swarmed with a huge army of ants that rippled with fear as German pilots made strafing runs. The mood was grim, both on the sand dunes where starving, exhausted Tommies waited for rescue, and in London, where even in Churchill's War Cabinet there was talk of a compromise peace with Hitler.

Churchill ended all such defeatist sentiment, telling his cabinet in an emotionally charged meeting on May 28: "I am convinced that every one of you would rise up and tear me down from my place if I were for one moment to contemplate parley or surrender. If this long island story of ours is to come to an end at last, let it end only when each of us lies choking in his own blood upon the ground."[4] Churchill's defiance was met with cheers and hurrahs. It was clear that he now had every one of his cabinet firmly on his side. "Quite a number," he recalled, "seemed to jump from the table and come running to my chair, shouting and patting me on the back . . . had I at this juncture faltered at all in leading the nation I should have been hurled out of office. I am sure that every Minister was ready to be killed quite soon, and have all his family and possessions destroyed, rather than give in."[5]

Just as the cabinet had rallied to Churchill, so would the nation. But first, something had to be salvaged from the disaster unfolding at Dunkirk. Senior commanders hoped that perhaps thirty thousand men, a fraction of the British Expeditionary Force, might be saved. In London, Ambassador Kennedy added his own assessment to the general air of doom, cabling President Roosevelt that: "Only a miracle can save the BEF from being wiped out or, as I said yesterday, surrender . . . the English people, while they suspect a terrible situation, really do not realize how bad it is. When they do I don't know what group they will follow, the do or die or the group that wants a settlement."[6]

But all was not yet lost. The seafaring nation was beginning to respond to a call for all available vessels to make the hazardous Channel crossing and evacuate men from the bloodstained beaches. All manner of craft, from private dinghies to Thames tugboats, were headed toward Dunkirk. Above the beaches, Fighter Command's Spitfire and Hurricane squadrons were also now in action, fighting with unprecedented aggression, many of their pilots furious at the sight of their countrymen being mowed down as they waded in long snaking lines toward rescue boats.

Even veteran Luftwaffe pilots, who had readily strafed columns of refugees in Spain and destroyed Guernica, soon began to sicken of the slaughter. For twenty-four-year-old Captain Paul Temme, flying at three hundred feet above his victims, it was "just unadulterated killing. The beaches were jammed full of soldiers. I went up and down 'hose-piping.' It was cold-blooded point-blank murder."[7]

The fighting over Dunkirk would be a prelude to the Battle of Britain, and the Luftwaffe and the RAF took careful measure of each other. For the first time, the Germans encountered the full force of Fighter Command, and it was soon clear that the RAF's Spitfires and Hurricanes were just as lethal as the Messerschmitt Me-109, the Germans' best fighter. Another thing was quickly obvious: the British pilots were as well disciplined and courageous as their foe in the air, confirming the warning of influential First World War veteran Theo Osterkamp: "Now we fight 'The Lords,' and that is something else again. They are hard fighters and they are good fighters."[8]

For many RAF pilots, Dunkirk was a chaotic and brutal baptism of fire. "The Me-109s were quicksilver," recalled one squadron leader. "It would have been ideal to come against them as a controlled formation, but the Germans always split up, so somehow you did, too. Then it was every man for himself—which was all right if you were good."9 Thankfully, some were very good indeed. They included twenty-eight-year-old Flight Lieutenant Frank Howell of 609 West Riding Squadron, a strikingly handsome, blond-haired former mechanic who, on June 1, 1940, was appointed a flight leader after two days of fierce combat.

In a remarkable letter to his brother, Howell provided a vivid account of what it was like to fly above the hell of Dunkirk: "The place was still burning furiously, a great pall of smoke stretching 7,000 feet in the sky over Belgium . . . Thousands and thousands of A/A [anti-aircraft] shells were bursting over the town . . . I looked down to see salvo after salvo of bombs bursting with terrific splashes in the water near some shipping, and there was a Heinkel, only 500 feet below going in the opposite direction so I did a half roll, and came up its arse, giving it a pretty 2 seconds fire . . . All the way back to England I flew full throttle at about 15 feet above the water and the shipping between England and Dunkirk was a sight worth seeing. Paddle boats, destroyers, sloops, tugs, fishing trawlers, river launches . . . anything with a motor towing anything without one . . . I am indeed lucky to have got away scot free. Dizzy was killed and five other chaps are missing. One was my flight commander so I am now in charge of A Flight, and will get another stripe, and it's a rotten way to get it."10

On June 1, Winston Churchill was back in Paris, again trying to rally the French and sharing with them the heartening news that more than 165,000 troops had been pulled off the beaches at Dunkirk. Distressingly, his exhortations to fight on to the very end appeared to fall on deaf ears.

Churchill's escort from Paris back to England was to be provided by 601 Squadron, otherwise known as the Millionaires' Squadron because several of its pilots came from wealthy families. "Winston was ebullient as ever," recalled an aide. "When we started back he insisted on pacing round the aerodrome to review [601's] nine Hurricanes, tramping through the tall grass in the flurry of propellers with his cigar like a pennant."11

British Major General Sir Edward Spears remembered "nine fighter planes drawn up in a wide semi-circle around the Prime Minister's Flamingo . . . Churchill walked toward the machines, grinning, waving his stick, saying a word or two to each pilot as he went from one to the other, and, as I watched their faces light up and smile in answer to his, I thought they looked like the angels of my childhood. These men may have been naturally handsome, but that morning they were far more than that, creatures of an essence that was not of our world: their expressions of happy confidence as they got ready to ascend into their element, the sky, left me inspired, awed and earthbound."[12]

One of these angels, Flying Officer Gordon "Mouse" Cleaver, remembered that morning somewhat differently.[13] The night before, the Millionaires had become rip-roaring drunk: "There assembled at Villacoublay just about as hungover a crew of dirty, smelly, unshaven, unwashed fighter pilots as I doubt has ever been seen. Willie [Rhodes-Moorehouse] if I remember right was being sick behind his aeroplane, when the Great Man arrived and expressed a desire to meet the escort. We must have appeared vaguely human at least, as he seemed to accept our appearance without comment, and we took off for England."[14]

By June 4, the evacuation of Dunkirk was officially over with an incredible 338,226 Allied troops removed from the beaches to England. Göring's promise that "not a British soldier will escape" had been ludicrous. He had simply been "talking big again" as General Alfred Jodl, Chief of Hitler's General Staff, was quick to point out.[15] In a week of almost constant combat above Dunkirk, the RAF had shot down 132 German planes for a loss of 99 of its own fighters, 5 from Flight Leader Frank Howell's 609 Squadron. It was a remarkable performance, or as Churchill described it to his War Cabinet, "a signal victory which gives cause for high hopes of our successes in the future."[16]

The British Expeditionary Force had been saved by some 693 boats of all sizes, many of them "little ships"—dinghies, pleasure yachts, skiffs, tugboats—a quarter of which were sunk. But now it had nothing to fight with. Almost all the BEF's armor and weapons had been left behind, leaving England practically defenseless. The evacuation of Dunkirk could certainly not be described as a victory, but it was nevertheless a powerful tonic to both the British people and the rest of the free world.

Across the Atlantic, some Americans were as inspired as the British themselves by the "miracle" of Dunkirk. Seeing the possibility of swaying public opinion in favor of outright support for Britain, Foreign Office officials initiated what would become one of the most sophisticated propaganda campaigns ever waged by the British. Churchill himself would soon add his own weight to the effort to convince America to come to Britain's aid. No matter how long Britain held out, he knew the war could not be won without American intervention. President Roosevelt, above all, was his great "star of hope."

One morning that early summer, the prime minister's son, Randolph, found his father shaving at 10 Downing Street, wearing just a silk undershirt that "left nothing to the imagination."

"Sit down, dear boy, and read the papers while I finish shaving," said Churchill.

Randolph did as he was told.

For a few minutes, Churchill scraped away with his Valet razor. "I think I see my way through," he finally said, continuing to shave.

Randolph was amazed. "Do you mean that we can avoid defeat or beat the bastards?"

Churchill tossed his razor into the sink and turned to face his son, towel in hand. "Of course I mean we can beat them."

"Well, I'm all for it, but I don't see how you can do it."

"I shall drag the United States in."[17]

Among the East Coast elites in America, there were already willing accomplices, including several of Roosevelt's intimates and influential newspaper editors. On June 4, the day the Dunkirk evacuation formally ended, a *New York Times* editorial concluded: "So long as the English language survives the word Dunkirk will be spoken of with reverence. For in that harbor, in such a hell as never blazed on earth before, at the end of a lost battle, the rages and blemishes that have hidden the soul of democracy fell away.

There, beaten but not unconquered, in shining splendor, she faced the enemy."[18]

Among America's isolationists, there was no such sentiment. Ambassador Joseph Kennedy and others had predicted annihilation for the British at Dunkirk. He and his fellow pessimists had been wrong, but after Dunkirk they were no less convinced of Britain's imminent defeat. Now America's chief representative turned his energies to getting first his family and then himself out of Britain before the Nazis came knocking at his embassy door. In direct contrast, Churchill seized the moment to inspire the whole nation and steel it for the bitter fight to come, telling Parliament in a speech that was printed on front pages around the globe: "We must be very careful to not to assign to this deliverance the attributes of a victory. Wars are not won by evacuations . . . Even though large tracts of Europe and many old and famous states have fallen and may fall into the grip of the Gestapo and all the odious apparatus of Nazi rule, we shall not flag or fail. We shall go on to the end. We shall fight in France, we shall fight in the seas and oceans, we shall fight with growing confidence and growing strength in the air; we shall defend our island whatever the cost may be."

And then came immortal words, intended for freedom-loving peoples everywhere, and in particular for Americans: "We shall fight on the beaches, we shall fight on the landing grounds, we shall fight in the hills; we shall never surrender; and even if, which I do not for one moment believe, this island or a large part of it were subjected and starving, then our empire beyond the seas, armed and guarded by the British fleet, would carry on the struggle, until, in God's good time, the New World, with all its power and might, steps forward to the rescue and the liberation of the Old."[19]

Meanwhile, in St. Nazaire, three hundred miles or so from the beaches of Dunkirk, Eugene Tobin was trying to find a way to get to Paris as fast as possible so that he could reunite with his friend Andy Mamedoff and Shorty. "Boy, did I learn about red-tape," he recalled. "After a five-hour wrangle with the immigration and customs, I found I still needed a special permit from the Commissariat of Police to travel by train to Paris. Lugging a heavy suitcase and an overloaded knapsack, I walked about five miles, looking for the right Commissariat. There were plenty of them, but each one specialized in something else. The one I wanted I found last, naturally."[20]

Tobin's status of indeterminate nationality was a problem.

"Doesn't Monsieur know what his nationality is?" asked an official.

"Of course. I'm an American."

"Aha, then why does Monsieur not possess an American passport?"

"Because they wouldn't give me one," replied Tobin. "The Neutrality Law doesn't allow it."

"Aha, aha, then Monsieur is not really an American at all. He is nothing."

Tobin had not spent two weeks dodging torpedoes only to be treated like an outlaw by the very people he had come to fight for.

Tobin banged his first on the desk. "Listen!" he shouted. "I've come here to fight for France. I'm a pilot, see? I'm going to fly one of your airplanes. Now give me the permit and let me get out of here right now—tout suite!"[21]

The bureaucrat did not comply: it took another four days before Tobin was issued a travel pass for Paris. Finally, he boarded a train, but after just a couple of hours it shuddered to a halt in Nantes. There would be yet another delay. Then a Red Cross train pulled into the station. Its passengers were wounded French soldiers, many of their faces deathly pale. Me-109s had recently strafed them, honeycombing some compartments with bullet holes. The last three cars in the train had been destroyed beyond recognition. Suddenly, Tobin realized that "there was another reason for being [in France] besides just wanting to fly behind 1000 horsepower."[22]

On June 4, at 6:30 a.m., Eugene Tobin's train finally pulled into the Gare de l'Est in Paris. He had slept badly, having spent the night on a cold platform in Nantes. "I went to a hotel to sleep," he noted in his diary. "Later I found out it was a whore house and for half a day it cost me 100 francs—was I mad . . . Found out where Andy and others are staying and I went to their hotel. I was sure glad to see them. All told there are eight American flyers staying in the hotel. The Germans bombed Paris yesterday and [one] bomb hit 456 feet from our hotel. That's too damn close for comfort. 45 people were killed within a three block radius of the hotel. All the glass is out of the windows around here—10 cars were hit, burnt like matchwood, holes all over the place—it was bad alright . . . Damn those squareheads."[23]

When Tobin spoke with his fellow American flyers at the hotel, he discovered that they were fast running out of patience with the French. "We've been here five days now," said an exasperated Mamedoff, "and every morning we go over to the Ministry and ask, 'How about it?' Then some nice polite officer replies, 'Any day now you are going to fly.' But so far, we haven't even taken a medical. Nuts!"[24]

All they could do was wait while the French Armée de l'Air got its act together. In the meantime, they decided that they might as well try to enjoy Paris, so that night they went to the home of an American correspondent for cocktails. But it was an awkward soirée: they had to be careful not to reveal why they were in France in case the reporter mentioned them in a story and tipped off the FBI.

The next morning, June 5, 1940, there was reason for optimism. Tobin was called into the French Air Ministry, where he passed his physical for entry into the French air force. He then headed out to the racetrack at Longchamps to bet on the horses. It wasn't long before he found himself discussing the war with some of the crowd: a Lithuanian air force captain, a Belgian refugee, and a Russian lawyer. They chatted away in their own languages, but one thing was understood by all. As Tobin put it: "If the allies [are] to win, America must enter the war . . . We won the last war for the [French and British] and we'll win this one for them— no kidding."[25]

That night, the flyers again went in search of fun, ending a drunken tour of the City of Light at the well-stocked bar of the

American Legion club in Paris. According to Tobin, they had a "big drinks fest then home, the boys all got a woman and went to bed."[26]

Then things turned sour. The next afternoon, Andy Mamedoff was arrested while sitting at a café with Tobin and Shorty on the Champs-Elysées. "The police came up and demanded his papers," recalled Tobin. "He showed them, but the police weren't satisfied."[27]

Perhaps his swarthy looks made him look suspicious. Or were the French authorities interested in talking to him about someone he knew back in Thompson, Connecticut? Ironically, given that he was about to fight the Nazis, Mamedoff was on intimate terms with one of most bizarre fascists in American history: his uncle, Count Anastase Vonsiatsky, was the leader of a White Russian supremacist movement that saw in Hitler a chance to return to power and reverse the Russian Revolution. Vonsiatsky had several well-connected followers in Paris, including embittered relatives of the slain Romanovs.

Back in the twenties, Vonsiatsky had jumped from flophouse to flophouse in Paris before latching on to a rich American heiress who was "slumming" in the city for a season, as was then the fashion among the New England elite with artistic pretensions. Twenty years Vonsiatsky's senior, Marion Ream was soon swept off her feet; to her family's outrage, the émigré and the impressionable heiress were quickly married. In 1924, not long after setting up home in Thompson, Connecticut, on a large estate called Nineteenth Hole, Vonsiatsky had invited his older sister Natasha and her husband, Lev Beck Mamedoff, to come join him in Connecticut. It had not been long before the childless Marion and Vonsiatsky began treating the Mamedoffs' only son—thirteen-year-old Andy—as their own.

With Marion's money, Vonsiatsky had given his sister and brother-in-law a new start in life, buying them a nearby 150-year-old farmhouse that the Mamedoffs quickly converted into a popular restaurant named after a famous establishment in St. Petersburg: the Russian Bear.[28] It had prospered throughout the thirties, drawing the likes of actor Alan Ladd and the well-to-do from across New England. Andy had often helped in the kitchen and served his parents' upscale patrons. He had inherited his plump mother's cheerfulness but looked more like his equally charming father, with his squat frame and thick black mustache.

After two hours of questioning, Mamedoff was released. "Oddly enough," recalled Tobin, "Andy wasn't amused."[29] The Americans had now been in Paris for over a week and had yet to hear from the man who had hired them—Colonel Sweeny. Why wasn't he there to help them?

Colonel Sweeny had fought hard to get the French Air Ministry to send his recruits into action. But his efforts had been stymied by infuriating lethargy, disorganization, and crippling bureaucracy. In his long career as a soldier of fortune, he had never been so frustrated. He had once fought against the Germans with the French and been impressed with their tenacity and sacrifice in defeating their invader. Now it seemed as if they were losing heart. And if there was one thing Sweeny couldn't abide, it was a quitter.

From an early age Sweeny had wanted to be a soldier but had been blessed with neither the temperament nor the patience to follow the conventional route. Although accepted into West Point, he had succeeded in being expelled twice from America's most prestigious military college, first aged nineteen for a hazing offense in 1900 and again the following year. "I was expelled for different reasons but I don't care to say what they were," he told *The New Yorker*. "They were glad to get rid of me."[30] Undeterred, he had then embarked on an alternative career as a high-profile mercenary. According to an American pilot called Jim Goodson, who knew Sweeny, his subsequent adventures soon "read like a chapter out of a *Boy's Life* magazine. A hero of freedom uprisings in Mexico, Venezuela and Nicaragua, he had become a colonel in the French Foreign Legion in the First World War and then an aide to the French General Weygand, supporting the Poles against the Russian Bolsheviks in 1920; an adviser to Kemal Ataturk in the Greco-Turkish war of 1922; a French Foreign Legionnaire fighting a Berber revolt in 1925; a military adviser to the Republican forces in the Spanish Civil War in the late 30s."[31]

Now Sweeny was on the run once more. Shortly before his recruits had arrived in Paris, he had been handed a note in the famous Crillon bar warning that, if he stayed in France, he would be tracked down and killed by agents belonging to the Abwehr, Hitler's secret service. It had been no idle threat. Rushing back to his apartment during an air raid a few days later, he had heard the crack of a pistol shot. Thankfully, the bullet had ricocheted off a stone wall a few feet away. After sprinting down a street and losing his would-be assassin, he returned to his apartment, where he had then spent the night pacing back and forth.

Just before dawn, he had peeked out his window and spied two men standing in the shadows, staking out the apartment block. Later that morning, he borrowed some clothes and, pretending to be a crippled old peasant, bent almost double with arthritis, he shuffled out of the apartment block, fooling the agents watching for him.

According to one account, Sweeny then escaped to Spain from France by fishing boat, leaving behind instructions for his pilots to follow him to London.[32] He was also able to arrange for most of them to receive directions through special radio transmitters set up in key cities and even aboard a fishing boat just off the coast of Bordeaux, in southwest France, farthest from the German onslaught. Unfortunately, in the chaos of early June 1940, several of Sweeny's recruits were not contacted. They included Eugene Tobin, Andy Mamedoff, and Vernon Keough.

The situation in Paris had become desperate. On June 10, Tobin and his fellow pilots woke to find a smoke screen blanketing the city. The French had lit fires and set off smoke bombs to shroud beloved quartiers and buildings in the hope of saving them from being destroyed by the Luftwaffe. "There was a feeling of depression and defeat we didn't like at all," recalled Tobin. "The sooner we got into a plane, the better."[33]

Tobin and Shorty, by now cursing the French at every turn,

tried to find a bar where they could get drunk. But almost every business in the city was closed. Back at their hotel, they learned that they would leave the next day, perhaps for a unit farther to the south, where they might finally be given the chance to fly. A harried official at the French Air Ministry added that the entire French government was abandoning Paris for Tours, a hundred miles to the southwest.

"That's fine," said Andy Mamedoff, "but how about some money to pay our hotel bills?"

"We have no funds here to give you," replied the official. "You pay and we'll reimburse you some other time, perhaps. We cannot say. We are busy now. *Au revoir* till Tours."[34]

The next morning, the Americans left their hotel without paying the bill, hailed a cab, and were driven to the Gare de l'Est. The station was a crush of evacuees. None seemed to care where they would end up as long as it was outside Paris, ahead of the German advance. The flyers struggled with their baggage onto a train so crammed with refugees that they were soon standing between cars so they could breathe fresh air. "It is a terrible situation indeed," noted Tobin in his diary. "I have never seen so much sadness in all my life."[35]

Around 1 p.m., they arrived in Tours, the new seat of what was left of the fractured French government. As the train pulled into the station, they heard the sounds of bombing; by now Tours was being pounded by the Luftwaffe on average four times a day. Exhausted and on edge, they finally reached their assigned base, five miles northwest of Tours. "We have very filthy quarters," Tobin jotted in his diary. "The whole French army is disorganized and everybody is lost."[36]

At first light, the Americans explored the base and examined the planes they had been assigned to fly. They were far from impressed. The machines were "old crates," obviously no match for the Luftwaffe's front-line fighters, such as the Messerschmitt Me-109 and Me-110. Other pilots agreed, among them several Czechs and Poles who detested the Germans with an unsettling ferocity.

Again the eternal wait to fly began. Around midday, just as the Americans were sitting down to lunch, they heard the terrifying high-pitched screams of Stukas diving at full speed. A bomb exploded close to the mess. Glass flew everywhere and explosions ripped across runways. As they took cover, the Americans looked up and saw other Stukas circling above, just out of range of the base's woefully inadequate anti-aircraft guns.

Shorty watched one of the Stukas dive almost vertically and open up with its machine guns. Then, out of nowhere it seemed, a French Potez 63 fighter attacked, its pilot firing six bursts of machine-gun bullets at the Stuka and scoring a direct hit. The Americans cheered as the Stuka fell and smashed into the ground in a ball of flame. A few minutes later, smoke from fires and explosions began to drift away, revealing runways pitted with shell holes and the smoldering ruins of the pilots' quarters and the officers' mess.

That night, the Americans were forced to sleep in a ditch. The following morning, as they lay in the sun, wondering what they should do next with just eighty francs between them, they heard the distant drone of German bombers. "Then the bombers came over," recalled Tobin. "About fifty of them, spread out perhaps twenty miles. One of them had a particular yen for our field. The first time he slouched over sort of nonchalantly at 10,000 feet and gave us the business, we stood up to watch him. But he wasn't very accurate. After a while we got used to him. Whenever there was a droning overhead, Shorty would open one eye and say, 'It's only Adolf,' then we'd go back to sleep again."[37]

For three more days, the Americans stayed on, hunkering down each night in their ditch. Shorty could no longer contain his frustration and began to take it out on any Frenchman in a smart uniform—the Americans had yet to be issued even a pair of fresh socks. Several times he marched up to senior French officers and in very bad French loudly demanded to be given a uniform. It was explained that no one was bothering to hand out uniforms anymore, and in any case they didn't come in his size.[38]

On June 13, 1940, as panzers surrounded Paris, the Americans learned that they had at last been cleared to fly. Their assigned "mount," declared a French pilot, would be one of several twin-engine Potez 63s, dispersed at a far corner of the base. On closer examination, it was obvious that the Americans would be lucky to get the single-seat fighter off the ground. "All the instruments in the cockpit of a French plane work backward; that is, all the controls are reversed," recalled Tobin. "The throttle is pulled back toward you for power instead of being pushed away."[39]

The French pilot tried to be reassuring. "We will try and find you some helmets, so that you can fly."[40]

The Americans followed him into a hangar. Thirty seconds later, they heard the now familiar sound of Stukas diving. The Potez 63 they had been assigned took a direct hit.

"Too bad," said the French pilot. "But tomorrow we will get another plane for you. Tomorrow you will fly, certainly."[41]

The Americans were not convinced. "Poor guy, it wasn't his fault," remembered Tobin. "So, just to show him there were no hard feelings, we put the bite on him for 100 francs."[42] After agreeing to spend the money in the best restaurant they could find, by midafternoon they had set off for nearby Tours. It was unfortunate that they did not stay at the airfield for the rest of that afternoon of June 13, 1940. Had they done so, they might have been able to meet the British prime minister, who was on a last-ditch mission to try to convince the French to carry on the fight.

Churchill's plane arrived in a thunderstorm over the pockmarked runway at Tours. With the prime minister that day was General Sir Hastings Ismay, secretary to the War Cabinet. "We landed safely and taxied around craters in search of someone to help us," he recalled. "There was no sign of life, except for groups of French airmen lounging about by the hangars. They did not know who we were, and cared less. The prime minister got out and introduced himself. He said, in his best French, that his name was Churchill, that he was Prime Minister of Great Britain, and that he would be grateful for a *voiture*."[43]

Eventually a car was provided and Churchill was driven to the center of Tours, where he sat down to lunch at the Grand Hotel while he waited for the French premier, Paul Reynaud, who had not yet arrived in the city. It was not long before Churchill was interrupted by the secretary of the French War Cabinet, Paul Baudouin. To Churchill's disgust, Baudouin talked solemnly of throwing in the towel while decent terms might still be negotiated.

After lunch, Churchill was driven to the local prefecture, but Reynaud was still nowhere to be found. The afternoon dragged on, Churchill's aides growing ever more concerned: the airfield at Tours had no lights, and takeoff with so many craters in the runway would be impossible after dark. At last Reynaud arrived and led Churchill to an office on the first floor of the prefecture, where he then broke the depressing news that his government would soon ask the Germans for an armistice. Could France be released from an earlier pledge not to negotiate a separate peace with Germany? According to one source, "tears streamed down Mr. Churchill's face" as Reynaud spoke.[44]

Churchill said he would have to confer with his War Cabinet colleagues and left Reynaud seated, solemn faced, behind a desk. In the prefecture's garden, Churchill discussed Reynaud's request with Lord Beaverbrook, the dynamic Canadian press magnate he had appointed to his War Cabinet, and Lord Halifax, his foreign secretary. Half an hour later, Churchill was again facing Reynaud. The answer was no. Reynaud must hold out.

"Is another week possible, or less?" asked Churchill.[45]

Reynaud made no reply.

There was one last hope—America. At the very least, pleaded Churchill, could the French not hold out until President Roosevelt made it clear where America stood? If America entered the war, the defeatists in Reynaud's cabinet would be silenced: there would be hope of eventually gaining victory, just as in the last war. Reluctantly, Reynaud promised that the French would not approach the Germans until Churchill had received an unequivocal answer from President Roosevelt. It was also agreed that in the meantime the French would hand over to the British four hundred Luftwaffe prisoners, most of them downed pilots such as Werner Mölders.[46]

Time was growing short if Churchill was to get back to the airfield in daylight. As he prepared to leave, Churchill saw General Charles de Gaulle standing in a doorway. Of all France's military leaders, de Gaulle had impressed him most with his determination to fight on, no matter the cost. Here was a man with the backbone so many of his countrymen lacked. Churchill caught his eye as he passed him and muttered: "*L'homme du destin* [the man of destiny]." And so it would prove.

A few minutes later, Churchill was seated beside Reynaud as they were driven back to the airfield outside Tours. "Don't give in, don't go over to the enemy," Churchill begged before parting. "Fight on!"[47]

It was late afternoon when the British prime minister's plane bounced along a rutted strip of grass under gray storm clouds and then lifted into the air. When he arrived back in London, Churchill cabled President Roosevelt as he had promised Reynaud, warning that: "If we go down you may have a United States of Europe under Nazi command far more numerous, far stronger, far better armed than the New World."[48] But it was to no avail: Roosevelt declined to come to Britain and France's aid. No American president in his right mind could suddenly take an isolationist, pitifully armed country to war at the drop of a hat, however much he sympathized and indeed agonized over the Old World's fate.

That evening of June 13, a deeply troubled Churchill drank champagne and tucked into jellied chicken and fresh strawberries with his family at Admiralty House. Four years would pass before he would see his beloved France again.

Back in Tours, in a small family-run restaurant, Eugene Tobin and his fellow flyers gorged on their first decent meal in a week and quaffed two-franc brandy.

Tobin recognized a couple of Czech pilots from their base at the next table.

"You will pardon us," one of them said, "but we realize you are in the same position as ourselves. We, too, have been waiting around for weeks to go into action. We think the French have lost heart for the war. But we have a scheme."

Their plan was to steal two Potez 63 planes and then hightail it across the Channel to England, where they would join the RAF. They intended to seize the planes at first light.

"You run two risks," the other Czech officer added. "One, the anti-aircraft guns may hit us if they get the alarm quickly—but that is doubtful. The other and more likely risk is that we might be chased by fighters. But we can avoid that if we get off the ground quickly and climb to fifteen or twenty thousand feet."[49]

Tobin looked at Mamedoff and Shorty.

"Sounds all right to us."[50]

Early the following morning, a Czech pilot crouched over Eugene Tobin and shook him awake. The silhouettes of two Potez 63 planes, several hundred yards in the distance, were just visible.

"My friend and I will run out and get into the planes first," whispered the Czech. "Give us about three minutes to get them primed up and ready. Then, when we start the motors, you can run out, pull the chocks from under the wheels, and jump in."[51]

Tobin watched as the Czech and his friend ran out to the planes. "They hadn't gone more than a hundred yards," he recalled, "when suddenly there was the sharp bark of a rifle, then another. One of the Czechs stumbled and fell. The other turned and ran back. As he knelt down, waving frantically at us to run, there was another shot and he slumped over the body of his friend. Then three soldiers crawled out from under the planes and advanced toward them with their rifles ready for action."

The Americans scrambled on all fours for several yards and then sprinted toward nearby woods, but before reaching them French guards opened fire. Bullets whistled through the air, gouging holes in the airfield perimeter. The Americans kept on running, through the woods and beyond, until they were out of breath. Thankfully, there was no sound or sign of pursuit: the guards must have given up and returned to examine the men they had killed. "We rested awhile, then sauntered over to the commandant's office, trying to look nonchalant," recalled Tobin. "There was plenty going on, they told us there. Fifty German soldiers dressed in Czech uniforms had tried to ambush the airport guard and set the planes on fire. The guards had driven them off after killing two officers. Also, German armored cars had been reported within a few miles of Tours. The station was being evacuated at once. As for us, we'd just have to get down to the south as best we could."[52]

There was even worse news. All of Paris was now in German hands. Earlier that morning, German General Fedor von Bock, the commander of Army Group B, had stood before two divisions of German storm troopers in the Place de la Concorde and made the "Heil Hitler" salute. In the distance, a swastika flew from the top of the Eiffel Tower. Signs declaring *Man Spricht Deutsch* [German Spoken Here] were already pasted on the entrances to bars and brothels across Paris.

The Americans began to walk south through Tours. That night, they slept in a hayloft. The next day, they traipsed seventeen miles on sore and blistered feet. "In every town they went to, Andy found a French girl he wanted to marry," recalled Harry Watts, a film director who would soon befriend the pilots. "And all the time [Tobin], the imperturbable, would act as general provider. What he couldn't scrounge he'd wheedle, using a weird combination of signs, grins, and bad French, even once throwing in a song and dance routine as good measure. He always got what he wanted."[53]

Finally, on June 17, 1940, the Americans arrived in the small town of Arcay in southwest France, three men among a throng of tens of thousands of refugees and countless deserters from the French army. In the town square, they learned that the French government had given up the fight. An armistice would soon be signed.

France had fallen in less than six weeks to the German onslaught. Britain now stood alone. "We shall do our best to be worthy of this high honor," declared Churchill in a short radio broadcast. "We shall defend our Island home, and with the British Empire we shall fight on unconquerable until the curse of Hitler is lifted from the brows of mankind."[54]

The following day, June 18, 1940, Churchill appeared before a packed House of Commons. Big Ben tolled midday as the prime minister rose to address his peers. After urging them not to seek scapegoats for the disaster in France, he stated that it would now be the RAF's pilots who would have the "glory of saving their native land, their island home, and all they love, from the most deadly of all attacks."

"What General Weygand called the Battle of France is over," continued Churchill before a deeply subdued House. "I expect that the Battle of Britain is about to begin . . . The whole fury and might of the enemy must very soon be turned on us. Hitler knows that he will have to break us in this island or lose the war . . . Let us therefore brace ourselves to our duties, and so bear ourselves that, if the British Empire and Commonwealth last for a thousand years, men will say, 'This was their finest hour.'"[55]

Back in Arcay that afternoon of June 18, 1940, Andy Mamedoff suddenly saw a French armored car speed down the main street. Its driver pointed behind him.

"*Le Boche!*" he shouted. "*Le Boche!*"[56]

The Germans were coming.

There was pandemonium for several minutes, but then it was announced that the Germans were indeed close but still several miles away. The driver of the armored car was a collaborator, spreading panic to aid the German advance. Knowing now that they were at most an hour or two ahead of the Nazis, the Americans rushed to the town's station and squeezed aboard the first train to leave, a freight carrying soldiers and supplies.[57] Legs aching, they lay down on a boxcar floor only to discover that it was covered in a thick yellow dust, which soon coated their dirty clothes, clogged their nostrils, and dyed their hair. "We got to keep moving or we'll be cooked pigeons," Tobin jotted in his diary. "And I ain't kidding. The car we are in has [a metallic powder] in it from its last trip and it sure is terrible stuff. It puts a terrible taste in your mouth and makes you sneeze like hell, your chest feels tight as a drum and it completely ruined all our clothing. I have never lived under such filthy conditions in my life."[58]

The next day, the agonies continued. "We're still on this damned train," Tobin wrote. "We travel about 15 minutes out of every three hours. The tracks are packed with trains and that's why it's so slow. We're traveling in *Grapes of Wrath* style—no clean clothes. Very little food and practically no water. It's really terrible but a damn good experience and I'll never forget it. All of the French soldiers are discouraged and the morale of the whole train is terrible. Bordeaux, our final destination, was terribly bombed yesterday. Everybody is griping like hell. I sure would like to hear something encouraging for a change."[59]

The one thing the Americans were not short of was cigarettes, and they chain-smoked to calm their nerves as the hellish journey continued, stubbing out their butts on sacks filled with the irritating yellow powder.

Suddenly, a Frenchman cried for them to stop smoking.

The yellow powder was dynamite.[60]

On June 22, 1940, the train finally arrived in Bordeaux, where the Americans managed to hitch a lift on a truck to St. Jean de Luz, a port not far from the Spanish border. Thousands of panicked families choked the town, trying to escape on one of the last boats out of France. Evacuees were dumping their bicycles, carts, and even trucks into the harbor or setting fire to them so the Boche couldn't make use of them. Mothers sobbed as they handed their children to relatives who had managed to secure passage to North Africa or England. For others, time was fast running out if they were to avoid a concentration camp.

Several hundred miles to the northeast, the most powerful Nazis in the Third Reich stood in a railway carriage deep in the forest of Compiègne. In 1918, the vanquished leaders of Germany had gathered in the same carriage, which had been preserved and kept at the same spot to commemorate French victory. Now Adolf Hitler, wearing a dark brown uniform and an Iron Cross on his chest, Foreign Minister Joachim von Ribbentrop, and Luftwaffe Chief Hermann Göring watched in glee as ashen-faced French representatives signed a new armistice and then bowed to their new Führer, the master of Europe at last.

PART TWO

Duel of Eagles

When you come right down to it, flying a fighter in combat is just about the greatest game in the world—even if you are playing for keeps. You're up there patrolling. Suddenly you sight those silvery specks coming toward you from across the Channel. You hold them for an instant framed in the circle of your gunsight against a background of blue sky. You can't help admiring the picture made by those 300 planes in tight formations. Then you remember those boys aren't out for a ride and you start climbing to get above them. From then on, as the old saying goes, you don't have to be crazy, but it helps.[1]

Eugene "Red" Tobin

4. Per Ardua ad Astra

Always a flamboyant young man, Billy named his sled Satan
and outfitted his teammates with yellow turtleneck sweaters.
A few days before the competition was to begin, Fiske added
another flourish. Each of the members appeared at a practice
session with a single letter sewn to the back of his sweater,
spelling out the name SATAN. This was too much for
US Olympic officials. After threats of barring the team,
Billy agreed to wear the official American Olympic uniform,
and to rechristen his sled USA II.[1]

Bud Greenspan, "He Was Absolutely Fearless"

All morning they shivered on the dockside in St. Jean de Luz
as a gale blew in from the Bay of Biscay. Finally, Eugene
Tobin, Andy Mamedoff, and Shorty Keough lost patience, pushed
past guards, and clambered aboard a large ship called the *Baron
Nairn*. Shorty was almost blown into the water, so fierce was the
wind, as he jumped down onto the main deck.

Tobin looked at his watch as the *Baron Nairn* sailed. It was 1:15
p.m. on June 23, 1940, as the British-registered boat's crew cast off
her moorings and the *Baron Nairn* began to steam out of the
harbor, the last ship containing refugees to leave defeated France.
An hour or so later, Tobin again pushed through a crowd of refugees,
this time to attend an impromptu Mass. By the grace of God, he
had escaped the Nazis just in time: less than two hours after the
Baron Nairn left port, the Germans seized St. Jean de Luz.

The *Baron Nairn* steamed out into the Bay of Biscay and turned
southwest, farther and farther into the blustery Atlantic, and then
north toward England through ever heavier seas. Conditions

aboard were horrendous: three thousand people filled every
gangway and deck on a boat designed to carry only a few dozen
sailors. There were just four lifeboats, which meant that if a
U-boat attacked, almost all aboard would drown. "It was plenty
rough and cold," remembered Tobin. "Nearly everyone was seasick.
The second day out we had our first meal, consisting of a dog
biscuit and a cup of some sort of dishwater. It was hot and it
might have been anything. We drank it out of a cold-cream
container borrowed from a woman passenger. I couldn't swallow
the biscuit, and as an experiment I offered it to the only dog
aboard. He turned it down."[2]

After forty-eight hellish hours, early on June 25, 1940, they
arrived in Plymouth, England. "What a difference in morale!"
Tobin noted. "The army and navy were disciplined and the civilians calm and businesslike . . . There were none of the signs of
fear and panic we had learned to spot in France."[3] They had
arrived in a country bonded as never before in its determination
to avoid becoming yet another slave state in the Greater Third
Reich. There was no doubting that the Germans would be resisted.
Some were actually looking forward to the invasion, so great was
their desire to avenge the humiliation of the BEF in France.

From Plymouth, the Americans took a train to London and then
went to the U.S. Embassy. "They had vague ideas that they might
be treated as heroes," recalled their friend, the film director Harry
Watts. "Instead they were treated as civil servants treat adventurers
the world over. They were classified as 'Distressed American Nationals'
and ordered home. When they talked about fighting they were
blasted by phrases like 'jeopardising neutrality.'"[4]

Eugene Tobin's twenty-two-year-old sister, Helen Maher, would
soon receive a letter from her brother explaining in detail what
happened at the embassy. "He wrote me that the American
Embassy gave him a bad time in London," she later recalled.
"The American Ambassador, Joseph Kennedy, was not a bit sympathetic. The only thing the Embassy wanted was to get them out
of England. Instead of helping Gene, the officials told him they
were going to put him on a boat back to America."[5]

Just a fortnight before, the U.S. Embassy had informed the four thousand Americans who had not already fled Britain that they should return immediately to America via neutral Ireland, adding that this might be their last chance before the Nazis invaded. Many had chosen to leave. Notably, seventy had done the opposite and formed the First American Squadron of the Home Guard, and were now wearing a British Home Guard uniform with a red eagle shoulder patch. True to form, Ambassador Kennedy was disgusted by this display of "militant Anglo-American solidarity," and warned one of its officers that the unit "might lead to all United States citizens being shot as francs-tireurs [mercenaries] when the Germans occupied London."[6]

Tobin, Mamedoff, and Shorty were issued travel passes to Ireland, from where they would be shipped home to America. To delay what felt like deportation, Tobin made an excuse about needing to get hold of his birth certificate because he had no passport. Ignoring the embassy's instruction to leave England, the three Americans flyers headed straight to the British Air Ministry. "The way we figured it, the RAF ought to be willing to take us on," recalled Tobin. "It looked as though they were going to need every pilot they could get before long."[7]

Tobin was right. The Battle of France had cost the RAF 435 pilots. Fighter Command was now 360 short of its full strength, officially stated as 1,450 pilots. Churchill was in fact so worried by this shortage that he had ordered pilots be culled from other services and headquarters to plug the gap. Even so, the British remained outnumbered almost five to one. Britain had 48 squadrons of 754 Hurricanes and Spitfires [roughly 16 planes to a squadron] against the Luftwaffe's 1,464 fighter planes and 1,808 bombers.[8]

Again, the Americans were out of luck. "We cannot possibly use you now, as you have had no combat training," an Air Ministry official told them. "We would suggest you go back and apply in Canada."[9]

"Well, I guess it's the RAF's loss," said Shorty bitterly. "If they don't want to win the war—okay, we'll go home."[10]

But not just yet. They had one last hope, or as Tobin put it:

"There was only one ace left in the deck ... On the boat coming over we'd met an English lady who told us to look up a certain member of Parliament [MP] if we ran into any difficulties." The name of that MP, which Tobin did not disclose at the time to protect his identity, was Roland "Robbie" Robinson, a member of the Conservative party who had apparently helped other foreign-born pilots get into the RAF. "They came [out of the embassy] into the street feeling pretty sick," recalled Harry Watts. "But they'd heard about [Robinson] so the three American kids, who only wanted to fight and fly against the Germans, and who had found it the most difficult job of their lives, went up to a London bobby [policeman] and asked him if he knew a place called the House of Parliament. And the bobby, in his tin hat and gas-mask, looked at their tattered and dirty store clothes and no doubt thought it was a funny time and way to sight-see, but he directed them."[11]

At the House of Commons, the Americans managed to track down Robinson, who arranged for them to be interviewed by a contact of his in the Air Ministry. They impressed the official and were soon being quizzed politely by an RAF recruiting officer.

Tobin was asked how many hours he had flown.

More than 2,000, he lied. In fact, he had 540 hours solo.[12]

Did Tobin have a logbook?

"I was in the French Air Corps," Tobin answered. "I had to leave everything—my logbook, my uniform, even my stopwatch—in France."[13]

A few days later, they pledged their allegiance to Britain's sovereign, King George VI, no easy thing for any patriotic American to do given that Americans had won their independence from King George III. Then they were formally sworn into the Royal Air Force. They were now committed to fighting for the British for the "duration of hostilities."[14] And they had effectively forfeited their citizenship to do so. According to the 1907 U.S. Citizenship Act, "any American citizen shall be deemed to have expatriated himself . . . when he has taken an oath of allegiance to any foreign state."[15] But to the Americans it seemed a fair trade: their nationality for membership in "the best flying club in the world" and the chance to fly a Spitfire.[16]

Unlike the French Armée de l'Air, the RAF wasted no time. They were soon being fitted with dark blue uniforms—the first they had ever worn. And then they set off to find somewhere to have a celebratory drink. As they sauntered through the heart of London, finally feeling like pilots again, they came across an RAF squadron leader. The Americans saluted for the first time, but the squadron leader looked annoyed. "I guess [the salute] looked more like a 'Hiya, pal,' than a good snappy military salute," recalled Tobin.

The squadron leader eyed the three of them suspiciously and then asked to see their identity papers. He was most perplexed by four-foot-ten Shorty Keough.

"What is he?" he asked. "A mascot?"

"Mascot!" replied Shorty. "I'm a pilot, you mug . . . I mean, sir."[17]

Thankfully, the squadron leader had a sense of humor.

Before being posted to a training course, the Americans dined in London with twenty-eight-year-old Charles Sweeny, Colonel Sweeny's London-based nephew. The younger Sweeny belonged to the First American Squadron of the Home Guard that had drawn Ambassador Joseph Kennedy's ire.[18] The Americans would eventually meet several other blatantly Anglophile compatriots, such as the burly, Brooklyn-born Quentin Reynolds of *Collier's* magazine, Scotty Reston of the *New York Times*, and the ebullient Harry Watts, who would direct the 1942 Hollywood film, *Eagle Squadron*.

Watts would vividly recall the three American volunteers: "They were handsome young animals with curly hair and magnificent teeth who talked a lot in a vivid, cynical vernacular that belied the sentimentality beneath. Andy was massive and broad. A Russian type with pale blue eyes in a puckish Mongol face. Shorty was a tiny dynamo with a shock of fair hair and an Irish temperament. Red was, perhaps, the most typical young American of the three. Tall and lanky, he had a grin that split his face in two, and a devastating vocabulary of wisecracks that was the delight of his friends and the despair of his seniors."[19]

On July 9, 1940, just a fortnight after arriving in England, the Americans were given rigorous physical tests and then informed they were to go without delay to Advanced Training Unit Number 7, at RAF Hawarden, near the port city of Liverpool. Finally, they were going to get back into the air. "Well, we'd made it!" recalled Tobin. "We were in at last!'[20]

Tobin, Mamedoff, and Keough had arrived in England just in time to fight in the Battle of Britain. But they were not the first from America to cross the Atlantic and enlist with the RAF. That distinction belonged to one of the most remarkable sportsmen in Olympic history: twenty-seven-year-old, two-time gold-medal winner, William Meade Fiske III.

Born on June 4, 1911, in Brooklyn, New York, the son of a wealthy banker whose ancestors came from English aristocracy, Fiske attended grade school in Chicago before moving with his family to France in 1924. He was then educated in Paris, spending summers in Biarritz and Christmas vacations in St. Moritz, the exclusive winter resort, where he learned to ski and then earned a reputation as a spectacularly precocious and cool-headed driver of the bobsled. At just sixteen, he won a place on the U.S. Olympic team, and on February 18, 1928, in one of the most thrilling finals of all time, he made international headlines by driving USA II to victory, becoming the youngest male to win a gold medal in the Winter Games. It would be 64 years before Fiske's record would fall—to Finnish ski jumper Toni Nieminen at the 1992 Albertville Games. Nieminen was just a day younger than Fiske had been.

At the Lake Placid Winter Games in 1932, Fiske carried the Stars and Stripes for the Americans at the opening ceremonies, presided over by Governor Franklin D. Roosevelt of New York. And he again led America to Olympic gold, doing so with chivalry and style. When the two German bobsleds at Lake Placid were involved in a stunning crash that destroyed both and injured some of the German crew, Fiske arranged for the Germans to be lent sleds while repairs were made.[21] He even went so far as to recruit a couple of German-Americans to stand in for the injured German team members.

By the time he graduated from Cambridge University with a degree in economics and history, Fiske was very much a European sophisticate—handsome, debonair, and sought after by Europe's classiest debutantes. After traveling extensively, particularly in the South Pacific, he decided to try his luck in Hollywood. In 1934, he co-produced the moderately successful *White Heat*, starring Virginia Cherrill, the fiancée of actor Cary Grant, and began to get a reputation as a ladies' man. According to one biographer, Grant suspected that Virginia was having an affair with Fiske and paid the operators at the Beverly Hills hotel to listen in on Fiske's calls to Cherrill.[22] It was also in Hollywood that Fiske learned to fly. One night in 1935, he and a fellow Cambridge graduate, twenty-one-year-old South African Charles Patrick Green, went to a screening of the movie *China Clipper* and were so inspired by its story of the quest to set up the first transpacific airline that they decided to take flying lessons. Fiske's first solo flight several weeks later was along the Pacific coast in an old Fleet biplane.[23]

In January 1936, Fiske returned to St. Moritz to win the famous Grand National championship on the legendary Cresta Run. To many people's surprise, he did not compete for a third gold medal at that winter's Olympic Games in nearby Bavaria, the birthplace of the Nazi movement. According to fellow Olympic medalist Irving Jaffe, he stayed away for political reasons: "Way back in 1932, after the Lake Placid Games, Billy was talking to me about his hatred for Adolf Hitler. Almost every day he would tell me how important it was that he won in Lake Placid, because that would be his last Olympics. He didn't want to compete in front of Hitler. When the United States Olympic Committee insisted he enter the trials, Billy had a graceful way of saying 'nothing doing.'"

The following winter of 1937–38, Fiske again broke several of his own speed records on the Cresta Run at St. Moritz. "As a

Cresta stylist," wrote one seasoned observer of the sport, "he was a joy to watch, taking the banks at the highest speed in perfect curves without the trace of a skid, and apparently without effort . . . Described as 'the right build, strong, safe, with great judgment and a wonderful starter,' he was a hero to everyone."[24] When not cementing his reputation that winter as the King of Speed—the title given to him on a celebratory cigarette card because of his record as the greatest bobsled champion of his generation—Fiske befriended several wealthy young Englishmen who belonged to White's Club in London and to the British Olympic skiing team: William Clyde, Gordon "Mouse" Cleaver, Max Aitken, Willie Rhodes-Moorehouse, and Roger Bushell. Like Fiske, they enjoyed dangerous sports and fast cars, but their greatest passion was for flying: all had already trained to be pilots and belonged to 601 Squadron, otherwise known as the County of London Auxiliary Air Force Squadron.

To a man, the Englishmen believed that the policy of appeasement had failed to contain a resurgent Germany and, notably, to prevent Hitler from amassing a vast new air force whose existence directly contravened the Versailles Peace Treaty. It seemed inevitable that they would see action as fighter pilots within the next few years. "If and when it breaks," Fiske told them, "I want to be in it with you—from the start."[25]

Following the Munich crisis in late 1938, Fiske hoped that the fast-rearming RAF would allow him to fly with his friends in 601 Squadron as a reservist, or weekend flyer, and he applied to join them. Unfortunately, his own country's recently passed neutrality laws made it illegal for him to serve in any British armed service. The RAF's official response was that "it was not yet in the interests of Britain to enlist American citizens."[26]

Bitterly disappointed, Fiske returned late in 1938 to New York and took a job with his father's company, the stockbrokers Dillon Read. By coincidence, Fiske's skiing friend from 601 Squadron, William Clyde, was working that winter in nearby New Jersey as a corporate pilot, and he and Fiske stayed in touch, often discussing the growing likelihood of war in Europe. It was Clyde who told

Fiske in August 1939 that he and 601's other reservists had been called up to active service. Soon after, the State Department announced that French and British visas on American passports would become invalid if war broke out.

Determined now to pass himself off as a Canadian to circumvent U.S. neutrality laws, Fiske cleared his desk at Dillon Read and booked passage with Clyde to England on the *Aquitania*. He left New York on September 1, 1939, the day that the Nazis invaded Poland. By the time the *Aquitania* docked in Southampton four days later, Britain was at war and its Royal Air Force had launched its first successful strike on the German navy.

Fiske then lost no time in reaching a British contact from the St. Moritz Tobogganing Club, Ben Bathurst, who promised to lobby several senior RAF officials on his behalf. A fortnight later, Bathurst came through: an interview was arranged with Wing Commander William Elliot, a forty-four-year-old World War I fighter pilot and now an assistant secretary to the War Cabinet. In his diary, Fiske noted that he "would have to make a very passable pretense at being a Canadian and of Canadian parentage. Having no identification papers other than an American passport, which was of no use at all, I had to make up some very watertight answers for any questions they might be expected to ask me."[27]

Before the make-or-break meeting with Elliot, Fiske played a round of golf to give himself "a healthy look . . . Needless to say, for once, I had a quiet Saturday night—I didn't want to have eyes looking like blood-stained oysters the next day."[28] Elliot was impressed and Fiske was formally admitted into the RAF on September 18, 1939. With just ninety hours solo in his logbook, he was posted to No. 10 Elementary Flying Training School in Wiltshire, southwest of London. In his diary, he wrote proudly: "I believe I can lay claim to being the first US citizen to join the RAF in England after the outbreak of hostilities."[29]

Fiske and his fellow trainees were a remarkably diverse group drawn from the far corners of the British Empire.[30] One of twelve New Zealanders on the course was a shepherd who, in Fiske's words, tried to bolster his confidence before flying "by whistling to his aircraft the way he did to his sheep in far away New Zealand."[31] Others were dangerously inexperienced: not long after his first solo flight on October 27, 1939, in a Harvard Trainer, Fiske was almost killed by a French-Canadian member of his "International Flight" who had agreed to rendezvous with him at four thousand feet to perform some basic maneuvers. "We met up all right—nearly head-on," wrote Fiske. "His idea, apparently, is that it doesn't matter how hard your wings hit each other as long as the motors themselves don't come into contact!"[32]

Another recruit, twenty-year-old Hugh Millar, recalled that Fiske was popular among his fellow pilots and respected because of his sporting achievements, especially on the Cresta Run. And he showed leadership skills within weeks of beginning the course. Fiske, Millar, and their fellow trainees had come to England to join as commissioned officers. "But then there was a ruling that none of us would be allowed to enter the RAF as an officer—we all had to be sergeants," explained Millar. "Billy and a bunch of Canadians said: 'Hey, you can't do this! We came over here to be officers. We don't want to be sergeants.' Billy then organized a meeting with a senior RAF official. The ruling was soon reversed."[33]

The bitterly cold weather that winter had grounded many training flights, so it wasn't until April 12, 1940, that Fiske gained his wings and became Acting Pilot Officer Fiske. According to one contemporary, he was now very much "the golden boy . . . good looks, wealth, charm, intelligence . . . he had it all. He was very American, but completely international at the same time. The English loved him, and he loved them . . . With his background it was natural that he 'got fighters,' and that he managed to get himself posted to 601 (Auxiliary) Squadron—known as the Millionaires' Squadron because of all the well-to-do pilots."[34]

One other American arrived in Britain just in time to fight in the Battle of Britain. Altogether different from Billy Fiske, though no less remarkable, twenty-seven-year-old Arthur Gerald Donahue had crossed the Atlantic that July to fight for England, believing it was his God-given mission to defeat the forces of Nazism, or what he preferred to call barbarism. A soft-spoken, Irish Catholic teetotaler, he had grown up in southeast Minnesota at the height of the Depression and had been cultivating corn on his family's dairy farm just days before leaving for Britain.

Flying and everything related to it had fast consumed Donahue as a boy. One school friend remembered him fitting an old apple box with flimsy wings and sitting in it, his imagination lifting him to the skies. Another noticed his superb eyesight, especially at night, when Donahue would sometimes shoot hoops in an unlit barn during the winter. At age fifteen, Donahue befriended a charismatic local pilot called Max Conrad, who had broken several long-distance records. Recognizing Donahue's passion for flying and potential, Conrad agreed to give him free flying lessons at an airfield in Winona, Minnesota. He later remembered his pupil's first solo flight at age sixteen: "We [Conrad and his girlfriend] got Art to take us to Rochester in a dual control plane and I threw out my control and put him on his own. He made a perfect cross-country flight and probably one of the best landings of his life, and I complimented him on it. He was sweating profusely. Art hadn't wanted to fly yet. He is a perfectionist, and didn't think he was perfect yet."[35]

After seriously considering the priesthood, Donahue had vowed to friends and family that flying would be his life, his only career. And so it proved to be. At nineteen, Donahue became Minnesota's youngest qualified commercial pilot. By the mid-thirties, he was helping Conrad run a flight-training school and scraping enough together as a mechanic and part-time truck driver to keep his first plane in the air. He also worked in Laredo, Texas, as an instructor for a while, and all across Minnesota as a barnstormer, landing anywhere that a small crowd gathered, be it a rutted field near a county fair or beside a work camp on payday.

As soon as war broke out in Europe, Donahue considered going to England to join the RAF: "I felt that this was America's war as much as England's and France's, because America was part of the world which Hitler and his minions were so plainly out to conquer."[36] But not wanting to worry his parents, he applied

instead to join the United States Army Air Corps Reserve. Rejected
after months of bureaucratic delay, he headed for Canada, where
in June 1940, according to a relative, "he was offered, and accepted,
a job in England to supervise the assembly of American planes
being shipped over, test-fly them, and instruct British pilots in
their operation."[37]

Ten days later, Donahue was aboard a passenger liner, painted
a dull gray to protect it from U-boat attack. After an uneventful
crossing, he arrived in Liverpool on July 7, 1940: a dreary, over-
cast Sunday that felt more like winter than summer.[38] Then he
took a train to London and was soon wandering in the blackout
around a defiant city that was still the heart of a British Empire
encompassing the globe. "There were a few very dim stop and
go lights, and here and there dim blue lights marking the entrances
to air-raid shelters," he later wrote. "These and the little lights of
cars, the glowing cigarette tips, and an occasional dimmed flash-
light were the only breaks in the darkness . . . Far overhead the
silvery barrage balloons hung silent and motionless, like sentinels.
The raids hadn't begun then, nor the devastation, but every one
knew they were coming; and London impressed me so much
with its greatness and beauty as it stood awaiting its trial, prepared
and unafraid."[39]

Throughout London, this courage and composure could be seen.
At train stations, mothers held back tears as they said good-bye
to their gas-mask-carrying children, who were being evacuated
to the country. Middle-aged veterans of the last war's bloodbaths
calmly picked up shovels and filled sandbags that soon scarred
Hyde Park. On the tiled walls of underground stations, patriotic
posters had been hastily pasted: "*Your* courage—*Your* cheerfulness—*Your* resolution—WILL BRING US VICTORY."

All of it profoundly moved Art Donahue, so much so that he
was prepared to die to protect and preserve it. "To fight side by
side with these people would be the greatest of privileges," he
explained. "Inquiries revealed that the way was wide open. I could
probably get where the fighting was heaviest if I wished. So in a
fateful moment on the day after my arrival, I held my pen poised

and then signed on the dotted line. I thereby surrendered my independence for the duration of the war. I also presumed that I was surrendering my citizenship, for I understood that the law was so interpreted at that time."[40]

As Art Donahue signed on the dotted line, his compatriot Billy Fiske was making final preparations to join 601 Squadron. At last he could call himself a fighter pilot, if yet untested. He had gained his wings. But others now had something very different in mind for the famous American: Fiske was already being touted by Lord Lothian, the British ambassador in Washington, and by others looking to undermine American neutrality, as an extraordinary asset. In their eyes, his celebrity was now a far more potent weapon than any plane he might fly. If they had their way, Pilot Officer Billy Fiske would not be sitting in a Spitfire's cockpit any time soon. He was far too valuable to waste in combat.

On July 11, 1940, the day before he was due to join 601 Squadron, Fiske was summoned to the Air Ministry in London for a meeting with no less than Air Minister Sir Archibald Sinclair, a close confidant of Winston Churchill and wily veteran of trench warfare.[41] Would Fiske be willing to go on a propaganda tour of the U.S.? It seemed that Fiske was in a double bind. If he refused to do what Sinclair wanted, his career in the RAF would surely be doomed and he would be barred from joining his friends in 601 Squadron. But if he accepted and returned to America, he could then be arrested for breaking neutrality laws and be out of the war for good.

"I've done nothing yet," said Fiske. "Why should the [American people] want to see me? Wait until I've shot down some Heinkels. Then, if you still want me to go, I'll go over."[42]

To Fiske's relief, Sinclair agreed that Lothian's propaganda campaign in America would be better served by a pilot who had actually seen combat. And so, on July 13, 1940, Billy Fiske joined 601 Squadron at RAF Tangmere, a bucolic airfield on the south coast at the front line of Britain's air defense system. Tangmere was also home to 43 Squadron, making it one of Fighter

Command's busiest bases, with sometimes more than a hundred sorties launched each day.

At all times during daylight at Tangmere, Hurricanes were positioned nose-to-wind, their engines revved every hour or so to keep them warm between sorties. The first fighters to break the 300 mph barrier back in 1935, these mainstays of RAF Fighter Command had been designed by Englishman Sydney Camm, who had fought tooth and nail to get them into production but tragically died before he could see how effective they were in combat. Wonderfully sturdy gun platforms, they now outnumbered less resilient but more elegant Spitfires by three to one.

Billy Fiske arrived at Tangmere with "no pretensions or illusions" and just in time: the Battle of Britain had officially started only three days before, on July 10, 1940, with major attacks on British shipping in the English Channel and its ports.[43] Intensely competitive by nature, Fiske was raring to join 601 in combat. But to go operational, he would first have to pass muster with 601's squadron leader, Max Aitken, son of Lord Beaverbrook, the Minister of Aircraft Production. Aitken had misgivings about "the untried American adventurer," as did other 601 stalwarts, including twenty-six-year-old Flying Officer Jack Riddle, whose brother Hugh also flew with 601: "When we heard that the whiz kid from America was coming over to the squadron, we wondered: 'Is he going to tell us how to fly airplanes and how to shoot down Germans?'"[44]

Soon after his arrival at RAF Tangmere, Fiske moved into a charming manor house near the base with his glamorous twenty-six-year-old wife, Rose Bingham, the "prettiest titled lady" in England according to the press.[45] The Fiskes had fallen for each other in St. Moritz in December 1937. Billy had been at the peak of his bobsledding career. Rose had been at her most beguiling and risqué, brows plucked and arched perfectly, dark brown hair tucked impishly beneath a ski cap as she cut back and forth across the trails.

Rose Bingham was certainly no innocent when she met Billy, having scandalized London by leaving her wealthy husband, the

Earl of Warwick, and their one-year-old son to pursue an acting career in Hollywood. In September 1938, less than a year after losing custody of her son in a bitter divorce case, she and Billy were married. The nuptials were reported in society pages around the world, and among the hundreds of guests were Fiske's friends from 601. Almost two years later, three now remained with the squadron at Tangmere: Gordon "Mouse" Cleaver, William Clyde, and Willie Rhodes-Moorehouse; the others—Paddy Green and Roger Bushell—had transferred to other squadrons.[46]

Late in the afternoon of July 20, 1940, Fiske flew for the first time in a 601 plane, making two patrols. During the next week, he completed several more over the rolling hills and quaint villages of southern Kent around Folkestone, Dover, and Lympne, a region soon to be known to Fiske and his fellow 601 pilots, who were rarely prone to exaggeration, as Hell's Corner. This area was the closest to France, so the Luftwaffe's aces could engage for longer than they could over London—as much as twenty minutes of dogfighting—because they had more fuel at their disposal.

Whatever their nationality, none who fought over Hell's Corner would ever forget the front line of the Battle of Britain: more German and British fighter pilots would lose their lives over this small patch of southern England than over all of the rest of the country.[47] For Billy Fiske, however, Hell's Corner proved at first to be a barren hunting ground. The Millionaires were scrambled, often several times a day, but not in time to intercept maddeningly elusive Dorniers and Stukas as they hightailed it back across the Channel.[48]

As each outing brought no result, not even the chance to get in a "squirt" (a short burst with machine guns), Fiske began to lose patience. "Too early for fun," he jotted in his logbook after yet another uneventful scramble. "We never saw one during [the] whole day . . . Frustration setting in badly."[49] His old skiing friend, Willie Rhodes-Moorehouse, Fiske's flight leader, vividly recalled one patrol when Fiske's frustration finally got the better of him: "You may talk of the dangers of war, but you can have small idea of what that means until you try coming back across the Channel in tight formation with 'Fisky'—in a rage because the Germans haven't stayed to fight—close on your tail with his jaw stuck out and his finger glued to the button . . ."[50]

Impatience aside, after barely a fortnight in the air, Fiske had impressed his British comrades. The commanding officer of 601 Squadron, Sir Archibald Hope, believed he had the makings of an ace.[51] "Unquestionably Billy Fiske was the best pilot I've ever known," he would later recall. "It was unbelievable how good he was. He picked it up so fast, it wasn't true. He'd flown a bit before, but he was a natural as a fighter pilot."[52]

Fiske had finally found a challenge to consume all his energies, more rewarding than winning Olympic gold on the Cresta Run or making a killing on Wall Street. According to contemporaries, he felt intensely alive and savored every new experience: watching dawn break before it could be seen from the ground; chasing other 601 pilots through the high cumulus and playing hide-and-seek among huge cottonballs of clouds; lounging in a deck chair between scrambles, reading about friends in the society pages of *The Times*; racing home to Rose each dusk after stand-down and then strolling with her through the grounds of a moss-covered church on his way to the Ship, a pub that overlooked the harbor in the village of Bosham. Other pilots often parked their sports cars on the beach a few yards away. If they had one too many pints, the "new lads" often returned to find their cars swamped by the incoming tide.[53]

As he knocked back cocktails in the Ship, Fiske got to know other 601 pilots, such as twenty-four-year-old Pilot Officer William Dickie, a Scotsman who had shared in the destruction of a Dornier bomber a couple of days before Fiske joined 601, and twenty-six-year-old Flying Officer James Gillan, a former instructor with colorful tales of postings to Egypt and Iraq in the late thirties.[54] And then there was Jack Riddle, who had shot down an Me-110 on July 11 and who often joined Fiske and Rose for a stiff gin and tonic or two. "Whenever we could get away from Tangmere," recalled Riddle, "we would go over to the Ship. My wife said to me one day: 'How does Billy manage to get to the

Ship so quickly? Why don't you get here as quickly as he does?' I had to explain to her that Billy had a super-charged Bentley [painted in British racing green] that went rather faster than my motor car."[55]

Whether racing through country lanes at 100 mph or coasting to victory after victory on the Cresta Run, it had always seemed as though Fiske had a split-second more than his opponents in which to make winning decisions: to steer one line or another around a bend; when to brake and when to let the sled ride. In combat, this gift would perhaps give him a vital edge. One thing was certain: when Fiske did finally come face-to-face with the enemy, he would need all the help he could get. Freshly minted pilot officers such as Fiske with their stiff new caps and unsoiled badges emblazoned with the RAF motto *Per Ardua ad Astra*—"Through Hardship to the Stars"—could expect to last just a few weeks before they were shot down and killed, drowned, or burned beyond recognition.[56]

Surprisingly little had been done to protect pilots from their worst nightmare—being trapped in a plane as it exploded into flames. When Fiske was seated on his parachute, strapped in by his Sutton harness, only a few feet were between him and a fuel tank containing up to eighty-five gallons of high-octane fuel.[57] One well-aimed incendiary bullet or cannon shell would be enough to toast him instantly in an inferno reaching several thousand degrees.

Meanwhile, back in Washington, Lord Lothian had not given up the idea of using Fiske for propaganda purposes. But he now agreed with Sinclair that Fiske would need to see combat if he were to have any credibility with the American press. "If you have one or two real ace fighters who need a rest and who could impress people here by their confidence through actual experience and superiority of our Air Force," he cabled Sinclair, "it would be a good thing to send them over for a fortnight."

Lothian added that there were few American politicians who believed Britain would survive the summer. "Defeatism, now rampant in high American circles, is strengthening the hands of those who are now trying to withdraw supplies promised to Britain for their own armament, on the ground that everything sent to us will be lost within a few weeks." Lothian recommended that the best way to convince America that Britain was worth supporting would be to "beat off the German attack" and make the argument that helping Britain would also be "best for American defense."[58]

Lothian had touched on the crucial question very much on the minds of Britons and Americans that July: Would the RAF, with around nine hundred fighters, be able to "beat off the German attack?" As one senior British civil servant pointed out: "It may well be that the continued existence of this country depends on a few thousand pink-cheeked young airmen."[59]

5. The Burning Blue

It helped to fly crudely, as I did, and not be bound by the rules.
The good pilots—often the squadron commanders—were
often killed quickly because they flew too well. If you went
skidding around the sky you were a more difficult target.[1]

Brian Kingcome, 92 Squadron

Werner Mölders walked onto a runway at the Rechlin Test
Flight Center, at the heart of the Third Reich, and then
toward a captured Hurricane and Spitfire, painted in gray
camouflage, their RAF roundels replaced by black crosses. He had
been invited by the brilliant Ernst Udet, Chief of Aircraft Procure-
ment and Supply, to test the enemy planes.[2] Mölders was only
too happy to interrupt three weeks of precious leave to do so.

After the fall of France, Mölders and a fellow JG 53 pilot,
Wolf-Dietrich, had been released—two of four hundred Luftwaffe
prisoners handed over following the armistice. Had the French
held out for just a few more weeks, as Churchill had urged, he
would have been sent to England and then shipped to Canada
to spend the rest of the war cutting wood as an embittered POW.
Instead, he was back in the fight and still several kills ahead of
his nearest rival in the contest to become the war's greatest ace.

It was obviously Mölders's destiny to return to the skies for
the Fatherland. And now he was getting an exclusive tryout of
the enemy's best fighters. God was indeed smiling on him. He
would now know Tommy's strengths and weaknesses—an invaluable advantage for an ace of Mölders's prowess. "The Hurricane
is a bit of a tugboat with a retractable undercarriage," he would
soon report to his former acolytes in JG 53. "In our terms both

are very easy to fly, the Hurricane particularly good-natured, steady as a rock in the turn, but well below the Me-109 when it comes to performance—it's heavy on the rudder and the ailerons are sluggish. Takeoff and landing of both types is child's play. The Spitfire is one class better, very nice to the touch, light, excellent in the turn and almost equal to the Bf 109 [the German designation for the Me-109] in performance, but a rotten dogfighter as any sudden dive and the engine cuts out for seconds at a time, and because the propeller's only two-pitch (takeoff and cruise) it means that in any vertical dogfight at constantly changing heights it's either continually over-revving or never develops full power at all."[3] The cockpits of both British planes smelled sweeter than that of the Messerschmitt, which had a sour odor from varnish and lubricants.[4]

Firepower between the German and British aircraft was comparable. The RAF's fighters had four Colt-Browning machine guns mounted on each wing, loaded with 2,660 7.7 mm bullets, many of the De Wilde incendiary type—hence the Spitfire's well-deserved reputation among Mölders's fellow pilots for actually "spitting fire." Mölders's plane, the Me-109, had two 7.9 mm machine guns, loaded with 1,000 rounds each and placed above a superlatively engineered Daimler-Benz engine, and two Oerlikon cannons, one on each wing. The cannons were particularly effective. Just one or two hits could blow the thin-skinned Spitfire to pieces. By contrast, it would sometimes require several hundred rounds of machine-gun fire for RAF pilots to destroy a Messerschmitt and thousands to take down a large German bomber.

It was not long before Mölders got the chance to try out his new knowledge of the enemy's fighters. Barely a fortnight after his test flights at Rechlin, on July 28, 1940, he took off on his first patrol since being shot down. Mölders was in a buoyant mood, having broken yet another record—he was now the youngest air commodore in the Luftwaffe after being promoted to lead all of JG 51. It had been almost two months since he had last killed, and he badly wanted to increase his score before others caught up with him.

Mölders's wingman that afternoon was Erich Kircheis, a squadron adjutant in JG 51. "The mission nearly over," he recalled, "Mölders ordered the other fighters to turn for home while he decided to fly some distance from the rest of the unit, perhaps so that he could observe things from a better position. Mölders and I thus found ourselves alone at [twenty-five thousand feet]. We knew that our situation was dangerous; we could be attacked by Spitfires, but even worse was the fact that it could get out that a Kommodore had flown over England alone with his wingman. Göring had personally written an order to forbid such a situation; he wanted to preserve his Kommodore!"

Meanwhile, twenty-nine-year-old Flight Leader Adolph "Sailor" Malan, a fair-haired South African, was flying in his customary position, ahead of the Spitfires of 74 Squadron. At 1:50 that afternoon, 74 had been scrambled from RAF Manston in 11 Group with orders to intercept JG 51 and other bandits.

Since the outbreak of war, Malan had turned 74 Squadron into a highly disciplined and ruthless unit, advising pilots that it was better to shoot the hell out of a bomber than to down it because having to pull severely wounded flying crew out of a crippled plane had a chilling effect on the Germans' morale.[5] The South African ace had also significantly increased his pilots' chances of survival by abandoning the RAF's standard V formation, the "vic," with its rear defender, the "tail-end Charlie," for a looser pattern similar to that devised by Mölders, which allowed every pilot to watch out for one another.

It was around 2 p.m. Mölders ordered Kircheis to turn back and head for their base at Wisant on the Normandy coast, midway between Calais and Boulogne. A few minutes later, just north of Dover, Kircheis saw a vic of three Spitfires flying five thousand feet below. His headset crackled to life.

"Let's shoot them down!" ordered Mölders.[6]

The Spitfires, with their brightly colored roundels, had not seen Mölders and Kircheis coming out of the sun.

Kircheis twisted and turned in his Messerschmitt's cramped cockpit, scanning the skies. Suddenly, he glimpsed several other planes far above, dark specks against the sun. He could not tell whether they were German or British.

"*Achtung!*" warned Kircheis. "A unit above us!"

"Be quiet!" snapped Mölders, totally focused on his prey below.[7]

Kircheis did as he was told. The legendary Mölders could do no wrong. "I trusted him: from afar, aircraft are only small dots and very difficult to identify," Kircheis later explained.[8]

A few seconds later, Mölders dipped his wing and then dived. Tracers and cannon spat through the air.

Mölders was back on form—Kircheis watched a Spitfire fall from the sky.

It was now around 2:20 p.m. Sailor Malan swooped down, closely followed by the rest of 74 Squadron, and soon Mölders and Kircheis were surrounded by Spitfires. There was no time for fancy footwork. Mölders opened his throttle and dived one way. Kircheis dropped his nose and went the other, losing thousands of feet in just a few blood-chilling seconds, and then looked around—there was no sign of his Kommodore. But there were still plenty of Spitfires in hot pursuit. Using all the skill he could muster, he dived, turned, dived again and pushed his plane beyond its specified limits until he was certain he had escaped his attackers.

Having lost his wingman, Mölders had meanwhile turned to face several Spitfires. One was soon in his sights. He opened fire. A few seconds later, another victim plunged in flames—Mölders's twenty-sixth kill. "But now I found myself in the middle of a clump of Englishmen and they were very angry with me," he recalled. "They all rushed at me and that was my good luck. As they all tried to earn cheap laurels at the expense of one German, they got in each other's way. Well, I managed to maneuver among them and made them even more confused."[9]

Mölders pulled away and climbed again, intent on taking down another Spitfire. There were still plenty to choose from. According to several accounts, he picked out Sailor Malan. It was not a good choice: Malan was no novice—he had seen Mölders and before the German could line up a shot he was pulling his Spitfire round.[10]

The Rolls-Royce engine roared as Malan kept the Spitfire

turning tight—tight enough to bring Werner Mölders into his sights.

Malan thumbed his firing button, spraying Mölders with a hail of lead.

"Bullets bespattered my aircraft," recalled Mölders. "The radiator and fuel tank were shot up badly and I had to make a getaway as quickly as possible."

Malan had also hit Mölders in the leg but not badly enough to cause serious blood loss. Mölders turned toward France, hoping that he would not have to ditch in the "shit canal," as many Luftwaffe pilots called the English Channel. Finally, chalk cliffs appeared below. He'd made it. But then the engine coughed and began to misfire. Mölders checked his instruments. His home base, Wisant, loomed in the distance. He tried to lower his undercarriage, but it was kaput. JG 51's "black men"—the ground crew—watched as their new Kommodore approached the airfield, wheels up, gliding toward the grass. To their delight, Mölders made a smooth belly landing.[11]

Mölders's wingman, Kircheis, also landed safely and then discovered that his engine had been hit twice. "I was very anxious to know what had happened to my Kommodore," he remembered. "As soon as I was on my legs, I was told that Mölders had already landed, but that he was wounded. At that very moment, he was on his way to hospital. Göring had already been informed of his fate. That same day, I was ordered to call him personally. I did it with considerable anxiety and I received the biggest bawling out of my whole life. Fortunately, Mölders was not long in coming back. We all remembered for a long time after that his first sortie with JG 51!"[12]

Once again, God had been on Mölders's side. He was wounded but alive. "My visit to hospital proved that I had three splinters in my upper thigh, one in the knee joint and one in my left foot," recalled Mölders. "In the heat of battle I had not felt a thing— the splinter in my kneecap is still there. On this occasion I experienced the fatherly solicitude of our Reichsmarschall once more; he had me flown to the [air force hospital] in Berlin. The eleven days at the [hospital] were a wonderful convalescence. I believe I was something of the 'showpiece' of the hospital and the sisters looked after me in a way that my own mother could not have bettered. Later on I sent the good people a sack of coffee."[13]

It would be another month before Mölders would return to the skies, hungrier than ever to increase his score and prove that he was, without doubt, still the Third Reich's top ace.

While Werner Mölders was recuperating, Art Donahue arrived at RAF Hawarden, near Liverpool, to join No. 7 Operational Training Unit.[14] A few days later, his fellow American volunteers—Eugene Tobin, Andy Mamedoff, and Shorty Keough—also turned up at Hawarden, all keener than ever to fly the fabled Spitfire.[15]

For any American pilot in 1940, being allowed to take up a Spitfire was a rare privilege. And for a first-timer, it was also a nerve-racking challenge. The "Spit" was much faster than even the best planes operated by civilian pilots. She could top four hundred miles per hour if pushed to her limits.[16] Vastly more powerful than anything the American trainees had handled before, her Rolls-Royce engine was capable of generating 1,500 horsepower at seven thousand feet; the last plane Art Donahue had flown, as an instructor in 1939, had boasted just 40 horsepower.

"Flying the Spitfire was like driving a sports car," wrote one young pilot. "It was faster than the old Hurricane, much more delicate. You couldn't roll it very fast, but you could make it go up and down much easier. A perfect lady. It wouldn't do anything wrong. The Hurricane would drop a wing if you stalled it coming in, but a Spitfire would come wafting down. You couldn't snap it into a spin. Beautiful to fly, although very stiff on the ailerons— you had to jam your elbow against the side to get the leverage to move them. And so fast!!! If you shut the throttle in a Hurricane you'd come to a grinding halt; in a Spitfire you just go whistling on."[17]

Not long after arriving at Hawarden, Art Donahue climbed into a Spitfire's cockpit and started her up. The sound of the Spitfire's twelve-cylinder Rolls-Royce engine was almost deafening but steadied into a throbbing hum when he closed the canopy and was airborne. Feeling more like a "passenger than a pilot," Donahue soon realized that the stories he had heard about the Spitfire were true: she was indeed a beautiful mistress but treacherous if scorned and terribly sensitive in the hands of a virgin.[18] "I was cruising along at about two hundred eighty and drew the control stick back about an inch, rather abruptly, to start my loop," he recalled. "Instantly the airplane surged upward in response, so hard that I was jammed down in the seat, feeling terribly heavy, feeling my cheeks sag downward and my mouth sag open from the centrifugal force on my lower jaw, and a yellowish gray curtain closed off my vision! I eased the stick forward again to stop the change in direction and my sight came back instantly."[19]

Donahue's fellow Americans had to show that they could handle the dual-control, American-built Miles Master before being allowed anywhere near the RAF's best fighter. "This kite is the closest thing there is to a Spitfire," Tobin's instructor told him. "If you can handle her, you're OK for anything."[20]

Tobin was determined to prove himself on the Miles Master so that he could advance as fast as possible to the Spitfire. To his delight, it was obvious that he was back in his element the moment he took to the air. "Boy did it feel good to be sitting in an airplane again! Although the Master was three times the size of anything I'd ever flown, she was easy to handle." Duly impressed, his instructor told Tobin to follow him to a corner of the airfield. They soon stood before a Spitfire: "Two and a half tons of flying heat with a 1,075 horsepower Rolls-Royce Merlin engine. What a plane!"[21]

As soon as Tobin sat in the Spitfire's cockpit, excitement gave way to absolute concentration. Then he was bumping along the grass, nose into the wind. Before he knew it, he was airborne, the Spitfire responding beautifully to the slightest touch. To his east stretched the heather and gorse-spotted hills and windswept summits of the Pennines. "For the first time in my life," he recalled, "I had a real taste for speed. I was booming along at a cool 240

[mph], the slowest cruising speed of a Spitfire, and I opened the throttle wide to make a steep climbing turn. The next thing I knew I was diving at a speed of about 430. Luckily, I came to with a couple thousand feet to spare."[22]

For Andy Mamedoff, taking off in a Spitfire for the first time was also an unforgettable thrill. "Flying one of these warplanes is something you just allowed yourself to think about back home," he explained. "The first time I was in a Spitfire I went so fast I kept getting lost—those long three-mile loops and rolling at 240 miles per hour without any trouble . . . When I saw the narrow landing gear they have, I thought it would be dynamite to land. But it didn't worry me at all when the moment came."[23]

Over the next fortnight, the Americans flew the Spitfire several hours a day, weather permitting. As they learned how best to handle their new "mounts" (planes), they also bonded with other trainees, many of them drawn from foreign shores, as had been the case on Billy Fiske's training course. "We were certainly an 'International Brigade': Belgians, Frenchmen, Czechs, Poles, South Africans—and two Englishmen," recalled Tobin. "And the English boys didn't like it at all when we dubbed them 'the foreigners.'"[24]

Of the 2,917 pilots who fought with Fighter Command between July 10 and October 25, 1940, most were British. But a fifth were not: 145 Poles, 126 New Zealanders, 98 Canadians, 88 Czechs, 33 Australians, 29 Belgians, 25 South Africans, 13 French, 10 Irish, 3 Rhodesians, and even 1 Jamaican pilot.[25] Among these 571 foreigners, 7 were officially Americans, according to RAF rosters released in 1940.[26] Of the many nationalities the Americans fought with, they were the only ones who did so against the laws of their country.

Art Donahue got on particularly well with the youngest member on his course at Hawarden: nineteen-year-old Englishman Peter Kennard-Davis, "a big dark-haired husky fellow." Kennard-Davis had joined the Royal Navy at sixteen to see the world and was far wiser and coolheaded than his age would suggest. Day after day, he and Donahue paired off to practice gunnery and aerobatics, dogfighting and flying in the RAF's tight vic formations, wing tips sometimes only a few yards apart.[27]

Donahue's nationality was not an issue with Kennard-Davis. But it was with others. Around two weeks into the Hawarden course, Donahue sat reading in the officers' mess. By now he had been nicknamed "America" by Kennard-Davis and his fellow trainees.

"When's your country going to give us some help, America?" asked a pilot.

"I don't know," replied Donahue. "They've sent me, haven't they?"

"Yes, but we're never sure whether that was helping us or Germany. Seriously, though, what do you think about it—don't they realize this is a world menace we're fighting?"

"Yes, most of them seem to realize it now. They seem pretty well agreed that if Hitler wins here it will only be a matter of time before their turn will come. But they'd rather have it that way, it seems, than take any chances of having their boys fight on foreign soil."

"What? You mean they'd rather wait and fight in their own country?"

"They say, 'What did we get out of helping England in the last war?'"

"They got rid of their menace, didn't they?"

"They forget that they ever had a menace then, and all they remember is that it cost them money."

"Do they think England got rich on it?"

"If you ask me," concluded Donahue, "they don't think very deeply."[28]

By late July the training was over. It had gone so quickly, perhaps too fast. For the princely sum of eighty dollars a month—half what Eugene Tobin had earned at MGM—the Americans could now call themselves pilot officers.

"We've made it," a relieved Tobin told Andy Mamedoff.

"Time will tell," replied Mamedoff, who had only just told his parents back in Thompson, Connecticut, that he was in England and had joined the RAF.[29]

In a matter of days, the Americans would be posted to front-line squadrons. Combat would require exceptional alertness and skill, but the Americans were confident nonetheless, aware that they enjoyed a marked advantage over most of the young men passing through Hawarden at that time. They had not been in a dogfight but they were experienced pilots, having flown for several years before even climbing into the formidable Spitfire. Donahue had logged more hours before even getting to England than any other American who fought in the Battle of Britain: 1,814 hours solo, and 4 hours of dual flying.[30] He also knew how to fly blind on instruments in bad weather, something every Minnesota pilot was forced to master.

If it was action the Americans were still yearning for, their graduation could not have occurred at a more opportune time. On July 31, with startling accuracy, General Raymond Lee, the military attaché at the American embassy in London, jotted in his diary: "Tomorrow, the first of August, is the opening day of the most critical month in history. If the British are standing upright on September 1, I will say there is a good chance of beating the Boche, no matter what may be happening elsewhere."[31]

The next day, Adolf Hitler issued his famous directive No. 17, calling for the total destruction of the RAF before launching an invasion of Britain: "The Luftwaffe will use all the forces at its disposal to destroy the British Air Force as quickly as possible. The attacks must in the first instance be directed against flying formations, their ground organizations and their supply organizations . . . Terror raids as revenge I reserve the right to order myself."[32] The plan to wipe out the RAF was code-named Attack of the Eagles, and it would begin on Eagle Day sometime after August 5, 1940.

6. First Blood

Statistically, a green pilot on either side going into action for the first time had three rolls of the die. First roll: four, five or six and you get back with your aircraft undamaged; one, two or three and your aircraft is hit. Second roll: four, five or six, and you bail out or force-land unhurt; one, two or three and you are injured. Third roll: five or six and you recover from your injuries; one, two, three or four and you are dead.[1]

Stephen Bungay, *The Most Dangerous Enemy*

When Art Donahue had signed away his nationality to join the RAF, he had hoped to be sent into combat as soon as possible. He was not disappointed. On August 3, 1940, less than a month after arriving in England, he was posted to RAF Kenley outside London, at the heart of Fighter Command's No. 12 Group. There was yet more good news: his friend, the young British pilot, Peter Kennard-Davis, was also being sent south with him to join 64 Squadron.

A charismatic twenty-seven-year-old Scotsman called Aeneas MacDonell led 64 Squadron. He later described how, despite heavy losses, his twenty operational pilots were in remarkably high spirits that early August and, like Donahue, raring to tangle with the Luftwaffe. It was difficult at times to rein them in. "It's like holding a team of wild horses when I keep them in formation when there are Huns near," explained MacDonell, who had taken over command of 64 only a fortnight before. "I'm almost afraid to give the 'Tally-ho' because I know I'll be alone about two seconds later! They just peel off like banana skins when they get the word to go after the Huns!"[2]

Slim, with fine wavy hair, a bushy mustache, and unforgettably piercing blue eyes, MacDonell was typical of the RAF's best squadron leaders: matter-of-fact, unemotional about combat, a natural leader, and fast on his way to becoming an ace, with three confirmed kills since July 25, when he had destroyed a Ju-87.[3] Sadly, during the same engagement near Dover, two 64 pilots had been lost, shot down in flames as they patrolled over British shipping. Understandably, MacDonell's "wild horses" were now hungry for revenge.

MacDonell did his best to prepare Donahue and Kennard-Davis for combat. It was important to maximize the Spitfire's advantages over the formidable Me-109. The Spitfire could not outclimb or outdive the faster Messerschmitt. On the turn, however, it was quicker, so long as Donahue and Kennard-Davis could stand punishing g-forces as they pulled round. In a dogfight, plane against plane, without the advantage of surprise, 64 Squadron had already proved it was the equal of the Luftwaffe's best. If they learned fast and kept their eyes peeled at all times, Donahue and Kennard-Davis should be able to "tune in" and joust with the Germans, and live to tell the tale.[4]

The same day that Art Donahue arrived at Kenley, his fellow Americans—Tobin, Mamedoff, and Keough—were posted to Middle Wallop, home to 609 West Riding Squadron, whose motto, "Tally Ho!" had been adopted as the RAF's official war cry. Unlike Donahue, the three Americans had joined the RAF looking to fly "hot machines," make a little money, and have a "million laffs" as Tobin often said flippantly. Now their commitment to fighting against the odds to save England, a country they barely knew, would be put to the test. To their delight, they were greeted warmly on the base. "The reception we received at the new station made up for everything that had happened in France and then some," recalled Tobin. "We were [about] to go operational in the RAF, and the boys figured that called for a celebration. And what a swell bunch of guys!"[5]

Two other pilots arrived at Middle Wallop with the Americans and brought 609 back up to full strength: Flying Officers Tadeusz

Nowierski and Piotr Ostaszewski. There was not the slightest doubt about their dedication to the cause. Both had fought to the bitter end with the Polish air force the previous September and had only just managed to escape ahead of the Nazis to England.[6] "They had undergone so much suffering and hardship," remembered Pilot Officer David Crook, a 609 stalwart, "and had lost almost everything in life that mattered to them—homes, families, money—that I think the only thing that concerned them now was to get their revenge and kill as many Germans as possible."[7]

Twenty-four-year-old Crook also recalled his first impressions of Tobin, Mamedoff, and Keough: "They were typical Americans, amusing, always ready with some devastating wisecrack (frequently at the expense of authority) ... Andy was dark, tough, and certainly rather good-looking with his black hair and flashing eyes. Red was very tall and lanky, and possessed the most casual manner and general outlook on life that I ever saw. I don't believe he ever batted an eyelid about anything."[8]

Before the war, 609 West Riding Squadron had been an auxiliary unit, comprising mostly prosperous sons of Yorkshire's factory and mill owners. Barely a year later, it was possible to count on one hand those from the squadron's original eighteen pilots who had survived the winter in France and the Dunkirk campaign. In just a week, four of 609's prewar stalwarts had been shot down.[9] Three more had been lost by June 22, when 609 had received a new leader, twenty-seven-year-old Horace "George" Darley, a no-nonsense Londoner who had joined the RAF at age nineteen. Darley had been sent to command 609, he recalled, because of his "awareness of problems peculiar to such squadrons, which were small squadrons of personal friends who had probably grown up together, and in which losses were particularly keenly felt ... The general atmosphere in 609 was depressed which did not help the younger pilots." The best way to raise the men's spirits, he believed, was to vastly improve 609's "kill/loss ratio."[10]

As the new boys, the Americans would train to become "tail-end Charlies," responsible for weaving behind their fellow pilots and protecting them from a surprise attack.[11] Flying in that role was no "piece of cake."[12] Many a first-timer was so focused on looking out for his fellow pilots that he forgot to watch his own back. As the veterans in both 609 and 64 knew only too well, the result was predictable: tail-end Charlies died instantly in a hail of machine-gun bullets.

It was not yet 6 a.m., but 64 Squadron's ground crew had already set up a couple of deck chairs, parked two Spitfires to form goal-posts, and were now playing a spirited game of soccer. Nearby, pilots listened to the radio and sipped mugs of strong tea. It was already too warm for flying suits. Today, they would go up in just their uniforms, yellow Mae West life preservers hanging limp across their chests, cockpits open to the elements, silk scarves tucked behind their starched collars to prevent neck burn from constantly swiveling their heads to scan the skies for bandits.

By coincidence, a celebrated American correspondent, Quentin Reynolds of *Collier's* magazine, was also at 64 Squadron's base on the morning of August 5, 1940. Reynolds had arrived before dawn and had then been introduced to Squadron Leader Aeneas MacDonell. The Scot had chatted blithely with Reynolds for a few minutes and had then called Art Donahue over, knowing Reynolds would be interested in meeting the squadron's only Yank.

As Reynolds and Donahue talked, a telephone in the dispersal tent rang three times.

The game of soccer stopped.

MacDonell answered the telephone.

"Twelve or more heading for convoy off Dover . . . Yes, sir."

It was 6:05 a.m.

"Scramble!"[13]

Donahue sprinted to his Spitfire and climbed into the cockpit. In seconds, his rigger had strapped him into his parachute and Sutton safety harness. Then he was pulling on his mask, turning the oxygen on. After a quick check of his oil pressure and fuel gauge and a thumbs-up to the ground staff, Donahue's chocks were away and his engine was roaring as he followed MacDonell across the grass. Then Donahue felt a "tremendous thrill . . . to be aloft with a fighter squadron for the first time." Soon he was raising the undercarriage by hand, correcting his course, climbing at two thousand feet a minute, throttle open, circling the airfield, waiting for all the flights to take up formation.

It was 6:09 a.m. as the last of 64 Squadron's Spitfires left the ground.[14] The squadron climbed to "angels ten"—ten thousand feet—and then MacDonell led the way toward the English Channel. Donahue's radio crackled to life and he heard 64's controller instruct MacDonell to relieve a squadron protecting an important Channel convoy.

"Bandits are approaching from the north!"

"All Tiger aircraft, full throttle!" ordered MacDonell. "Full throttle!"

Donahue had so far been totally focused on flying in tight formation and following MacDonell's crisp orders. Now he realized he was finally going to engage the enemy. "My pulse pounded and my thoughts raced," he remembered. "This was it!"

MacDonell again led the squadron in a fast climb. Donahue pushed his emergency boost and heard the engine growl with extra power as he tailed MacDonell upward. The first rule of combat was always to try to gain an advantage in height. Making sure he was not caught unawares by a "Hun in the sun" was what most concerned every pilot, and now compelled each member of 64 Squadron to soar toward the thinner air, spurred on by their emergency boosts. "Trembling with excitement, trying to realize that this was actually happening and I wasn't dreaming," recalled Donahue, "I pulled the guard on my firing button. For the first time in my life I was preparing to kill! The button was painted red, and it looked strangely grim now that it was uncovered. I turned its safety ring, which surrounded it, from the position which read SAFE to the position which read FIRE."[15]

Donahue then turned on his electric gunsight. An orange light, in the form of crosshairs, glowed on a six-inch square piece of glass tilted at forty-five degrees in front of his nose.

"Steer one-three-zero and climb to twenty thousand feet."

The squadron was now nearing the coast of France. It was Donahue's first sight of the country—enemy-occupied territory.

"Circle your present position."

"Watch to the left."

"Believe enemy is now heading south and passing behind you."

Suddenly a black dot appeared in the distance and then several bandits took form. Donahue dived after one of them. The wind shrieked against his canopy, his airspeed indicator moved beyond 400 mph, his controls stiffened. He pulled on the stick and raised his Spitfire's nose. The bandit grew bigger . . . five hundred yards away . . . four hundred . . . a "barbarous swastika" soon visible on its tail.[16] It was Hitler's best fighter, the Me-109 E, and it belonged to JG 54's I Group, one of the Luftwaffe's most experienced and lethal units, nicknamed the "Green Hearts."[17]

There was an explosion. Donahue was stunned.[18] His plane had been hit by a cannon shot. Then machine-gun fire followed. Swiveling his neck, Donahue saw two Germans on his tail, spitting bullets through their propellers. He pulled his Spitfire over and then tried to out-turn his pursuers. G-force quickly crushed him, so he planted his feet forcefully in his g-stirrups and then he was diving, rolling, standing the Spitfire on its tail, doing aerobatics he'd never attempted as a barnstormer back in Minnesota.[19]

Donahue heard machine-gun fire. Bullets passed close by. Again, he pulled his Spitfire round. The sun scorched through his closed hood and his heart raced as he then dodged his adversaries along the jagged French coastline. Finally, he got behind one of the German planes from I Group. But just as he was about to fire, he realized his gunsight was broken. "During the next few minutes I think I must have blacked out at least 20 times in turns," he recalled. "I remember starting to spin at least once from turning too violently. I wanted to flee but couldn't get my directions straight because I was maneuvering so fast. My compass couldn't help me unless I'd give it the chance to settle down. It was spinning like a top."[20]

Donahue finally managed to shake off the enemy. He had survived his first dogfight. But then he saw yet more Germans from JG 54. They were following him across the Channel toward England. He turned to face them head-on, and to his relief saw them bank away and return to France, no doubt low on fuel, red lights flickering on their tank gauges. Shaken and very much sobered, he set course for 64 Squadron's base at RAF Leconfield. It was only now that he realized that a cannon shell had cut several cables, making the Spitfire barely operable and explaining why the gunsight had not worked. There was a large hole in the fuselage behind his cockpit. Part of his RAF roundel was missing.

The Channel stretched away into the distance. A long stripe of white appeared: the high, chalky cliffs of Beachy Head and Dover—home.

Donahue landed back at Leconfield and taxied to the end of the field, noticing that most of 64's planes were already down. Armorers ran toward him, carrying trays of machine-gun bullets. As he shut down his Spitfire, they yanked off covers below and above his guns and rearmed. Donahue then joined the rest of his squadron in time to hear Squadron Leader MacDonell brief 64's intelligence officer on that morning's combat: "We met them about halfway over the Channel at 14,000 feet. There were about twenty Heinkels and at least twenty-one 109s and 110s. We came out of the sun and got fairly close. I sent a four-second burst at one of them." MacDonell had destroyed an Me-109 and damaged another. "[Then] there were no enemy aircraft in sight. We came home."

"Is that all?" asked the intelligence officer.

"Yes, except that Isaac failed to return. He got separated from the rest of the squadron."

A Welshman with an uncanny resemblance to the movie star Errol Flynn, twenty-four-year-old Lewis Isaac had flown with the squadron for less than a month as a tail-end Charlie.

"I saw him," said a nearby pilot. "I saw him with two 110s on his tail. By the time I got to him they had gotten him. He went down. Had no chance to bail out."

"He must have seen some Messerschmitts coming up to attack

the squadron from behind and turned back and engaged them," said MacDonell. "I noticed that we *weren't* attacked from the rear."

Isaac had sacrificed himself to save Donahue and his new friends.

Donahue went to check on his plane. He was still examining several bullet holes when Squadron Leader MacDonell found him later that morning.

"You put up a great show," said MacDonell. "When did you get hit?"

"Just when I was on the tail of an Me-110," replied Donahue. "I felt a little jar and then all my controls went haywire. I sent one burst at the [Messerschmitt] but didn't get him. Even my sights were acting funny. But it was fun while it lasted."

Donahue beamed, high on his first combat, and then turned toward the damaged Spitfire. "It's a beautiful plane. I never saw anything handle quite so sweet."[21]

MacDonell walked away, and soon Donahue was lying in the grass beside his friend from training school, Peter Kennard-Davis.

"Will you do me a favor?" Kennard-Davis asked.

"Sure. What is it?" replied Donahue.

"Let me have your notebook for a minute and I'll tell you."

Donahue handed over a notebook he'd bought in a small town in Wisconsin three months before. Kennard-Davis jotted down the name of his girlfriend and her telephone number.

"If anything happens to me, will you telephone this number and tell her the story? And then if it's possible, I'd like to have you see that she gets this."[23]

Kennard-Davis pointed to a wristband on his left hand.

Donahue nodded.

"Okay."

It would be forty-eight hours before Donahue and his nineteen-year-old friend, 64's youngest pilot, would return to the skies. Then they would be involved in the fiercest fight yet above the Channel between the RAF and the Luftwaffe—a midday mêlée so costly that it would eventually be seen by the German pilots involved as marking the true beginning of their Battle of Britain.

7. The Channel

The really good fighter pilot had a gift. He could scan the
skies, take it all in, know how long he had to do something,
and then do it. Very few people had that gift.[1]

Flight Lieutenant Frederick Rosier, 229 Squadron

Art Donahue watched the blue flames in wonder. They flared
from the exhausts of 64 Squadron's planes as he and his
fellow pilots flew in formation to their advance base near the
coast, having left RAF Kenley well before dawn. It was the most
beautiful flight he had ever experienced. "We seemed to hover
motionless," he recalled, "except for the slight upward or downward drift of one machine into another in relation to the rest,
which seemed to lend a sort of pulsating life to the whole formation . . . we were like a herd of giant beasts in some strange new
kind of world."[2]

The Germans were now concentrating all their energies on
destroying Channel convoys, thereby drawing the RAF into costly
engagements above the cold waters. So confident were some of
Göring's top fighter pilots of imminent triumph, they were advising
subordinates to take leave in a few weeks' time, or at most a
month, when the war would be over.[3] The previous day, August
7, JG 51's commanding officer, Werner Mölders, had told one of
his young pilots: "Why marry now when there is only England
left? Marry later to celebrate the victory."[4]

Earlier that morning of August 8, the Germans had tracked the
progress of a convoy of mostly coal-bearing merchant ships—
code-named Peewit by the RAF. Wanting to prove that the
Luftwaffe now controlled airspace above the Channel, Herman

Göring ordered that the convoy be destroyed. Soon, Major General Baron von Richthofen, the First World War ace's cousin, was barking at his Stuka pilots: "This convoy must be wiped out!"[5]

By midmorning, Richthofen's 8th Flying Group was above Peewit. William Dawson, captain of a five-hundred-ton coaster, the *John M.*, watched as several Stukas broke from the clouds and screamed down in almost vertical dives. "I saw a blinding flash, followed by a heavy explosion in the starboard column of the convoy," he recalled. "A second later the same thing happened out in the port column. The explosions rocked the ships and I could smell the cordite fumes blown over on the wind. Down came more bombs, flinging up great columns of water nearly one hundred feet high."[6]

Fortunately for Dawson and other British seamen, thick cloud cover prevented most of Richthofen's Stukas from attacking the convoy accurately. Only a few tenacious and brave pilots managed to drop their bombs on target. Peewit steamed on, bloodied but unbowed. Exasperated, Göring's lieutenants ordered a second attack. This time, around thirty Me-109s of JG 27 would escort three units of Ju-87s, approximately three hundred planes in all, under orders to obliterate the slow-moving convoy no matter how thick the clouds. Here was the Luftwaffe's opportunity to prove beyond a doubt that it could close the Channel to British shipping.

The strike force was first identified by the RAF's forward radar station at Ventnor, on the Isle of Wight. Such stations provided the RAF with perhaps their greatest advantage over the Luftwaffe —a system of detecting, through small blips on radar screens, any aircraft flying toward Britain from any base along the Normandy coastline. This information was quickly relayed to controllers at various operations rooms, where WAAFs (members of the Women's Auxiliary Air Force) then plotted the enemy's exact whereabouts on large tables.[7] "In battle we had to rely on our own human eyes," recalled one German ace. "The British fighter pilots could depend on the radar eye, which was far more reliable and reached many times further."[8]

It was around 11 a.m. in the operations room of Sector 11 Headquarters. Air Commodore Keith Park, the forty-four-year-old New Zealand–born head of Sector 11, turned calmly to his controller and ordered him to scramble Art Donahue's 64 Squadron and several others.

The unflappable Park, recognizable to many of his pilots because of his frequent visits to their bases in his own Hurricane, was perhaps the greatest air commander of the Second World War. Tall, impeccably groomed, thin-faced, and ascetic, he had spent more than a hundred hours in the air during the Dunkirk evacuation and therefore understood exactly what his men needed and confronted. There was no doubting his resilience and courage. He had fought at Gallipoli in World War I with his fellow Australians, had been carried, badly wounded, on a stretcher from the muddy killing fields of the Somme, and then had wangled his way into the Royal Flying Corps before ending the war as a widely respected squadron leader with twenty kills.

At 64's advance base, there was an ominous click and then a black Bakelite telephone rang. Squadron Leader MacDonell picked up the receiver, nodded as he was given orders, and then turned to his pilots: "Operations just called to tell us to be on our toes. There's a lot of activity on the other side, and they have a 'fifty plus' raid plotted, coming across farther down the coast. It may turn our way though."[9]

Donahue was soon strapped into his Sutton harness and pressing his starter button, trembling with excitement, hearing other Spitfires cough to life as engines turned over. "We roared off like a stampeding herd of buffalo, climbing steeply and wide open," he remembered. "'Two thousand feet, four thousand—there were thick fluffy clouds at five thousand, and we flashed up through their misty chasms, caverns, hills and valleys; and then they were dropping away below us and forming a snowy carpet for us to look down on."[10] Maintaining radio silence, Donahue and his fellow pilots glimpsed Channel ports through gaps in the cumulus. And then they were above the choppy English Channel. It was around 11:30 a.m. when they spied the Peewit convoy below.

Pilot Officer Richard Jones belonged to Donahue's flight. Sixty-four years later, he would vividly recall arriving over Peewit's beleaguered ships and then circling them: "We were waiting for the dive-bombers. Art Donahue got a bit near to the convoy and of course all hell opened up at him. We had to shout out: 'Christ almighty, Art, get out of there, they're shooting at you!' It didn't matter to the gunners on the convoy what nationality you were. If they saw an aircraft above, they opened up on you. I didn't blame them. We had a rule never to get too near unless we saw the enemy."[11]

Donahue opened his throttle and joined Jones at a safer height. "We were about eight thousand feet up, patrolling over the Channel, and for a couple of minutes we had received no new orders," recalled Donahue. "The sun was very hot, and I wished I hadn't worn my tunic."[12]

Donahue's radio whined. There were new orders to intercept incoming bandits, as many as three dozen, heading toward the Kentish coastline near RAF Manston. Breaking away from Peewit, 64 Squadron flew east. Two other RAF squadrons had in the meantime been scrambled for the same purpose. It was around 11:40 a.m. when the bandits—belonging to JG 51 and JG 26— spied neat vics of Spitfires in the far distance and several thousand feet below.[13] The British had, it seemed, been vectored too late and too low, and were now terribly vulnerable.

Leading JG 26's III Group that day was twenty-eight-year-old Major Adolf Galland. It was high time he bagged another of the Lords, as some of his colleagues called the RAF's pilots. Whether his prey was a Lord or a giant stag mattered little to Galland, described as a "shit" by some and a gentleman by others. The hunt was what counted—the primeval, life-affirming thrill of the chase.[14] His mission—the aim of every fighter pilot, he believed— was simply "to attack, to track, to hunt and to destroy the enemy. Only in this way can the eager and skillful fighter pilot display his ability. Tie him to a narrow and confined task, rob him of his initiative, and you take away from him the best and most valuable qualities he possesses: aggressive spirit, joy of action and the passion of the hunter."[15]

Many said Galland was supernaturally gifted. Others were less charitable. "Galland was very pretentious," recalled Hugo Dahmer of JG 26, who had survived several dogfights by flying as if he had been badly hit. "He made himself a 'star' but in fact he was not as exceptional as has often been described. He used aircraft especially equipped for flying at high altitude, the same as flown by our squadron, the Hohenstaffel [high-cover squadron]. However, the other pilots in his unit had no such aircraft so that when he sighted a possible target and accelerated toward it, they were unable to keep up with him. Galland, therefore, was always first to reach the enemy and the first to be presented with an opportunity to shoot him down. None of the pilots in Galland's flight had this same advantage. They remained behind him and protected his back."[16]

In 1938, as a Condor pilot in Spain, Galland had completed more than two thousand sorties, often flying in just his bathing trunks, and had contracted a severe case of "throat-ache"—the Luftwaffe's term for every young ace's yearning to wear an ever more grandiose decoration at his neck: the Knight's Cross, the Knight's Cross with Oak Leaves . . . and ultimately the Knight's Cross with Oak Leaves, Swords, and Diamonds. He now vied for the ultimate prize of being the war's highest scoring ace with an exalted group of the Luftwaffe's best: JG 53's burly Karl-Hans Mayer; the dashing twenty-five-year-old Helmut Wick of JG 2, touted as the rising star of the Jagdwaffe, the German equivalent of the RAF's Fighter Command; wily Captain Wilhelm Balthasar of JG 27, with no less than twenty-three kills to his name; and last but not least, his good friend Werner Mölders.

With poor old Mölders injured, seated behind a desk in Caffiers no doubt fingering his rosary beads, the time for Galland to catch up had arrived. The rudder of his Me-109 already boasted seventeen carefully painted white stripes, but he would need to add another nine to match Mölders's tally.

Galland checked his instruments and the electric gunsight in his cramped cockpit—the only one in the entire Luftwaffe fitted with a cigar lighter so he could puff on one of his beloved black

Havanas as he glided home after a kill.[17] He was now fast approaching several Spitfires from one of the RAF squadrons sent to intercept the Germans. Galland waited for the right moment to attack. It was crucial to bounce, guns blazing, and then peel away. In a full-throttle dive, he knew from experience, the Messerschmitt could not be beat.

At some point in the next few minutes, both Galland's JG 26 and JG 51 struck from greater height, taking numerous tail-end Charlies by surprise. As a mass dogfight soon developed, 64 Squadron's Art Donahue suddenly heard his radio transmitter crackle to life.

"Bandits astern!"[18]

Squadron Leader MacDonell reacted instantly, leading Donahue and others in a violent turn.

Donahue saw several bandits flash past.

"Tal-l-l-ly–ho-o!" said MacDonell, his voice calm and reassuring, and then he dived after the Germans.

An Me-109 appeared in Donahue's reflector sight. He thumbed his firing button and watched as bullets sprayed across the German plane. Then he broke away, afraid that he would be surprised by another bandit. "When Donahue broke off his attack," recalled fellow 64 pilot, Richard Jones, "he was doing the right thing. If you were in a dogfight, you never stayed more than a few seconds on the enemy's tail because there was always someone on your tail. So you kept moving every second, all the time. Invariably you found that those who wanted the kill and followed an enemy plane down ended up with a kill to their credit but also got shot up in the bargain. Getting a confirmed target did not matter as much as living to fight another day."[19]

Another Me-109 was soon in Donahue's crosshairs. Donahue opened fire. At the sound of eight Brownings letting rip, his confidence surged: "They sounded terribly capable and completed the steadying effect of our leader's voice on my nerves." Turning sharply, he didn't have time to see whether the bullets had caused any damage. Then, suddenly, a Messerschmitt was snarling toward him at over 350 mph, head-on, spitting four white tracers.

Fortunately, they arced over his head and then the bandit flashed by. The sky was now crowded with darting and diving machines, glinting like silverfish as they caught the sun. "We seemed to be milling about like a swarm of great gnats in this giant eerie amphitheater above the clouds," recalled Donahue. "Sets of long white tracers crisscrossed the air and hung all about, like Christmas decorations! They stay visible for several seconds after they're fired." [20]

Donahue twisted and turned, sweltering in his cramped cockpit, looking for his next target and watching his tail. Then another Messerschmitt attacked, again head-on, "his guns blazing out their tracers and his cannon firing through a hole in the center of his propeller, puffing blue smoke for all the world like a John Deere tractor! It wasn't a pretty sight. Two of the tracers erupted from guns on either side of its nose, at the top, and two from the wings."[21] Donahue jerked his control stick, turning sharply away from the tracers.

In the meantime, 65 Squadron had been scrambled and then vectored toward the mass dogfight. It joined the scrap around 11:45 a.m. And that's when an excited shout of "*Horrido!*" filled the Germans' headsets—the shout of victory, the call required of all Luftwaffe pilots claiming a kill. A few seconds later, 65 Squadron's twenty-one-year-old Sergeant David I. Kirton and his Spitfire were falling in flames. Adolf Galland and his wingman, Lieutenant Joachim Müncheberg, quickly fastened on to the tail of another 65 pilot—thirty-one-year-old Flight Sergeant Norman T. Phillips, a former carpenter. It wasn't long before Müncheberg had riddled Phillips with bullets and sent yet another Spitfire to the seas below, trailing black smoke.

Galland pulled back on his control stick to regain precious height. It was around 11:55 a.m. when he spotted Gerhard Grzymalla, another of JG 26's brightest young talents. Grzymalla was glued to another Spitfire's tail, letting rip with cannon and machine-gun fire.[22] A few minutes later, Galland ordered his flight to break away and follow him up into the sun. Meanwhile, the dogfighting between 64 and 65 Squadrons and JG 26's other flights had stretched for more than twenty miles above the Kentish coastline.

Over several minutes, Art Donahue managed to get shots in at several bandits, aiming at their crosses as they flashed across his glowing gunsight. But he did no significant damage. Then, to his horror, he glimpsed yet another Messerschmitt on his tail, firing tracers at him. Donahue pulled over in a vertical turn, but the black-crossed hunter stayed with him.

Donahue had only one option: to try to out-turn his assailant. Round and round he pulled his Spitfire. Finally, he eased out of the turn. It had worked—now he was the hunter with his opponent in his sight. Donahue opened fire.[23] And then three times more, each time thumbing the button for a second. His victim appeared dead center in Donahue's crosshairs. Again he "pressed the tit," now for three consecutive seconds, the clattering staccato from his guns making his plane quiver slightly.

Bullets exploded across the bandit, which then went into a spin. "He disappeared into the clouds below, diving straight down, and although he might have gotten home he certainly wasn't headed [there] right then," recalled Donahue. "Two more were following me down closely, and in pulling out of my dive I plunged momentarily through the clouds and then up out of them, turning to meet these two. The powder smoke from my guns smelled strong, and I felt good. This was battle royal! But my newest opponents failed me. As I zoomed up out of the clouds I saw them just disappearing into the clouds and heading homeward. Another diving out of nowhere took a snap shot at me as he went by and down into the clouds, also heading for home. Recovering from the shock that gave me, I looked around and found no more planes of either nationality in view. I appeared to be in sole possession of this part of the battlefield. This was well out over the Channel and I knew I must be nearly out of ammunition, so I headed for shore and our advance base."[24]

As Donahue made for home, Squadron Leader MacDonell and a fellow 64 stalwart, twenty-six-year-old Sergeant Jack Mann, were readying for the kill. JG 26's Lieutenant Oehm, at the controls of a state-of-the-art Me-109E-4, didn't stand a chance. The 64 duo, flying with as much ferocity and tenacity as Galland and his wingman, stuck to Oehm "like terriers" and then opened fire, peppering the German's plane with bullets before watching him spiral into the Channel four miles from Dover.[25]

It was around 1 p.m. when Art Donahue landed back at 64's forward base. As he taxied toward the dispersal tent, he noticed that one of 64's Spitfires was missing. It belonged to Peter Kennard-Davis. Donahue braked, brought his Spitfire to a stop, reached down and switched off two magneto switches at the bottom of his instrument panel, climbed out of his Spitfire, greeted his fitter and rigger, and was soon "comparing notes" with other 64 pilots. Several had seen JG 26's Oehm spin down and crash into the Channel.[26]

"Texas Shorty," as Donahue was now called, did not express the same passions as his English comrades after combat. According to MacDonell, he had "almost the detachment of a war correspondent."[27] That was about to change: concerns grew over the fate of Kennard-Davis. One of the 64 pilots told Donahue that during the morning's mass dogfight he had seen the white canopy of a parachute, but he didn't have any idea whether it was German or British. Soon MacDonell was calling around nearby bases to ask whether Kennard-Davis had landed there rather than at 64's advance base. He also ordered the rest of the squadron to fly back to its home base at Kenley without him while he tried to locate Kennard-Davis.

Meanwhile, across the Channel, Werner Mölders of JG 51 and every other senior Luftwaffe commander received the following order:

FROM: REICHSMARSCHALL GÖRING
TO: ALL UNITS OF LUFTFLOTTES 2, 3 & 5.
RE: OPERATION ADLER
WITHIN A SHORT PERIOD YOU WILL WIPE THE BRITISH
ROYAL AIR FORCE FROM THE SKY
HEIL HITLER[28]

Back at RAF Kenley, Art Donahue was so worried about Kennard-Davis that he couldn't eat that night's supper in the mess. Finally, word came of the nineteen-year-old's fate: At 12:05 p.m., his Spitfire had been badly shot up by machine-gun fire over Dover. Although suffering from severe shock and acute blood loss from several bullet wounds, Kennard-Davis had managed to pull back the hood on his damaged plane and bail out. His Spitfire, L 1039, had crashed and blazed for several minutes in a field near the small village of West Langdon.[29] He was admitted to the Royal Victoria Hospital in Dover, where he was reported to be "in wonderful spirits, cursing the Huns and spoiling for another go at them!"[30] According to the doctors treating Kennard-Davis, he would make a full recovery if he could survive his first twenty-four hours of hospitalization. Donahue went to sleep that night feeling confident that his young friend would pull through.

As far as Galland and his fellow Jagdwaffe aces were concerned, it had been an excellent day's hunting: they claimed to have shot down forty-nine British fighters, a record number. At airbases all along the Normandy coastline, there was also reason for celebration: the entire Luftwaffe's Luftflotte 3 had been involved in the fighting and had succeeded in virtually wiping out the Peewit convoy of twenty ships. Only four boats arrived at their destination, Swanage in Dorset.[31]

The next two days were quiet for 64 Squadron. Art Donahue caught up on his correspondence. Other pilots lounged around in deck chairs, played skittles and Ping-Pong, and listened to scratched records, hoping the black Bakelite telephone in the dispersal hut would stay silent for another hour, then another until finally the sun set and they were able to stand down and head to the local pub.

The inactivity obviously meant something big was brewing, and pilots on both sides knew it. Hans Joachim Marseille, a young pilot with the JG 27's I Group, was one of many who had a gut feeling that the fight to defeat Britain was about to reach a decisive stage. Exhausted after daily combat in July, he sunbathed and slept as much as possible, steeling himself for the final challenge of the war—destroying the RAF. "Word had got around that the Führer had endorsed a plan of [the] invasion of England and we all believed that this to be somewhere on or about the 10th or 12th of August . . . this period of quiet that we were experiencing was to get all our aircraft in 100 percent operational condition. Many trucks were seen arriving at our base and we could only assume that they were bringing in fresh supplies of fuel and ammunition. Everyone seemed to know that the planned invasion of England was near."[32]

Art Donahue also had time to recuperate and reflect before returning to the fray. "I took stock of the events of the week in relation to myself, and decided it hadn't been bad," he later wrote. "I certainly wasn't sorry I had come here. Although I was pretty scared while on patrol I felt that, given a little more time to get used to it, I'd be all right. I'd been through two good engagements and felt quite sure that I'd already accomplished a little for the flag I was fighting under."[33]

Then tragedy struck. Shortly after breakfast on August 10, 1940, while Donahue was visiting 64 Squadron's adjutant, an orderly arrived carrying a telegram. The adjutant read it and then handed it to Donahue. The telegram was from the Royal Victoria Hospital. Nineteen-year-old Peter Kennard-Davis had died from his bullet wounds earlier that morning. His mouth dry and in a state of shock, Donahue struggled to convince himself that this news was just what he needed: it would toughen him for the inevitable losses to come. Somehow, he kept his deep grief in check. "I kept trying to tell myself, in the dazed moments that followed, that this was good for me . . . and somehow that seemed to help me keep control of my pounding heart and wild emotions. When I was alone I murmured aloud: 'I'll make it up for you, pal. I'll get the ones you won't be getting now. Wait and see if I don't.'"[34]

The German onslaught resumed the next day, Sunday, August 11, 1940. "I didn't get to go to Mass," recalled Donahue. "There were some other blood sacrifices being made, to the ambitions of a hate-crazed, power-maddened little man who wanted to take the place of God."35 It was early morning when 64 Squadron was scrambled. Perhaps there was no time to check his instruments properly or maybe he forgot to do so, but in any case as Donahue climbed at full throttle, following Squadron Leader MacDonell toward Dover, he realized his oxygen apparatus was not working. He informed MacDonell, who told him he could continue but should leave the formation if it went above fifteen thousand feet, at which height he would begin to be seriously affected by altitude sickness.

For several minutes, Donahue flew on MacDonell's wing at around ten thousand feet. But then Kenley's controller ordered 64 to fifteen thousand feet, and then to twenty thousand. A large formation of bandits had been picked up by radar and was climbing fast, heading for home. As the Germans crossed the coast, 64 Squadron was to intercept them. Donahue, hating to do it, had to break away and lose height. He decided not to return to base, however, hoping any fight would work its way lower, where he could then rejoin 64. So he listened carefully to the Kenley controller's crisp orders to MacDonell and followed the same instructions, only at ten thousand feet rather than a brain-starving twenty thousand.

Then it began. Donahue heard one of 64's pilots over his radio: "Many bandits approaching from the starboard!"

"Look out!" cried another pilot. "There's more of them behind and above!"

"All right!" called MacDonell. "Tally-ho!"36

Donahue's radio went silent. He knew 64 was engaged in a terrific fight and that it was close, but he could see no sign of it. Puffs from anti-aircraft fire dotted the sky a few miles to the east over Dover. Donahue opened his throttle and closed on them. The Germans had attacked the anti-aircraft balloons, suspended above the port to ward off attack. Donahue looked down and saw scarlet flames rolling upward from one of the damaged balloons. A few minutes later, having spotted no enemy fighters, he turned back toward Kenley. At around seven thousand feet, as he neared the base, he saw a dot in his rearview mirror. The dot became a plane. It looked like a Spitfire. Donahue flew on, the Spitfire now on his tail. Tracer fire whizzed past him: the Spitfire was in fact a Messerschmitt Me-109.

Donahue turned away from the fire and to his relief saw the bandit dive and then disappear into clouds. He checked his instruments. He had been hit—the airspeed indicator wasn't working. A few minutes later, he was on the ground, examining his plane with his ground crew. A bullet had cut through his wing and severed his airspeed indicator pressure tube.

Donahue's fellow pilots returned one by one, having split up during a prolonged dogfight with Me-109s over the Channel. Squadron Leader MacDonell had shot down a Messerschmitt and hunted another almost all the way to France but had then been forced to turn back, out of ammunition. In all, the squadron had claimed four of the enemy. "We had one more patrol, which proved uneventful," recalled Donahue, "and then our shift was over and we returned to our home airdrome. Our C.O. [Squadron Leader MacDonell] went to visit Peter Kennard-Davis's parents that afternoon, so before he left I told him the request Peter had made me about his wristlet and he said he would have it taken care of. The funeral was to be Tuesday morning, and I planned to attend."[37]

It was also an action-packed day for 601 Squadron at RAF Tangmere on the southern coast. Early that morning, Billy Fiske learned that he had been designated number three—the tail-end Charlie—to 601's Blue Section. His skiing friend, Willie Rhodes-Moorehouse, had been told to stand in for Sir Archibald Hope and lead the squadron.

It was 10:25 a.m. when the Millionaires were scrambled for the first time that day. They were soon aloft and then ordered to intercept a bomber fleet and dozens of escorting Me-109s over Hell's Corner. The second, increasingly violent, phase of the Battle of Britain was about to begin. The Luftwaffe had changed strategy: no longer was the emphasis on attacking shipping, thereby drawing the RAF into a war of attrition over the Channel. Now the aim was to destroy Britain's key defenses on the ground. Göring's new targets were naval bases such as Portsmouth and Portland, airfields such as Tangmere and Middle Wallop, and early-warning radar stations.

One of the young Germans headed Fiske's way was blond-haired, twenty-two-year-old Rudolf Rothenfelder, an Me-109 pilot with JG 2. Rothenfelder was flying above his fellow Germans at thirty thousand feet, acting as a lookout, breathing steadily from his oxygen, the southern coast of England spread before him. Attached to his leg were a flare pistol and a yellow-dye pouch, which could be used to indicate his position to search-and-rescue planes if he ended up in the sullen waters far below. The pouch also contained rations: caffeinated chocolate, Pervitin (amphetamine) tablets, and a small bottle of cognac, which Rothenfelder invariably knocked back before takeoff.

"It was a truly uplifting sight to see what we had assembled in the air," recalled Rothenfelder. "There were fighters [Me-109s] and Zerstorer [Me-110s] which were flying at various altitudes toward the Isle of Wight. We could see, in the far distance, that our fear that the British would not come up and engage us was groundless. Over Portland, there was already an intensive combat in progress and we could see the first parachutes drifting to earth. In the water below, we recognized green patches which indicated our pilots."[38]

It was around 10:35 a.m. when Tangmere's station controller announced that bandits were close by. A few minutes later, at angels twenty, fifteen miles south of Portland, Billy Fiske and his fellow Millionaires spotted at least two dozen Me-110s and prepared to intercept. Pilot Officer Jack Riddle recalled what happened next: "The boys had seen the enemy, were all ready to intercept, but then Willie Rhodes-Moorehouse's aircraft coughed [because of engine trouble] and he had to turn back for Tangmere. It was left to Billy to lead the squadron into combat, which he did without a flinch of course."

Fiske and his flight were soon set upon from all directions by

Me-109s escorting ZG 2, a heavy fighter unit of around a hundred Me-110s, formidably armed with two cannon and five machine guns, one rear-facing. The sky was quickly latticed with tracer fire. Fiske saw an Me-110 and gave chase. Then, for the first time, the enemy appeared in the glowing amber crosshairs of his reflector gunsight. He thumbed his firing button and eight Vickers .303 burst into life. Bullets spattered across the bandit's long wings. It started to fall, one of its two engines on fire, but Fiske could not claim it as a confirmed kill because he did not see it crash—he was too busy escaping another Me-110 that was soon fixed on his tail, blazing away with its machine guns.

Within minutes, nine RAF squadrons, around a hundred planes, were fighting against overwhelming odds—some five hundred German machines according to JG 2's Rudolf Rothenfelder. The sky over Portland was crisscrossed with vapor trails; parachutes drifted among falling planes belching smoke and flame. It was the largest and fiercest fight so far between fighters of the RAF and Luftwaffe in the Battle of Britain.[39] To many of the Spitfire and Hurricane pilots battling Rothenfelder and his comrades, it seemed that the Luftwaffe owned the skies: however high they climbed, wherever they turned, there was another swarm of black-crossed bandits.

None of Fiske's fellow 601 pilots later recorded their emotions during the battle, but perhaps most would have concurred with Peter Townsend of 85 Squadron, who also fought that day: "In the mounting frenzy of battle, our hearts beat faster and our efforts became more frantic. But within, fatigue was deadening feeling, numbing the spirit. Both life and death had lost their importance. Desire sharpened to a single, savage purpose—to grab the enemy and claw him down from the sky."[40]

Fiske and his flight were lucky to escape with their lives. The other flight of 601 Squadron was not so blessed: twenty-four-year-old Pilot Officer J. L. Smithers, a popular Etonian and stockbroker before the war, was last seen crashing into the sea around 10:45 a.m. Five minutes later, Flying Officer R.S. Deme-triadi, brother-in-law of Willie Rhodes-Moorehouse, was hit by machine-gun fire and instantly killed or so badly wounded that he did not bail out: his Hurricane R4092 splashed into the Channel off Portland and quickly slipped beneath the waves. Even the most skillful pilots did not survive for long: twenty-six-year-old Flying Officer J. Gillan, a former instructor at Brize Norton, was shot down at the same time. Gillan and his aircraft were never found. Five minutes later, at 10:55 a.m., William Dickie was also swallowed by the gray waves.[41]

All but Gillan had belonged to 601 before the war, back when Willie Rhodes-Moorehouse had whipped out a checkbook and bought a local gas station so that the Millionaires need not worry about filling up their Bentleys and Triumph motorcycles because of strict rationing; back when Fortnum and Mason had delivered picnic baskets every lunchtime and the weekend flyers had dined on the grass next to their twin-engine Bristol Blenheims.

After returning to Tangmere late that morning, Fiske was credited with a probable kill. In his flight log, he jotted: "Terrific fight—Terrified but fun—had to lead the squadron in. Willie's engine failed."[42] Then, one after another, four of his friends failed to return. By sundown, Fiske and his fellow Millionaires were trying to come to terms with the news that 601 had suffered its greatest one-day loss of the war. Fiske had flown with both Gillan and Dickie only the day before.[43]

Across the Channel, the day's fighting was regarded as the ideal dress rehearsal for Eagle Day—Göring's planned coup de grâce to finish off the RAF. There had been thirty-eight German and thirty-two British losses. Six planes from Rudolf Rothenberger's JG 2 and ten Me-110s had failed to make it back across the Channel.[44] Given the extent of the fighting and number of sorties, it was no great blow to the Luftwaffe. For Britain's Fighter Command, by contrast, the day's score was deeply troubling; 601 Squadron and others had been lured into the kind of dogfights that Adolf Galland had been arguing for since the fall of France. Freed of its role as escort to lumbering bomber fleets, the Jagdwaffe had jubilantly thrown off its chains and fought as it had been trained, machine against machine, ace against ace. If that bloody

Sunday were to become the norm, there would soon be too few RAF pilots, let alone 601 Millionaires, to fend off the ever more aggressive Luftwaffe.

It seemed that there had never been a summer in England with such glorious weather, day after day of bright sunshine and mostly cloudless skies with often only the faintest hint of a breeze—the perfect killing season. "You were awake long before daybreak," recalled one pilot, "busy in your cockpit as the first chill slivers of light thrust up out of the enemy's domain in the east . . . Scramble—climb—vector—buster! Your life was packed with action, the breathless, throbbing sensation of intense danger. You flew and fought the death-long day."[45]

Monday, August 12, 1940, was such a day.

It was late in the afternoon when Art Donahue's 64 Squadron was scrambled and ordered to intercept eighteen Do-17s of KG 2 that had just bombed RAF Manston, causing severe damage and sending clouds of smoke and chalk dust spiraling several thousand feet into the air. "I guess we were all feeling a little subdued," recalled Donahue. "We knew that if we intercepted we'd be fortunate if there was more than one other squadron at the most with us in the fight."[46]

64 Squadron did not intercept KG 2. Instead, it ran into the bombers' escorts—thirty Me-109s of JG 26. Within seconds, fighters were wheeling and diving, it seemed, across the entire horizon. Donahue closed on a bandit, throttle wide open, thumb crooked over his firing button. But then either Sergeant Gerhard Grzymalla or Lieutenant Heinz Ebeling of JG 26's III Group spotted Donahue and swooped down. Both were superb pilots and highly experienced; Ebeling had already shot down two Hurricanes that day.[47]

Donahue saw a yellow-nosed Messerschmitt in his rear mirror.[48] It was firing at him. "The familiar sound of exploding cannon shells wracked my eardrums and my plane shook," recalled Donahue. "Shrapnel banged and rattled and white tracers streamed by . . . The firing lasted only a second, but I expected it would start again." Donahue pushed his stick forward to dive. Nothing happened. His elevator cables had been shot to pieces. He pumped back and forth on the rudder pedals. They had gone limp. It was soon a battle simply to keep his Spitfire in the air.[49] "This was bad. I could smell powder smoke, hot and strong, but it didn't make me feel tough this time. It was from the cannon shells and incendiary bullets that had hit my machine. Smoke from an incendiary bullet was curling up beside me. It was lodged in the frame of the machine and smoldering there."

Donahue pulled open his cockpit and felt the wind tear at his goggles and helmet. Then there was another ear-splitting bang. Parts of his instrument panel were breaking up. "Smoke trails of tracer bullets appeared right inside the cockpit. Bullets were going between my legs, and I remember seeing a bright flash of an incendiary bullet going past my leg and into the gas tank. I remember being surprised that I wasn't scared anymore. I suppose I was too dazed . . . Then a little red tongue licked out inquiringly from under the gas tank in front of my feet and curled up the side of it and became a hot little bonfire in one corner of the cockpit. I remembered my parachute, and jerked the locking pin that secured my seat straps, and started to climb out just as the whole cockpit became a furnace."[50]

Donahue felt a blowtorch-intense burst of heat as he lifted himself up in the open cockpit. Then he was yanked out by a 200 mph wind. Dimly aware that he was falling, he reached for the rip cord on his parachute and pulled it.[51] There was a surreal silence now after the din of the battle. He noticed that one of his trouser legs was missing. His lower leg was blistered and badly burnt. The skin had come off in several places; around his ankle it flapped freely.

"Well, Art, this is what you asked for," he said out loud. "How do you like it?"[52]

Perhaps a minute after bailing out, as he fell through thick clouds, he heard a fighter nearby. The parachute obscured his view. The Luftwaffe had strafed Polish pilots who had bailed out over Poland. Would they do the same over England? Donahue began to panic as bullets zipped through the air.[53] "My parachute canopy quivered with each shot," he recalled. "It lasted for perhaps a second. I could think of nothing but that a Hun was firing at me and hitting my parachute canopy. I knew that if I pulled the shroud lines on one side it would partly collapse the canopy and I would fall faster, so I just went hand over hand up the shroud lines on one side until the canopy was two-thirds collapsed—I wasn't taking any halfway measures! That changed my position so I was looking up and could see the canopy, and I was surprised that there didn't seem to be any bullet holes in it. Then another volley sounded and the canopy quivered in the same way, and still no bullet holes appeared in it."[54]

Donahue looked down. The bullets were from an anti-aircraft gun on the ground. Then the earth was rushing up to meet him and he landed in a field of oats. Before long, a group of Home Guard soldiers approached, rifles at the ready. Donahue struggled to his feet, his burns agonizing now as the shock wore off. The men lowered their guns, recognizing the RAF blue of what remained of his uniform, and helped him toward their barracks. Halfway across the field, Donahue's knee buckled and he had to be carried the rest of the way.

In the soldiers' barracks, a young medical orderly was soon tending to Donahue's burns.

"You'll get about a six weeks lay-up out of this, sir."[55]

"Don't be silly!" replied Donahue. "This won't keep me laid up more than two or three days, will it?"[56]

"Well, you've got a couple of pretty nasty burns there on your leg and your hand. The one on your face isn't so bad, but the other two ought to take a month to heal. Then you'll get a spot of sick leave of course—yes, I'd make it all of six weeks before you're fit again."[57]

A British Air Ministry communiqué issued early the following day, August 13, reported: "It is now established that sixty-one enemy aircraft were destroyed in yesterday's air fight over our coasts. Thirteen of our fighters were lost, but the pilot of one of them was saved."[58]

Because of his injuries, Art Donahue was unable to attend his young friend Peter Kennard-Davis's funeral as he had planned. He would spend a month being treated for his burns near Canterbury before returning to 64, by which time it would have moved to the far quieter 13 Group area so that its pilots could get some desperately needed rest.

For Arthur Gerald Donahue, the Battle of Britain was over. For his fellow Americans in 601 and 609 Squadrons, however, it was only just beginning.

8. Tally-Ho!

Scarcely had I dropped off when I was in my Hurricane
rushing head-on at a 110. Just as we were about to collide
I woke up with a jerk that nearly threw me out of bed. I was
in a cold sweat, my heart banging wildly. I dropped off again—
but the nightmare returned. This went on at intervals of about
ten minutes all night. I shall never forget how I clung to the
bed-rail in a dead funk. If there is ever a choice between
physical and mental pain, I'll take physical every time.[1]

Paul Richey, No. 1 Squadron

Eagle Day dawned. It was August 13, 1940—the date set by
Göring for his knockout attack on Britain's airfields and defensive installations. At Tangmere, Billy Fiske and his fellow 601
Squadron pilots went to their dispersal hut, flying jackets hanging
around shoulders to fend off the chill, wet grass slicking flying
boots stuffed with maps. Aircrews warmed up 601's Hurricanes,
props blowing away the dew from the Perspex windscreens,
revealing the usual specks to be wiped away so pilots didn't suddenly
mistake a piece of grit for a Messerschmitt.

Fiske could not have been more content. "Life has never seemed
so good," he told family and friends.[2] It was as if he had found
his true calling. And he now fit into 601 perfectly. The squadron's
stalwarts had all heartily accepted him as one of their own: a
throwback to a more chivalrous age, a fellow aristocrat who also
cultivated an air of suave nonchalance in the face of danger, a
"jolly good sport" who had quickly seen to it that a scarlet silk
lining was sewn into his RAF uniform—the RAF's dark blue was
not sufficiently flamboyant. "They wore red linings in their tunics,

and mink linings in their overcoats," wrote Fiske of his fellow Millionaires. "They were arrogant and looked terrific, and probably the other squadrons hated their guts."[3] Rumor had it among Tangmere's ground crew that it cost a hundred pounds [around four hundred dollars] to get a stake in a 601 poker game while awaiting the call to scramble.[4]

It was 10:25 a.m. when the Millionaires were scrambled for the first time on Eagle Day. Climbing steeply, they heard that bandits were in the vicinity. Around 10:45 a.m., they spotted several slow-moving Ju-88 bombers, the spearhead of KG 54. Large swastikas emblazoned their tails.

Fiske picked out a target, closed until the German plane loomed in his reflector sight, and then fired. The German plane's engines began to stream smoke. Then it rapidly lost altitude, but Fiske did not follow it down. There were other bandits to watch out for, other machines to destroy. Soon his bullets were ripping into two more gray Ju-88s, yet they were somehow able to limp on. One was credited to Fiske as a probable and was later seen spewing black smoke as it struggled south over the Solent, the four-mile blaze of water separating Portsmouth from the Isle of Wight.[5]

Low on ammunition, Fiske returned to Tangmere where his Hurricane was quickly refueled. At 11:50 a.m., the telephone in the dispersal hut rang again. Fiske once more ran to his plane and was soon in formation. A few minutes after noon, he spied around forty Me-110s flying in what he described as a "defensive circle" to protect each other's tails. It was the standard tactic for flights of the two-seater fighter touted by Göring as unbeatable.[6] The German pilots used a different term for the defensive maneuver— the "circle of death."[7] And so it proved to be that day.

The Millionaires tore the invaders to pieces. Fiske fired on two Me-110s from LG 1[8] but then cannon fire smashed into an aileron, jamming it.[9] Perhaps he had flown too straight for too long, making himself an easier target for one of the Me-110s armed with four forward-firing machine guns and two cannons.[10] Thankfully, his other controls worked fine. Fiske set course for

Tangmere. Soon, he could see the airfield in the far distance. He eased off on the throttle, and saw his clock (airspeed indicator) fall and the glow of a green light, which indicated that his undercarriage was down. At last he was safe, his wheels bumping along the turf.

Although he had been in combat for just a few minutes, Fiske was exhausted—the strain of a dogfight was immense, and at twenty-eight he must have felt it more than most of his fellow pilots, whose average age was just twenty-two. It was the kind of fatigue that made even the toughest pilots feel like simply sitting and staring at flies on the dispersal hut's wall, speechless, as they tried to unwind. Fiske's fellow American, Art Donahue, already knew it: "I didn't want to sleep, but I didn't want to move, or talk, or fly, or anything else either, just relax. As nearly as I can describe it, it is a sensation of being drained completely, in every part of your body, though I don't know what of. But you seem to just want to surrender to relaxation, sitting or lying inert and absorbing whatever it is back into your system. I've heard many other pilots say they get the same feeling."[11]

The stress of combat was now taking its toll on every fighter pilot, especially those like Fiske who were still learning to master the Hurricane. Throughout Fighter Command, nerves were fraying and tempers were on a hair trigger. As pilots were strapped into their Sutton harnesses, their cheek and eye muscles twitched. Anything unexpected, any sudden sound or movement, however banal, could fill even the most unflappable with rage: the sight of an airman running for no good reason to a plane; the sound of a bicycle bell; a lukewarm cup of tea after a sweat-soaked dawn patrol; a "streamlined piece"—a well-proportioned young woman—who turned up late because the trains weren't running on time. Constant tension and fear wore down even the most experienced pilots and within a few weeks made them gaunt. "Sprogs"—young recruits—suddenly looked like their fathers.

Lovers and wives suffered perhaps just as much nervous strain. They could not experience combat but they could easily imagine how it might end. They also awoke on soaked sheets. They too knew the nightmares: falling, unable to pull the cockpit hood back, clawing at the Perspex; yanking a rip cord and then seeing the parachute not open; blowtorch flames melting eyebrows, the face, leaving soft lips feeling like a beak; mangled limbs amputated after a wreck.

Like every other pilot's wife, Rose Fiske worried constantly, but it was perhaps easier for her to say good-bye and wish her husband good luck each morning than it was for other spouses. Living with a fighter pilot was not so terribly different from being the lover of a bobsled champion who daily risked life and limb on the ice at St. Moritz. When she had married Billy, he had made it clear that he would not stop testing himself to the limit. He had always admired men who lived "at full blast" and wanted to emulate them, even if it cost him his life. "So many nice people have died in the last few years," Fiske wrote in a letter to his family that year, "one is assured of pleasant company on the other side of the pearly gates—and I bet they are all laughing like buggery at us poor mortals."[12]

Rose was one of the top debutantes of her generation, so striking that her portrait was hung in the Royal Academy in London that long hot summer. But there was no haughtiness about her. Without complaint, she quickly adapted to her new circumstances. "Rosie is the most efficient settler-iner and house-keeper I've ever seen," Fiske told his family proudly. "She works like a Trojan from dawn till dark and is as happy as a clam."[13]

One morning, however, Rose Fiske was not up at dawn. It was long after first light when her mother, who had moved down to Tangmere from London to provide emotional support, woke her and told her to jump out of bed, put on a robe, and run outside. A German bomber was passing low overhead, tailed by a Hurricane. Rose ignored her, rolled over, and fell back asleep.

An hour later, the telephone rang. Rose answered. "Maybe you're not interested, but we fought a terrific battle over the Channel," said Billy angrily. "One of the Huns, badly shot up and out of ammunition, headed toward Tangmere to force-land. I line up alongside to bring him in, take all the trouble to push him five miles off the course in order to bring him over the house and show him to you, and you can't even be bothered to get out of bed and look."[14] Apparently, it was a rare outburst. As with most couples in wartime, for the most part the Fiskes avoided argument and instead squeezed as much joy from their limited time together as possible.

The urge to make every moment count was particularly strong that summer of 1940, and it was reflected in radio plays and films as well as on the best-seller lists. The most popular book, selling more than three hundred thousand copies in hardback in just a few weeks, was a long and patriotic poem by Alice Duel Miller, titled *The White Cliff*. One of its stanzas read:

> Lovers in peace-time,
> With fifty years to live,
> Have time to tease and quarrel
> And question what to give;
> But lovers in war-time
> Better understand
> The fullness of living,
> With death close at hand.[15]

The Fiskes understood only too well.

Thanks to foul weather, August 14 had so far been a quiet day at RAF Middle Wallop, now dubbed "Center Punch" by Eugene Tobin. During recent lulls, 609's pilots had tried to distract themselves as best they could. The Polish duo, Tadeusz Nowierski and Piotr Ostaszwski, nicknamed Nowi and Osti, often lay on their bunks watching flies climb up a wall, working their eye muscles, improving their long-range sight.[16] Andy Mamedoff preferred to gamble, wagering any spare cash in card games. Tobin sometimes joined in but usually opted to be 609's disc jockey, playing over and over the Bing Crosby records he had brought all the way from California.

Around 4 p.m., the black telephone rang in 609's dispersal hut.

The squadron's adjutant, Flying Officer Dick Anderson, was on the line, asking for Red Tobin.

Tobin soon picked up the receiver.

"Hey, Red," Anderson said, "if you hop down to Hangar Five, there's a Spit to deliver to Hamble."[17]

Tobin grabbed his flying gear, stuffed a few maps into his boots, and headed out of the hut on yet another ferrying mission. Hopefully, it would be a more successful flight than his last one, on August 9, when he had taken Squadron Leader Darley's bullet-holed Spitfire to Hamble to get it repaired but had then wrecked its prop by pushing the stick too far forward on takeoff for the return flight. From Hamble it had been a long journey back by road to Middle Wallop, where he had had to explain, shamefaced, what he had done to Darley's plane. "Blast it!" had been Darley's only recorded response.[18]

When on earth would he see some real action? The evening before, he had listened to story after story about 609's best day yet in combat—on Eagle Day, August 13, 1940, the squadron had intercepted fifty-two Ju-87s of Major Graf Schonborn's StG 77 as they hightailed it back toward France.[19] The pilots of 609 had heard the Germans' terrified shouts of "*Achtung, Spitfeuer!*" over their radios as they tore into the infamous hook-winged bombers, whose maximum speed was 250 mph, 100 mph less than the Spitfire's. The ensuing "Stuka party" had been like swatting flies for Osti and Nowi, who had claimed two planes each,[20] and so thrilling that Johnny "Dogs" Dundas joked that although he had missed the famous "glorious twelfth" grouse shoot in Scotland, the "glorious thirteenth" had been "the best day's shooting" he had ever had.[21] Osti and David Crook had also engaged the Stukas' escorts from the Ace of Spades, and given Werner Mölders's boys a bloody nose, shooting down two Messerschmitt Me-109s, one crashing into Weymouth Bay, the other into Poole harbor.[22]

Tobin hoped he would soon be able to share in the spoils, but first he would have to convince Squadron Leader Darley that he should go operational. Not crashing another Spitfire on today's ferrying mission would be a start. And looking on the bright side, the daily run to Hamble and back left him with plenty of time to flirt with English girls and practice his wise-cracks. With this no doubt in mind, Tobin decided to look in on the operations room and its WAAFs with their neatly pinned hair, black stockings, and saucy smiles.[23] Then he would stroll over to Hangar Five, at the opposite end of the Middle Wallop base, and fly to Hamble.

Tobin found the girls hard at work, with no time to laugh at his jokes today. Bandits had been detected and were heading toward the area. With a fellow pilot, thirty-two-year-old Flying Officer Alexander Edge, Tobin hurried toward the hangar where his Spitfire was being warmed up. But then, around eighty yards from the hangar, he heard the drone of a fully loaded bomber and looked up to see a Ju-88 of the Luftwaffe's elite Lehrgeschwader (LG) 1 unit sneak below the clouds. Edge began to run away, but he doubled back and sprinted directly beneath the bomber after Tobin yelled for him to follow him instead. "The bombs landed near enough, but we were unharmed thanks to Red's better under-standing of ballistics," recalled Edge. "A row of craters lay right across my original line of escape."[24]

The bombs kept falling. Edge and Tobin dived to the ground as one landed on Hangar Five, destroying it, killing every man inside, and stunning everyone within fifty yards. "My head was spinning," recalled Tobin. "It felt as though I had a permanent ringing in my ears. I felt the blast go over me as I lay there flattened on the ground. I got up and my instinct was to run toward the hangar. It was carnage. I saw one overalled person with his foot and half a leg blown off, another had a great red patch on his chest with a load of mess hanging from it, another was rolling in agony with one of his arms missing. The door of the hangar was only half closed and just inside I could see the bodies of four overalled men on the ground with one seemingly splat-tered against the edge of the door. I felt sick. I almost threw up there and then . . . other air force personnel came into the hangar [and] they just seemed to go about their business in a respectable and calm manner with no sign of panic. Then I remembered what

I was told about the British, 'no matter how bad the situation, they will always keep that stiff upper lip.'"[25]

Meanwhile, 609's only sergeant pilot, twenty-eight-year-old Alan Feary, had managed to get airborne. Thirty seconds after LG 1 had struck, he was banking sharply, his wings at ninety degrees to the ground, chasing the offending Ju-88 over Boscombe Down as it fled for the nearest clouds. Slamming open his throttle, the Derbyshire-born pilot closed fast and soon had the bomber exactly where he wanted it—250 yards ahead of him, at the center of his reflector sight. Feary opened fire. Over two thousand rounds ripped along the bomber's undercarriage, tearing its belly to shreds and killing all but one of the crew. The bomber appeared to "hang in the sky" before plunging to the ground, five miles away, at North Charford near Romsey.[26]

Back at Middle Wallop, as soon as the all-clear sirens sounded, Eugene Tobin rushed to 609's dispersal hut. "[Tobin] turned up grinning as usual," recalled David Crook, "but with his clothes in an awful mess and covered in white chalk because he had to throw himself several times into a chalk pit as the Huns dropped out of the clouds."

"Aw hell," Tobin grinned, "I had a million laffs."[27]

The Luftwaffe had so far failed miserably to land a decisive blow even though Göring had thrown the best of his dive-bombers at the British day after day. Between them, 609 and 601 Squadrons had destroyed more than twenty Stukas on August 13 alone, making them the RAF's most successful squadrons on Eagle Day.[28] Such losses could not be sustained, so Göring reluctantly agreed with his senior commanders to withdraw the highly vulnerable Stuka from the battle as soon as possible.[29] The pride of the Luftwaffe, having terrorized troops and massacred countless civilians from Poland to Plymouth, had finally been neutered.[30]

On the evening of August 14, at Fighter Command HQ, Chief Air Marshal Hugh "Stuffy" Dowding and Sector 11 Commander Sir Keith Park pondered the Germans' next move. "They're playing games at the moment," said Dowding, "they're not going to achieve anything by these scant and random attacks . . . Something is building."

"What damage they have done to the airfields has been a setback but they're still operational," replied a confident Park. "Middle Wallop is [already back] at full strength . . . We will be ready for them."[31]

9. That England Might Live

High summer at Tangmere. I shall never forget those stirring
days, when it seemed the sky was always blue and the rays of
the fierce sun hid the glinting Messerschmitts; or when there
was a high layer of cirrus cloud (although this filtered the
sun and lessened the glare, it was dangerous to climb
through it, for your gray-green Spitfire stood out against the
white backcloth); when the grass was burnt to a light brown
color and discolored with dark oil-stains where we parked
our Spitfires, and when the waters of the Channel looked
utterly serene and inviting.[1]

Air Vice-Marshal "Johnnie" Johnson

It was still dark when 601 Squadron's pilots sat down the next
day, August 15, 1940, for their usual breakfast: bacon and eggs
and jam on toast, washed down with mugs of piping hot, strong
tea. Dawn heralded gray skies, but as the morning wore on the
sun burnt off the cloud cover, and by 10:30 a.m. the conditions
were ideal for dropping bombs on England. The first scramble of
the day came around 11 a.m.: 601 Squadron was ordered to prevent
the attack of sixty Ju-88As of LG 1, escorted by forty Me-110s of
ZG 2, on the airfields at Middle Wallop and Worthy Down.

By midday, the Millionaires had destroyed five Ju-88s and
returned to Tangmere to refuel. A fine morning's work but not
without cost: Fiske's close friend Billy Clyde and another pilot
officer had been shot down but were unhurt; another of his prewar
skiing friends, Gordon "Mouse" Cleaver, had been almost blinded
from pieces of his Perspex cockpit hood and had only just managed,
with great bravery, to nurse his badly damaged Hurricane home
to Tangmere. Cleaver would soon be awarded the Distinguished

Flying Cross and eventually regain his eyesight but would not fly
again with 601. Fiske himself had been in particularly fine form,
managing the difficult task of "maneuvering a straggling Ju-88
into the Portsmouth balloon barrage, having exhausted his ammunition" as the squadron records put it.[2]

It was obvious now to 601's pilots that the odds were heavily
stacked against them if they were to continue fighting as they had
in the past few weeks. "We all knew it was like a game of roulette,
backing black all the time," recalled Flight Lieutenant Tom
Hubbard, who had shot down a German search-and-rescue
seaplane a month before. "Our luck wouldn't come up forever."[3]

By nightfall, the Luftwaffe had completed its largest attack to
date, hitting targets the length and breadth of England, but at the
loss of seventy-five aircraft, causing its shaken pilots to dub August
15 "Black Thursday."[4] Tangmere had been singled out by the
Germans for attack but, just as with the raid on Middle Wallop,
only a few bombers had penetrated Fighter Command's defenses
and the base remained operational.

Undeterred, Göring ordered the Luftwaffe to return en masse
and wipe Tangmere and other 11 Group bases off the map the
following day—August 16, 1940. The Reichsmarschall was certain
of success this time—so much so that he ridiculed the concerns of
escalating losses expressed by his senior commanders, Kesselring
and Sperrle, and shrugged off the previous day's serious bruising
as simply bad luck. He had not been outsmarted by Fighter
Command. Only three hundred RAF fighters were left, according
to Beppo Schmid, the Luftwaffe's chief of intelligence. With the
right protection from the Jagdwaffe, his bombers would now finish
off Park's force.

Conditions were once again ideal as Göring marshaled every
available fighter and more than half his bombers. Among the 1,720
German aircraft directed to give the RAF "the big lick" was a
flight of courageous young Stuka pilots. Around noon, they left
their base in Normandy with orders to attack Tangmere. Ten
minutes later, they were approaching the middle of the English
Channel, nervously scanning the skies, painfully aware that at just

250 mph—the Stuka's maximum speed—they were sitting ducks if they came across Spitfires.

At Tangmere, meanwhile, an informal party was under way. In the officers' mess, several young WAAFs mingled with a dozen or so of the base's pilots. Suddenly, the station commander rushed into the room. "Girls, get in your cars and out of here!" he shouted. "Leave everything—get out! 601 Squadron, readiness!"[5]

Ground crews jumped into action. Among them was twenty-year-old Airman William Higgs. He had been on duty for fifty-two hours at a stretch for several weeks and was so tired these days that he often fell asleep on the grass near an assigned plane as soon as he had serviced it.[6] Now, yet again, he and his mates quickly readied 601's Hurricanes for combat.

It was 12:25 p.m. In Tangmere's operations room, a young WAAF named Anne Turley-George heard a warning of bandits approaching across the Channel and went to work: "We felt we were a part of things at last, transmitting directions and logging messages."[7] It usually took no more than two minutes to get all twelve of 601's Hurricanes off the ground, but that lunchtime the scramble was twice as long because of craters left in the grass runways from the previous day's raid. Knowing they had lost precious time, Fiske and his fellow pilots then climbed as fast as possible to intercept the incoming German bombers.

As 601 soared toward the sun with throttles wide open, one of the most extraordinary episodes of individual heroism during the Battle of Britain was unfolding. At around 1:45 p.m., 249 Hurricane Squadron's Flight Lieutenant James Nicolson spotted three Ju-88s and attacked. Suddenly, an escorting Me-110 opened up on him. Cannon fire ripped his canopy apart and he was partially blinded by blood from a wound to his forehead. A second explosion set his cockpit on fire. Machine-gun bullets then riddled his Hurricane from nose to fin, hitting him in the left leg. Yet Nicolson somehow controlled his plane and then, incredibly, set off after the Me-110.

The glass on his burning instrument panel had soon popped and shattered in the intense heat, but Nicolson still gave chase.

Finally, he got the enemy in his sights, fired, and watched as his tormentor spiraled down to the English Channel. Nicolson then found the strength to get out of his blazing cockpit. He was in such a state of shock from severe burns that he dropped five thousand feet before he remembered to pull the rip cord on his parachute. When he landed, he noticed that blood was gushing through the lace holes of his left boot. The glass on his wrist watch had melted. But he had the satisfaction of having destroyed a German plane. And his courage would soon be rewarded with the only Victoria Cross—Britain's highest award for gallantry— of the Battle of Britain.[8]

Meanwhile, 601 Squadron had been scouring the skies and listening carefully to the Tangmere controller as he plotted the German advance. Many bandits were now closing fast on Tangmere at twenty thousand feet.[9]

"You are only to engage the Little Boys [fighters]," the controller instructed. "On no account must you attack the Big Boys [the Stukas]."[10]

There they were: small gray dots at first, around fifty Stukas from StG 2 in the hazy distance, flying without escort in a diamond formation. They were crossing the coast. A few minutes later, they were nearing Tangmere itself.

Sir Archibald Hope, 601's squadron leader, reported to Tangmere's controller: "There are no little boys but plenty of big ones. Permission to attack?"

"No."

They were to engage only escorting fighters.

Then Hope heard the high-pitched whines of several Stukas beginning to dive on Tangmere.

"To hell with this," said Hope. "I'm going after the bombers."[11]

Disobeying his controller, Hope ordered 601 to attack. But it was too late. The Big Boys had got through. Dipping his wing to swing around and give chase, to his dismay Hope saw a bomb explode less than fifty yards from 601's dispersal hut, narrowly missing his car.[12] Below, Airman William Higgs heard the whistle of another bomb as it fell toward him. "I took off like a rocket for the nearest shelter which was just outside the barrack block," he recalled. "I got to it just in time—just as another airman behind me was hit by splinters and a soldier was badly wounded in the back. The shelter was rocking and swaying and earth was falling from the roof. Fortunately, it stayed in one piece."[13]

Shelters, the officers' mess, and two hangars were hit as more gull-winged Stukas swooped down out of the sun. Seven Hurricanes on the ground were quickly destroyed—they had not been dispersed around the base. "After the first stunned disbelief," recalled WAAF Anne Turley-George, "we tumbled into the shelters whilst they beat and hammered us into the ground . . . The squadrons thundered off the ground tirelessly. Off they pelted . . . those glorious, radiant boys."[14] Nearby, Gunner J. J. Ingle of the 98th Heavy Anti-Aircraft Regiment watched in mounting frustration: "Neither we or the ground defenses on the airfield could open fire as our fighters were taking off as fast as they could and were mixed up with the Germans."[15]

Tangmere's doctor, twenty-seven-year-old Dr. Courtney Willey, had just gone on duty when a bomb landed on his sick quarters. "I was suddenly aware that it was disintegrating around me," he recalled. "Luckily, I was standing behind a chimney stack with a tin hat on. That took the brunt of the fall. It was lucky that we were in a single-story building. Although the ceiling fell in on me, I was able to get out unaided. Immediately adjacent to the sickbay was a bomb-proof shelter with a red cross on it. The sick were in there and none had been hurt."[16]

The airfield was now dotted with craters. In many places, the earth bulged, indicating delayed-action bombs. After a brief lull in the bombing, yet more Stukas attacked, killing two more airmen. "Their bodies were being placed on a tarmac path as some captured German aircrew were marched through the gate," stated the official squadron history. "One of the Germans was imprudent enough to laugh when he saw the bodies, and a senior RAF officer who was walking to meet them lengthened his stride and punched the German on the nose."[17]

At last, the all-clear siren sounded. Ten RAF personnel and

three civilians lay dead. Twenty others were wounded. Airman William Higgs emerged from his shelter to find utter devastation. "The whole area was a mass of bricks and rubble. We had taken quite a beating in such a short time. In one place, airmen had taken shelter in a tanker shed [which] had nine-inch-thick walls, a steel shuttered door, and about a one-foot-thick roof. A bomb had burst close by and the blast from it had blown the walls out, the roof crashing on those below."[18]

The pilots of StG 2 had struck with devastating accuracy. Now it was 601 Squadron's turn. Leading the hunt, determined to avenge Tangmere's losses, was Billy Fiske's flight: his close friend Billy Clyde, by now one of 601's leading aces; working-class twenty-one-year-old Sergeant Norman Taylor; twenty-eight-year-old Hugh Riddle, later to become a celebrated portrait artist; thirty-one-year-old Michael Doulton, reputed to be the tallest pilot in the RAF; and Sergeant Pilot Alexander S. MacDonald, who had risen fast through the ranks, having joined the RAF as a lowly airman in 1937. To a man, they attacked with unflinching courage, flouting fierce volleys of rear-gunner fire to pepper the cumbersome Stukas as they fled across the Channel, sometimes just a few hundred feet above the water, straining to get above 200 mph.

It is thought that Billy Fiske dipped his wing and soon fixed on a Stuka, its hooked wings looming in the glow of his reflector sight. Fiske may then have opened fire only to see the Stuka's rear gunner shoot back at him. What's certain is that at least one bullet, perhaps an incendiary, struck Fiske's reserve gas tank in front of his cockpit and set it ablaze.

Fiske reported to the controller at Tangmere that he had been hit.

"Bail out!"

"No, I think I can save the kite," replied Fiske. "I'm coming in."[19]

Flames were licking up his legs and then scorching his hands and the exposed parts of his face. As Fiske struggled to bring the Hurricane home, the flames roasted the skin around his ankles, causing horrific third-degree burns, leaving his feet looking like stumps.

Pilot Officer Jack Riddle had landed, refueled, and was now

taking off to go "bash" the Boche again when he saw "an aircraft coming in with smoke pouring out of her back."[20] It belonged to Fiske, who somehow managed to fly over the airfield's boundary and then touch down.[21]

Twenty-year-old nursing orderly Jeffrey Faulkner and his friend, Corporal George Jones, set off in an ambulance, a so-called "blood bucket," ringing its bell constantly. "We got to Fiske's Hurricane on the western boundary of the airfield," recalled Faulkner. "The plane was damaged but it wasn't on fire."[22] Fiske was conscious but in a terrible state as Faulkner reached into the cockpit, pulled him out, and then removed his flying jacket, helmet, and earphones. "His burns were really horrific. When we took his gloves off, the skin just sort of fell away from his hands."

Faulkner knelt close to Fiske and tried to comfort him.[23] "It was a marvelous thing that he had brought his plane in. He could have turned upside down and bailed out. But if he had been attacked below a thousand feet, he probably wouldn't have had time. In which case he may have just torn back to the aerodrome and landed. I noticed that Fiske's plane was shot up and the fabric of the plane was split. The only thing I remember him saying was 'goddamned thing.' He swore at the aircraft in no uncertain way."[24]

The next man on the scene was Sir Archibald Hope, who had been returning to refuel and rearm when he spotted Fiske's damaged Hurricane near the airfield's boundary. "Fiske's plane was on its belly, belching smoke," he remembered. "It must have got a bullet in its engine. There were two ambulance men there. They had got Billy Fiske out of the cockpit. He was lying on the ground. They didn't know how to take his parachute off, so I showed them. Billy was burnt about the hands and ankles, so I told them to put on Tanafax, the stuff we were supposed to put on burns."

Hope leaned over Fiske.

"Don't worry," he said. "You'll be all right."[25]

Hope returned to his Hurricane and then taxied toward 601's dispersal hut. Meanwhile, Faulkner placed blankets around Fiske to keep air from his burns, gave him a shot of morphine, lifted him with Jones on a stretcher into his ambulance, and then drove back to the sick quarters, where Dr. Willey was waiting.[26]

"Hello, Billy," said Willey calmly. "What have you been up to?" Fiske did not reply.

Willey administered another painkiller.

"There's nothing more I can do," he told Faulkner. "Get him in the hospital as fast as you can."[27]

It was twenty minutes later when an ambulance arrived to take Fiske to the St. Regis Hospital in nearby Chichester. "Some people say that there was a woman in the ambulance," recalled Faulkner. "Perhaps the operations room had phoned his wife Rose who lived not far from the aerodrome. And she may have come and then sat in the ambulance with him."[28]

Fiske was admitted to the St. Regis near death and still wearing his scorched flying boots. There was little hope of him surviving but then, by some miracle it must have seemed, he began to make a startling recovery. When 601 Squadron's adjutant visited the hospital later that afternoon, he found Fiske "sitting up in bed, perky as hell."[29]

The tension was yet again almost too much to bear at Fighter Command's 11 Group operations room in Uxbridge. Prime Minister Winston Churchill sat impatiently in the gallery overlooking a large plotting board. It was around 6 p.m. when he saw the WAAFs below push several markers across the board that dominated the room and then place them mid-Channel: yet another mass raid was headed England's way. Seated at Churchill's side, "sick with fear," was General Sir Hastings Ismay, secretary to the War Cabinet, and a glum-looking, blue-suited Lord Beaverbrook, Minister of Aircraft Production.[30]

All three were soon transfixed by a display panel across the room. Red bulbs indicated that every squadron was either in the air or unavailable. Britain's fate appeared to hang in the balance, the margin between victory and defeat excruciatingly narrow. The Luftwaffe's targets were now London's perimeter airfields. The minutes passed slowly as Park issued crisp commands; Churchill appeared not to move a muscle.

The wall display finally showed that some of Park's squadrons were available and that the German raiders were turning and heading back across the Channel. Visibly weary, Churchill stood up and then walked quickly to his waiting Humber staff car, deep in thought. A few minutes later, he and Ismay were on their way to Chequers, the British premier's country retreat.

Ismay turned toward Churchill.

"Don't speak to me," snapped Churchill. "I have never been so moved."

They passed neat gardens, suburbia, and leafy parks in the gathering dusk.

Several minutes later, Churchill broke the silence: "Never in the field of conflict has so much been owed by so many to so few."[31]

Ismay was speechless.

Back at Tangmere, RAF ground crew and other personnel struggled to get the base operational again. Sandy Johnstone, 602's squadron leader, recalled driving to the airfield that evening and finding it "in utter shambles, with wisps of smoke still rising from the shattered buildings. Little knots of people were wandering about with dazed looks on their faces, obviously deeply affected by the events of the day. I eventually tracked down the station commander standing on the lawn in front of the officers' mess with a parrot sitting on his shoulder. Jack was covered with grime and the wretched bird was screeching its imitation of a Stuka at the height of the attack! The once immaculate grass was littered with personal belongings that had been blasted from the wing which had received a direct hit. Shirts, towels, socks and a portable gramophone—a little private world for all to see . . . Rubble was everywhere and all three hangars had been wrecked."[32]

That evening, Fiske's fellow pilots waited for news about his condition. He was no longer as "perky as hell." In fact it was now questionable whether he would make it through the night, and if he did, he would never race a bobsled or fly again unless he learned to use prosthetic limbs—below the knees his legs would probably need to be amputated to prevent gangrene.

Rose Fiske apparently stayed at the St. Regis Hospital throughout that long night as doctors and nurses worked to save her husband. But his heart and lungs could not cope with the massive trauma caused by such terrible burns, and sometime after dawn twenty-eight-year-old Pilot Officer Billy Fiske passed away.[33] He was the first American pilot to lose his life in the Battle of Britain, eighteen long months before his own country was attacked at Pearl Harbor and finally joined the fight against Hitler. As one of his contemporaries later recalled, his had been a life of many notable firsts.

The news of Fiske's death spread fast through fashionable London society, and then across the Atlantic and around the world. The celebrated CBS broadcaster, Ed Murrow, was one of many American correspondents in London who paid tribute.[34] The British writer and advocate for women's rights, Vera Brittain, wrote perhaps the most poignant epitaph: "In smoke and flame the most highly trained young airmen of two nations have fallen from the sky, and with them a youthful American, gay, fortunate, brilliant, an only son whose best years should have lain before him."[35]

In the cafés of the Reich's capital, and all across conquered Europe, that summer's hit song was "Bombs on England." The macabre ditty saddened Adolf Galland as much as it stirred the Nazi faithful sunning themselves that Saturday, August 17, on the sidewalks of the Unter den Linden and on the lawns of the Tiergarten. But what really depressed him was the sight of his fellow Germans carrying on with not a care in the world as he was driven that morning in a Horch staff car from the center of Berlin to Karinhall, Herman Göring's country retreat forty miles northwest of the capital. Indeed, Galland would never forget his profound sense of alienation on arriving back in the Fatherland for the first time during the Battle of Britain. Unlike the British, the German people clearly had not the faintest idea what the conflict entailed, how fierce and unrelenting it had become.

By now, even some of the hardiest pilots in Galland's JG 26 threw up their breakfasts before sorties. And at JG 51, Werner

Mölders's unit, the first stop after a briefing was often not the dispersal hut but the toilet. "I had come out of a battle of life and death," recalled Galland, "the brunt of which so far had been borne by the fighter force . . . we guessed fairly accurately that the battle we were fighting on the Channel was of decisive importance to the continuance and the final outcome of the struggle. The colossus of World War II seemed to be like a pyramid turned upside down, balancing on its apex, not knowing which way to lean. And for the moment the whole burden of the war rested on the few hundred German fighter pilots on the Channel coast."[36]

The dark pine forests separating Berlin from Karinhall seemed to stretch endlessly. Eventually, the Horch slowed and then Galland's identity was being checked by a phalanx of guards at the entrance to the sprawling estate. Galland was expected and was quickly flagged through razor-wired fences fitted with photoelectric devices to detect any movement from unwanted visitors. Then the Horch was cruising along a two-mile avenue, edged with marble lions, toward a building that resembled a Swedish hunting lodge—Karinhall, built in 1931 to honor Göring's deceased Swedish wife.[37]

Galland stepped out of the Horch. Young staff officers in white-and-red-striped trousers scurried to greet him. Werner Mölders waited nearby. There were the usual pleasantries. His leg wound had healed nicely. He would be back in the air soon.

Galland and Mölders entered Karinhall together. When they had arrived in Berlin, it had been disorienting, but walking now along Göring's main hallway was disturbingly surreal. Silk hangings adorned the walls. Massive crystal chandeliers, shimmering in the light, dangled from the wooden rafters high above. The ascetic Mölders and even the *bon viveur* Galland—with his shiny new silver Mercedes, film-star friends, and ostentatious falconer's gloves—were unnerved by the excess. It was grotesque, too far removed from reality: the mud and sandbags of Caffiers airfield, dubbed Devil's Village by Galland's fellow JG 26 aces. There were too many monuments to Göring's ego, too many hunting trophies, too many pelts strewn across the marble floors.

Mölders and Galland hurried on down the entrance hall, flanked by long carved tables bearing decanters filled with France's best vintages. Their commander arrived to welcome them, dressed in one of his specially tailored uniforms. He pointed to the decanters.

"Fine wine for my bold eagles!" Göring quipped and then belly laughed.

Galland looked at Mölders, who remained silent.

The five-foot-nine Reichsmarschall had a powerful handshake. Up close his clear blue eyes were equally forceful. There was no doubting his formidable charm.

Servants dressed like medieval courtiers were soon at the aces' sides, holding silver trays bearing Havana cigars and flutes of champagne.

Göring was in high spirits. Little did Galland know that his commander was now taking thirty paracodeine tablets a day, his addiction to the narcotic as hard to shake as his reliance on morphine in the 1920s. And Göring was also his usual loquacious self. The decanters held fine wines, he explained, but far inferior to cases now on their way from Bordeaux and Lyon. If the Luftwaffe hadn't been so busy recently, the best vintages would have already been flown in.

Again the belly laugh as Göring rocked back and forth on his heels.

Galland and Mölders took their place in Karinhall's vast banquet hall with a group of senior Luftwaffe officers. Göring was soon holding court. As Hitler often did, he began a rambling lecture on the battle, on its broader implications for the Reich and how Britain would soon be defeated in the air. The other officers nodded, not one daring to interject.

Mölders and Galland hid their boredom. Göring was telling them nothing new. But the atmosphere of confidence and enthusiasm was somehow seductive. Galland began to wonder whether he had too narrow a view of the battle. Perhaps Göring was right: victory was not far off. Maybe Galland had spent too long analyzing the war from a cockpit.[38]

Göring announced a break in proceedings. To their surprise,

ABOVE: Art Donahue, far left, with his first plane, St. Charles, Minnesota, 1934. Donahue's father stands at far right. *Courtesy Donahue family.*

LEFT: "The first latch-key kid in Los Angeles." Eugene Tobin with father, Los Angeles, October 9, 1927. *Courtesy Helen Maher.*

Eugene Tobin in Los Angeles at
the height of the Depression.
Courtesy Helen Maher.

Eugene Tobin with one of the cars he serviced as a mechanic,
Los Angeles, 1930s. *Courtesy Helen Maher*.

Eugene "Red" Tobin,
MGM pilot, Los Angeles,
late 1930s.
Courtesy Helen Maher.

Eugene Tobin's girlfriend,
Anne Haring, standing before
his plane, Los Angeles, 1930s.
Courtesy Helen Maher.

ABOVE LEFT: Billy Fiske, "The King of Speed," sits at the
wheel in front of the 1932 U.S. Winter Olympics bobsled
team. Fiske won his second gold medal with the team.
Getty Images.

ABOVE RIGHT: "No. 42."
Celebratory cigarette card
detailing Fiske's unrivalled
record as a bobsled
champion. *Author's
collection.*

TO WHOM IT MAY CONCERN:

I hereby certify that Eugene Tobin has exhibited
to me a certificate of birth indicating that he was
born at Salt Lake City, Utah, United States of America,
on January 4, 1917, and a Pilot's License issued by
the United States Department of Commerce, bearing his
photograph, as evidence of his identity.

This document is issued to enable him to travel from
London to the United States, travelling via Eire and
sailing from Galway on the SS Washington.

John G. Erhardt
Consul General of the United
States of America.

LONDON,
July 2, 1940.

Travel pass issued to
Eugene Tobin by the
American Embassy in
London. Tobin did not
use it, opting to join
the RAF instead.
Courtesy Helen Maher.

Eugene Tobin's
travel papers,
summer 1940.
Courtesy Helen Maher.

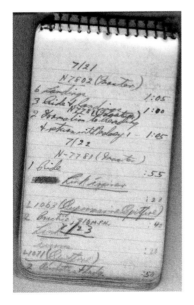

Art Donahue's log book
during training, July 1940.
Courtesy Donahue family.

The "Bulldog." Winston Churchill, Britain's prime minister, during her finest hour. *National Archives*.

"The Fat One." Luftwaffe chief Herman Göring, far right.

ABOVE: Watching for the Luftwaffe.
Civilian aircraft-spotter, London, 1940.
National Archives.

The enemy. JG 26's Adolf Galland,
one of the Battle of Britain's greatest
Luftwaffe aces.

The greatest. Werner "Daddy" Mölders,
the Third Reich's finest fighter pilot
and air combat commander.

Spitfire being re-armed during the Battle of Britain. *Imperial War Museum.*

609 Squadron takes a "tea break" between scrambles at RAF Warmwell, August 1940. *Courtesy Chris Goss.*

Eugene "Red" Tobin, right, relaxes between scrambles, Middle Wallop, August 1940. *Courtesy Mark Crame.*

"He was in a terrible state."
Geoffrey Faulkner, 601 Squadron
airman who pulled Billy Fiske
from his badly damaged plane.
Courtesy Geoffrey Faulkner.

The last journey. Billy Fiske's coffin, draped in the Union Jack and the Stars and Stripes, is carried to his final resting place. *Author's collection.*

Art Donahue takes a short break from the war with an
English friend. *Courtesy Donahue family.*

Children in the ruins of the Blitz. *National Archives.*

St. Paul's Cathedral surrounded
by flames during the Blitz.
Imperial War Museum.

The "Canadian."
Pilot Officer Hugh Reilley was born
in Detroit, Michigan, but pretended
to be a Canadian to circumvent
strict U.S. neutrality laws.
Imperial War Museum.

Vapor trails left during a dog-fight over the English Channel. The French coast
is visible in the distance. *Courtesy Donahue family.*

Pilot Officer Phillip Leckrone, from Salem, Illinois, fought during the Battle of Britain. *Imperial War Museum.*

OPPOSITE ABOVE:
Werner Mölders, left, and his friend and rival, Adolf Galland, on the hunt.

OPPOSITE BELOW:
Adolf Galland, second from left, listens to Werner Mölders, far right, during a break from fighting.

The farm boy from Minnesota.
Pilot Officer Arthur Gerald Donahue after
recovering from his burns, late 1940.
Courtesy Donahue family.

The "Few." Some of Art Donahue's fellow fighter pilots.
Courtesy Donahue family.

The first Eagles. Eugene Tobin looks on as Andy Mamedoff places Eagle Squadron patch on Vernon "Shorty" Keough's uniform. *Imperial War Museum.*

Ready for action. Mamedoff, 71 Squadron adjutant, Tobin and Keough, Church Fenton, 1940. *Imperial War Museum.*

Eugene Tobin leads fellow Eagle pilots on a practice scramble.
Winter 1940–41. *Imperial War Museum.*

LEFT: Andy Mamedoff finds time
to get his hair cut while on duty.
Courtesy Helen Maher.

OPPOSITE BELOW: Some of the
first Eagles during an early briefing,
late 1940. *Imperial War Museum.*

71 Squadron, the first all-American unit in RAF history. Andy Mamedoff, fifth from left, beside Eugene Tobin, sixth from left. *Imperial War Museum.*

Eagle pilots watch
their compatriots return
from a scramble.
Imperial War Museum.

Andy Mamedoff with fellow
Eagle pilot, Bill Hall, 1941.
Courtesy Helen Maher.

Phillip Leckrone's final resting place.
Imperial War Museum.

Eagle pilots wait for the call to scramble in their dispersal hut, March 1941.
Imperial War Museum.

A visit from royalty. The king and queen inspect 71 Squadron.
Imperial War Museum.

The Eagle Squadron mascot—an eagle with boxing gloves.
Imperial War Museum.

The Eagles watch a flyby of their
fellow American pilots.
Imperial War Museum.

Art Donahue, center,
with fellow pilots.
Courtesy Donahue family.

Art Donahue looks on as his sister examines part of a downed Messerschmitt, March 1941. *Courtesy Donahue family.*

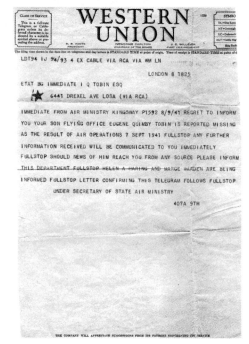

The dreaded telegram. Tobin reported missing in action. *Courtesy Helen Maher.*

BUCKINGHAM PALACE

The Queen and I offer you our heartfelt sympathy in your great sorrow.

We pray that the Empire's gratitude for a life so nobly given in its service may bring you some measure of consolation.

George R.I.

I. Q. Tobin, Esq.,

Condolences from the king.
Courtesy Helen Maher.

Eugene Tobin's grave
in France, late 1941.
Courtesy Helen Maher.

Art Donahue's log book shortly before the fall of Singapore, February 1942.
Courtesy Donahue family.

Art Donahue in 91 Squadron Spitfire, 1942. "Message from Minnesota"
is painted on his fuselage. *Courtesy Donahue family.*

Mölders and Galland were then invited into the Reichsmarschall's library and awarded the Pilot's Badge in Gold with Diamonds: the most prestigious award they could hope for, devised by Göring himself. Only thirty-eight others received this utmost honor during the entire span of the Third Reich.

Having softened up his eagles, Göring now began to berate them, imitating the primitive tactics that Hitler used on the Reichsmarschall himself to great effect. Cruel words followed: the Jagdwaffe was not trying hard enough. Its tactics were far too cautious. Too many bombers were being shot down and it was all the fighter escorts' fault. The bombers were what mattered, not the fighters.

When Göring finally ended his rant, Mölders tried to explain the operational difficulties he and his men faced. They were flying over enemy territory, with only ten to twenty minutes' supply of fuel. London was the limit of their operational range. Having to get back across the Channel after a sortie was often as treacherous as combat. And sticking close to bombers made the Jagdwaffe a slow-moving, easy target. Shooting down Spitfires and Hurricanes was what really mattered. After they had been destroyed, Göring's precious bombers would always get through.

Göring again tried to blame the fighters for the failure to bring the RAF quickly to its knees.

Galland had heard enough and was about to speak his mind when Mölders cut in quickly, explaining diplomatically that dogfights at 400 mph were different from combat with the Richthofen Squadron—the Red Baron's Flying Circus—back in the good old days when Göring had been the squadron's leader.

Göring nodded in agreement. Yes, of course, it was different now. But some things never changed. Just like in the last war, the ablest pilots needed to be promoted to high command to ensure victory. What the Jagdwaffe needed was new blood, new leadership. Mölders had already done a fine job commanding JG 51. Galland would be just as successful in charge of JG 26.

Galland protested. He was already in the best position, leading JG 26's III Group in the air. He didn't want nine squadrons and a desk job ordering around a hundred fellow pilots. He was a fighter pilot, not a pen pusher.

"My group is a pleasure to me and the responsibility sufficient," said Galland. "I am also scared of being tied to the ground and not seeing enough action."

"Don't worry," said Göring.

Galland could still fly. Of course he could. But he would also lead all of JG 26.

Göring concluded the meeting by asking whether Mölders and Galland had any requests.

"Yes, Herr Reichsmarschall," said Galland, "to remain a group commander."

Göring refused.

It was pointless to argue further. Galland had been promoted and could still fly. It was best to leave it at that.

By late afternoon, Galland and Mölders were in the Horch winding its way back through the suburbs of Berlin. Galland complained to Mölders about his new role. It would inevitably hamper him. He would not be as free to hunt and kill. Mölders was not in the least sympathetic. He relished the role of fighter pilot but also high command. "Brilliant though Mölders was as a fighter," recalled Galland, "his actual abilities and ambitions lay more in the field of tactics and organization."[39]

Galland said that Mölders could be the Oswald Boelcke—the grand tactician of the last war—of this conflict. Galland would be the ace of aces—the Richthofen of the Second World War.

"Well," said an indignant Mölders, "you *can* be the Richthofen . . . I prefer to one day be its Boelcke."[40]

As long as Galland focused his anger on the enemy and not on his superiors, added Mölders, he might even go one better than Richthofen by actually surviving the war.[41]

Rose Fiske followed behind young men in dark blue uniforms. At Rose's side was her mother, Lady Rosabelle Brand. It was all too easy for her to imagine how her daughter was feeling. Her first husband, an officer in the Coldstream Guards, had been killed in action in 1914 when Rose was a baby. Her second husband had passed away in 1929, leaving mother and daughter twice bereaved. And now it was happening all over again.

The Central Band of the Royal Air Force accompanied the funeral cortege as it wound its way through the small village of Boxgrove. Locals bowed their heads. An old man was seen to salute as the bier carrying Fiske's coffin—draped in the Stars and Stripes and Union Jack—moved into the moss-covered church-yard of St. Mary and St. Blaise. The service that followed was short but packed with emotion as twenty-eight-year-old William Meade Fiske, America's youngest ever Olympic gold medal winner, was lauded as a selfless sportsman as well as a skilled fighter pilot.

Then Billy Fiske began his last journey. His fellow pilots carried him into the graveyard, to a spot at its far corner, a stone's throw from the airfield he had died protecting. It was thought that this was where he would have wanted to be interred, his headstone overlooking Tangmere.[42] Buglers played a final farewell for the "supreme artist of the run"[43] and then a firing party cracked the silence with parting shots.[44]

Among the wreaths then placed on Fiske's grave was one from Lord Beaverbrook, the Minister of Aircraft Production, and another delivered that very morning to the station headquarters at Tang-mere. "There was a card with it," recalled Jeffrey Faulkner, the airman who had pulled Fiske from his Hurricane. "I can't remember exactly how it was worded, but it was definitely from Winston Churchill. I told the medical officer. He said, 'Good God!'"

Having sent flowers with a personal message to Fiske's funeral, Winston Churchill addressed the House of Commons that same day—August 20, 1940: "The gratitude of every home in our island, in our empire, and indeed throughout the world, except in the abodes of the guilty, goes out to the British airmen who, undaunted by odds, unwearied in their constant challenge and mortal danger, are turning the tide of the world war by their prowess and by their devotion. Never in the field of human conflict was so much owed by so many to so few."[45]

PART THREE

The Narrowest Margin

My first emotion was one of satisfaction, satisfaction at a job adequately done, at the final logical conclusion of months of specialized training. And then I had a feeling of the essential rightness of it all. He was dead and I was alive; it could easily have been the other way round; and that would somehow have been right too. I realized in that moment just how lucky a fighter pilot is. He has none of the personalized emotions of the soldier, handed a rifle and bayonet and told to charge. He does not even have to share the dangerous emotions of the bomber pilot who night after night must experience the childhood longing for smashing things. The fighter pilot's emotions are those of the duelist—cool, precise, impersonal. He is privileged to kill well. For if one must either kill or be killed, as now one must, it should, I feel, be done with dignity. Death should be given the setting it deserves; it must never be a pettiness; and for the fighter pilot it never can be.[1]

Flight Lieutenant Richard Hillary, *The Last Enemy*

10. Huns in the Sun

Hardly a day was now passing without some striking event
taking place. The death of a friend or enemy provided food
for a few moments' thought, before the next swirling dogfight
began to distract the cogitating mind from stupid thoughts
such as sadness or pity—remorse had long since died. It was
the act of living that perhaps became the most exciting form
of occupation. Any fool could be killed; that was being proved
all the time. No, the art was to cheat the Reaper and merely
blunt his Scythe a little. After all, it was only a game and he
was bound to win, but it was fun while it lasted.[1]

Geoffrey Page, DSO, OBE, DFC, and BAR

The long wait was over. Finally, the 609 Yanks were to go operational. On August 16, 1940, the same day Billy Fiske was shot
down, his fellow Americans in 609 Squadron learned that they were
to alternate weaving behind 609's two flights, A and B, watching
for surprise attacks by the swarms of German Me-109s that were
now escorting bombing raids on Fighter Command's 11 Group
bases.[2] "If you want to go chasing a DFC [Distinguised Flying
Cross] all over the deck, go somewhere else," Squadron Leader
Darley warned them. "We go up as twelve and we come down as
twelve—if we lose even two, the odds are shortened immediately."[3]

Tobin had been assigned to be the tail-end Charlie to A flight's
commander, Frank Howell, a Dunkirk veteran, and his wingman,
Geoffrey Gaunt, a tall and gregarious character brimming with
humor and life. "He was one of the best-looking fellows I've ever
seen," recalled Tobin. "He had a rosy complexion, a big set of
white teeth, blond wavy hair, and a perfect English accent."[4]

Before dawn, 609's pilots gathered in their dispersal hut, a small brick bungalow on the edge of Middle Wallop's airfield. It was always the worst time of day on the airfield: pilots were tired, anxious, and increasingly tense as they waited for the call to action. Since the wisecracking Americans had arrived, however, plenty of laughs had lightened the mood. Even the most exhausted and depressed pilots couldn't help but smile when Shorty had to be given a leg up into his Spitfire.

"Shorty was the smallest man I ever saw," recalled David Crook, "barring circus freaks, but he possessed a very stout size in hearts. When he arrived in the squadron we couldn't believe that he would ever reach the rudder bar in a Spit; apparently the Medical Board thought the same and refused to have him at first, as he was much shorter than RAF minimum requirements. However, Shorty insisted on having a trial, and he produced two cushions which he had brought all the way from the States via France, especially for this purpose. One went under his parachute and raised him up, the other he wedged in the small of his back, and thus he managed to fly a Spitfire satisfactorily, though in the machine all you could see of him was the top of his head and a couple of eyes peering over the edge of the cockpit."[5] According to Crook's fellow pilot officer, Michael Appleby, Shorty was so short because he had had two vertebrae removed after a parachute accident.[6]

The day wore on. By night-fall, 609 Squadron had been scrambled several times, but had seen no action. Yet again, Shorty Keough and his fellow Americans were left wondering when they would finally meet the enemy.

Back at Tangmere, 601's pilots were determined to avenge the attack on their home base, in whose defense Billy Fiske had been killed. On August 18, late in the afternoon, the squadron was directed to intercept eighty or so dive-bombers from StG 77, which were heading to attack radar stations and airfields along the southern coast. Pilot Officer Carl Davis, a South African born of American parents, was on superb form, taking down a Stuka and an escorting Me-109E. But that day's combat also saw the loss of two more 601 pilots, both sergeants, who had fallen prey to the German fighters. There were also unsustainable losses in several other front-line squadrons: twenty-seven planes shot down, ten pilots killed, and eighteen badly wounded.

In fact, 601 Squadron was now nearing the breaking point, having been in continuous action since the spring.[7] "The chain of reactions from 'scramble' [takeoff] to 'pancake' [landing] which were the fabric of the pilots' lives was taking its toll of their ability to remain constantly alert and responsive to danger," recalled the squadron's official history. "On August 19, therefore, in exchange for No. 17 Squadron, 601 was withdrawn from the southern battle skies to Debden, just north of the inner ring of fighter stations around London. Here the fighter pilot's life, though active, was more peaceful than over Hell's Corner."[8] But there was to be little respite for the badly battered unit. A few days after the exhausted pilots got to Debden, the Germans intensified their attacks on bases in 11 Group, so 601 was once again in the thick of things, protecting other airfields farther south.

Now began the hardest time for both sides—a battle of attrition above England that would soon be decided by simple numbers: the victor would be the air force that shot down more than it lost. At a similarly critical period, at the battle of Waterloo, the Duke of Wellington had urged the British to greater feats with the famous words: "Hard pounding gentlemen! Let us see who pounds the longest."[9] By the last week of August 1940, both sides were pounding harder and harder. But it was the Luftwaffe who looked like they would pound the longest. More RAF pilots were being lost than could be replaced. In some squadrons, the veterans were too tired to be effective. With novice pilots now being lost at five times the rate of veterans, the strain felt by flight commanders and squadron leaders was immense, and no relief was in sight. Every one of them knew that they would have to fly on to the bitter end, which could not be far off.

For 609 Squadron, the last week of August started with a visit from royalty in the form of the Duke of Kent. "The Americans were very intrigued," recalled David Crook, "being good Republicans, they are always much impressed by royalty. Shorty said, 'Say, what do we call this guy—dook?' We hastily assured him that sir would be sufficient. Anyway, the 'dook' arrived, shook hands with each of us, and spoke to us, and had a particularly long chat with Shorty [who was] immensely gratified."[10] In his diary that night, Tobin wrote: "He seemed like a nice guy, but he looked mighty tired. We had one scramble at 25,000 ft over Portsmouth but we didn't see anything. Went to the Mucky Duck and had a good time drinking and listening to some Crosby records."[11]

The following day, August 24, was Andy Mamedoff's twenty-eighth birthday. Tobin had decided not to give him a present, perhaps having lost to him at poker. By mid-morning, the skies were a perfect blue. There were no clouds, not even a wisp of cirrus. According to Mamedoff's flight leader, Flight Lieutenant James "Butch" MacArthur, it was impossible to get a sunny, warm day if one took leave, but it seemed that this was no problem at all during a battle when "every fine day simply play[ed] into the hands of the German bombers."[12] Clear skies also meant that the chances of survival—of cheating the "Grim Reaper," as MacArthur put it—decreased dramatically for pilots who were suddenly bounced by Me-109s diving out of the sun.

MacArthur was something of a swashbuckling character, with a thick mustache and slicked-back hair, and the squadron's royal blue scarf always draped around his neck. He had held the record for the fastest flight from London to Baghdad in the thirties and had been a civil pilot before joining the RAF in 1936. Posted to Middle Wallop on August 1 as B Flight commander, he had already taken down two Ju-87s and several Messerschmitts, making him one of the squadrons' deadliest aces.

By lunchtime, 609's pilots were seated in deck chairs or lying in the grass, basking in the sunshine, still waiting for the black Bakelite telephone in the nearby dispersal hut to ring.

It was around 1 p.m. across the Channel when several young German pilots belonging to JG 53 gathered around and listened to the crisp commands of their squadron leader, twenty-nine-year-old Hans-Karl Mayer, one of the leading aces of the battle with fifteen white stripes on his Me-109's tail fin. For the last week, the Ace of Spades had not seen much action, mostly because of adverse weather. There had been plenty of time to catch up on much-needed sleep, write letters home, and gorge on lobster and oysters in Mayer's favorite seafood restaurant in Rennes.

Mayer had learned how to fight in the air from none other than Werner Mölders. Like his mentor, he had served in the Condor Legion in Spain, gaining vital experience. A fellow JG 53 pilot, Werner Karl, recalled that Mayer "was so tall [that] he used to cram himself in his cockpit and when on missions used twice as much oxygen as the rest of us." Karl had recently seen Mayer shoot down an RAF fighter. The British pilot had bailed out, to Mayer's delight, but then Karl had seen the pilot fall and "an orange glow getting bigger and bigger—the parachute was on fire and soon collapsed and the British pilot fell to his death. On landing, I told Captain Mayer what he had not seen . . . he was genuinely upset."[13]

Today's mission would be a big one: JG 53 would be part of a huge escort of three hundred German fighters, protecting fifty bombers bound for Portsmouth. They would fly to the airfield at Cherbourg-East and refuel, so the fighters would be able to fly at their maximum range, before meeting up with the bombers over the Channel. The British were certain to pick up the raid as it crossed the Channel, so Mayer's pilots were more than likely to be engaged by several squadrons of Spitfires. It was crucial that they maintained their height above the bombers. Mayer would choose when to attack. The moment they started to get "thirsty"— low on fuel—they were to turn around and head for home.

It was 1:30 p.m. as Mayer and his men took off from their base in Rennes and headed toward Cherbourg-East to refuel. At Cherbourg-East, Mayer again gathered his flight, his so-called dog pack, around him. He assigned two pilots the role of lookout pair. Then he asked his men to synchronize their watches.

Twenty-two-year-old Josef Broker made certain he was in time with his leader. He was about to go on his first operational sortie with the Ace of Spades's highest-scoring squadron, which he had joined just over a week ago. Moreover, he was to fly as Mayer's wingman. Mayer would expect him to stay with him at all times, watching for Tommies, protecting his tail.

In all, eighty-one Messerschmitts from the three groups of JG 53 now stood, their engines idling, in neat rows on Cherbourg-East's airfield. Suntanned and shirtless, the ground crew crawled over the planes, starting batteries, cleaning canopies, making sure the fuel tanks were full to the last drop and their warning lights were working.

The Aces of Spades went to their planes. Props whirred and dust flew as the German pilots climbed into their cockpits. The ground crew pulled away chocks, shielding their eyes from the blasts of dirt, clothes flapping in the prop-wash, and covered their ears as the growl of eighty-one Daimler-Benz engines became a roar.

Hans-Karl Mayer checked his instruments and then signaled that he was ready.

A member of JG 53's ground staff pointed a flare pistol toward the sky.

Hans-Karl Mayer released his brakes and pushed a yellow knob to the left of his control stick. His engine responded and he began to move forward.

"We're off!" Mayer called to his men. "All the best!"[14]

A green flare exploded, signaling takeoff, and then one after another JG 53's flights took to the skies.

Back at Middle Wallop, 609's pilots still basked in the sunshine.

Around 4:10 p.m. the squadron was scrambled and was soon heading toward Portsmouth under orders to patrol above the city at ten thousand feet. Other squadrons would be doing the same but at a far greater height. "We were the luckless ones sent low down to deal with any possible dive-bombers," recalled David Crook. "We hated this—it's a much more comforting and reassuring feeling to be on top of everything than right underneath."[15]

Eugene Tobin and Andy Mamedoff were now at the rear of

their sections, nervously performing their role as tail-end Charlies. Mamedoff's job was more difficult because he was flying the oldest plane in the squadron, which had been with 609 since a few days before the outbreak of war. Soon, Tobin could see that Mamedoff was having trouble keeping up with the rest of his flight as it climbed above an intense barrage from anti-aircraft guns below. To one of the pilots, the barrage looked like a "large number of dirty cotton-wool puffs in the sky."[16] Every gun anywhere near the port of Portsmouth appeared to have opened up.

It was now around 4:40 p.m. Squadron Leader Hans-Karl Mayer scanned the skies, squeezed into his cockpit with barely enough room to move his legs—he was over six feet and around 230 pounds. Five thousand feet below, Mamedoff continued to weave behind his flight. "We were flying at 2,300 feet and going into the sun," he recalled. "I was told to investigate a plane below and behind us and I flew off, but found it was one of our own. I tried to rejoin the squadron but I had lost them."[17]

Hans-Karl Mayer spotted Mamedoff and was soon on his tail, thumbing the firing button on his control stick, letting rip with 20 rounds of 20 mm cannon and 140 rounds of machine-gun fire, watching as Mamedoff's plane disappeared in a shower of tracer puffs, explosives, and pieces of fuselage. "There was just one burst but it was enough," recalled Mamedoff. "Eight bullets went through the prop, twenty through the fuselage and one through the armor plating . . . I tried some violent evasive tactics and pulled out at 8,000 feet. My plane wasn't too good after that, as you can imagine, but I flew it all right."[18]

An utter professional, Mayer did not hang around to see what had happened to Mamedoff. Instead he turned back, concerned about his wingman, Josef Broker, and the rest of his squadron, and led them safely to their base in Rennes, where he would incorrectly claim his sixteenth victim. Meanwhile, Mamedoff struggled back to Middle Wallop. With great skill, he somehow managed to land despite intense pain and extensive damage to his Spitfire. His rigger, Flight Sergeant "Tich" Cloves was soon examining the plane. According to Cloves, a 20 mm shell had "entered the tail of the aircraft, [gone] straight up the fuselage, through the wireless set, just pierced the rear armor plating and presumably dented the pilot's uniform."[19] Fifty percent of the starboard elevator had been ripped away and the wings and fuselage peppered by Mayer's 7.92 mm machine-gun bullets. The plane was a write-off.

Remarkably, Mamedoff's only injury was a badly bruised back. No other pilot was hurt in 609's first tangle with JG 53.

Like many other tail-end Charlies that summer, Mamedoff had been taken completely by surprise. "He never saw [Mayer] following him, and [Mayer] put a lot of bullets into Andy's machine," remembered David Crook. "He was very lucky to get away with it."[20]

That evening, in a local pub, Eugene Tobin commiserated with his fellow American. "For a week after, [Andy] looked like the Hunchback of Notre Dame," Tobin later wrote. "It was Andy's birthday so we drank to the present he'd received from the Krupp factory."[21]

As 609 slept that night, several frightened pilots from KG1 were making a break for Germany in their Heinkels, hoping British night fighters had not been scrambled to give pursuit. The pilots had attempted to bomb the Thameshaven oil terminal on the far eastern outskirts of London, but they had fouled up and their bombs had landed wide, hitting densely populated streets in the working-class East End and ruining the church of St. Giles in Cripplegate. It was a momentous mistake. Hitler had explicitly stated that London itself was not to be bombed.

The following morning of August 25, the British War Cabinet agreed to send a reprisal raid to Berlin. It was an abject failure, with the only damage inflicted on a summerhouse in a suburban garden. The Germans responded by hitting at the outskirts of London the following night. For the first time, air-raid sirens sounded throughout the city. At Downing Street, Winston Churchill, wearing a dressing gown emblazoned with golden lions, paced back and forth, listening to the distant thuds of explosions. The next morning, he sent a note to the chief of the air staff:

"Now that they have begun to molest the capital, I want you to hit them hard, and Berlin is the place to hit them."

The RAF's next visit to Berlin killed just eight people, a minuscule toll in human lives when contrasted with the firestorms that would eventually engulf cities such as Hamburg and Dresden. But the raid's psychological effect was enormous. Berliners were stunned. Göring had vowed that the city would never be hit, and naively they had believed him. Suddenly, they felt vulnerable. Hitler was no less surprised and returned from the Berghof to the Chancellery in Berlin as soon as he was informed about the raid. The following day, he lifted his restriction on terror bombing of London.

The Luftwaffe's next targets would be millions of defenseless civilians.

11. Achtung! Spitfeuer!

If you are on fire do not open the hood until the last moment,
as it will draw flames into the cockpit. If your clothes are
soaked in petrol, switch off the engine switches and leave the
throttle open, otherwise as you get out sparks from the exhaust
may act like the flint in your cigarette lighter.[1]

Air Ministry instructions to pilots on bailing out, 1940

Among Eugene Tobin's fellow pilots, there had been a lot of
bellyaching of late. Life at Warmwell, 609's advance base, was
awful. The accommodations were so pitiful that Tobin and others
had opted to sleep under dirty blankets in the dispersal tent, a
long walk from running water and toilets. A road ran close to the
tent, and most of the pilots now relieved themselves there rather
than be caught short in the officers' mess. "One risked either prosecution for indecent exposure," recalled Squadron Leader Darley,
"or returning too late for a scramble."[2]

The station commander had been less than helpful. When Darley
had asked him to improve 609's living arrangements, he had
responded by locking the officers' mess except at assigned meal-
times, hoping this would encourage 609's pilots to arrive on time
for supper. "All our efforts to get the Luftwaffe to respect meal-
times having failed, deadlock occurred," recalled Darley. To make
matters worse, the civilian cooks had then gone on strike, refusing
to get up at 3 a.m. to prepare breakfast.[3]

That morning, some of the ground crew had used a Primus
stove at the dispersal tent and done a first-class job with the bacon
and eggs. Later on, another airman had gone over to the cookhouse to scrounge a cup of tea and to his amazement had found

a "mountain of eggs, tea, sugar, tins of Nestlé's milk and packets of Kellogg's cornflakes" waiting for him. It had taken three trips in Pilot Officer Johnny "Dogs" Dundas's flashy Lagonda to cart the booty over to the dispersal tent. Several airmen working in the cookhouse had pooled their rations to show that they thought 609's pilots were marvelous, even if the civilian cooks did not.[4] Rumor had it they'd also procured barrels of beer.

It was now late afternoon on August 25, and once again Eugene Tobin had had nothing to do all day except bask in the sunshine. With any luck, the station commander would call through in a couple of hours and order 609 to stand down. Then Tobin could retire to the pub for a pint with the chaps.

It was too much to hope for. Suddenly, 609 Squadron was scrambled. Tobin was soon seated nervously in his baking cockpit, as if trapped in a sauna, waiting for Squadron Leader Darley to open his throttle and taxi across the sunburnt grass. Finally, RAF ground crews pulled away the chocks. Darley's Spitfire shuddered for an instant and then sped across the airfield.[5] Tobin and the rest of 609's pilots followed in sections of three.

"Patrol Channel at twenty-five thousand feet," announced the Middle Wallop controller.

The squadron climbed fast, throttles wide open, knowing every angel—thousand feet—gained could be invaluable. Tobin looked out of his cockpit as they reached the assigned height above the English Channel. Below, a convoy showed as minute specks in the middle of a stretch of gray separating southern England from the French coast. Such convoys usually attracted plenty of German attention.

Heading toward Tobin were around 350 bandits, some intent on destroying RAF Warmwell, 609's advance base. They included Hans-Karl Mayer's JG 53, more than a hundred of Göring's much-vaunted Me-110s, and thirty-five bomb-laden Ju-88s. Mayer was once more with young Josef Broker as his wingman. After the previous afternoon's nerve-jangling combat, Broker was glad to be at his squadron leader's side.

Flying with the huge formation of twin-engine Me-110s were ZG 2's Lieutenant Westphal and his rear gunner, Corporal Brief.

In recent weeks, their unit's morale had plunged as the RAF had ripped them apart. Now every time they left their base in Guyancourt, they knew the odds of returning were less than fifty-fifty. The heavy Me-110 was simply no match for the more maneuverable Spitfires and Hurricanes. Pulling an Me-110 around in a tight turn took enormous strength—the controls went infuriatingly stiff at relatively low levels of g-force.

Meanwhile, Eugene Tobin was doing a fine job of weaving behind his section as it climbed higher and higher above the Solent. He looked at his clock—fifteen thousand feet, high enough for him to be breathing oxygen. He reached to turn on his supply but nothing happened. There was no head-clearing whiff, just a grogginess that grew as he flew to twenty-five thousand feet. If he dropped back behind Darley, he could soon find himself unable to catch up and flying alone. Darley had drummed into his head that sticking together was paramount—stragglers never lasted long. What should he do: fly on and perhaps black out with altitude sickness, or break off and risk being bounced by some Messerschmitt prowling several thousand feet above, its better designed prop biting the even thinner air with ease?

Tobin now felt light-headed. Thankfully, he heard Darley order 609 to drop down to nineteen thousand feet. The loss of altitude cleared his head a little, but he was still too high. He had better ask Darley if he could break for home. "Breathing the thin air at that altitude wasn't very pleasant," he recalled. "But it didn't bother me for long."[6]

More than fifty Me-110s of ZG 2 emerged from clouds two miles away.

Thank God 609 was higher. Darley ordered 609 to form up line astern. Then came the call to attack. The squadron dived.

"Break left!" screamed a German rear gunner, Corporal Walter Wotzel, as he opened fire.[7] Wotzel's pilot, Staff Sergeant Siegfried Becker, reacted but not quickly enough. 609 pilots Geoffrey Gaunt and Noel Agazarian snapped off the first of several quick bursts, riddling the Germans' plane. The port engine caught fire. The other jammed. Then Becker and Wotzel were bailing out.

Tobin and Squadron Leader Darley picked out another bandit: the Me-110 of ZG 2's Lieutenant Westphal and his rear gunner, Corporal Brief. In a few seconds, Tobin and Darley were on their tail, the Me-110's fifty-six-foot wingspan soon appearing in the orange glow of their reflector sights. Both opened fire, Tobin aiming just ahead of the Me-110's nose. "The stream of tracers raked his fuselage," recalled Tobin. "The [plane] climbed almost vertically as though [Westphal] was trying to loop. For an instant it seemed to remain motionless, pointing to the sun. Then it fell off to the right and disappeared."[8]

Tobin did not follow the stricken bandit down. "There were too many planes in the air, and if I started down, it would leave me wide open to a tail attack," he explained. "It's always nice to know whether you've scored a bull's-eye. But you're worth more alive than dead."[9] Tobin had indeed scored a bull's-eye. He and Darley had killed Lieutenant Westphal and his rear gunner, Corporal Brief. Not long after, the Germans' plane crashed and exploded at Winfrith, East Chaldon, near RAF Warmwell.[10]

Tobin broke away, following Darley, and then looked around. Fighter Command had scrambled 87, 213, and 152 Squadrons and they were now attacking from all directions, tearing into the Me-110s and firing tracers into the dark gray bombers below.

Meanwhile, Hans-Karl Mayer had been leading his JG 53 pilots across the Channel.

"Everyone attack!" ordered Mayer.

It was around 5:25 p.m. as Mayer dropped like a hawk onto the tail of a Hurricane and let rip with his cannon and 7.9 mm machine guns.

"*Horrido!*"

The Hurricane exploded in flames and Mayer saw its pilot bail out, apparently unharmed. The sky was now a chaos of diving fighters and panicked Ju-88 bombers, breaking formation, turning tail, and diving low, throttles open, their crews praying they would make it home.

Mayer's radio crackled. It was his wingman, twenty-two-year-old Josef Broker. "*Achtung!*" There were bandits above and behind.

Mayer took evasive action. Then his radio hissed to life again. "I've been hit!" cried Broker. "I've been hit!"[11]

Broker was spinning as he called out, burning planes falling past him, and then there were glimpses of water and suddenly green fields surging toward him.

"Bail out or crash-land," Mayer replied calmly.

Busy watching Mayer's tail, Broker had not seen a Hurricane from 152 Squadron behind him. By the time he realized that he was being followed, the Hurricane had opened fire, hitting his engine and causing him to stall. Rapidly, like circling sharks, other Hurricanes had then attacked as Broker had lost control and gone into a violent spin.

Around three thousand feet above England, Broker pulled on his stick. It responded. Somehow, he eased out of the spin. But his engine had gone dead. He had no choice but to glide down and crash-land. At 5:30 p.m., he did so in a field a few miles north of Weymouth. Above, 609's David Crook circled and watched Broker coolly get out of his stricken plane, pull out a box of matches, soak his scarf in gasoline, light it, and fling it into his fuel tank. The plane exploded, burning Broker on the face and hands. He staggered away and collapsed not far from the roaring fighter, its Ace of Spades insignia consumed by the blaze.

609 fought on in the skies above, all across the Solent from Weymouth to the Isle of Wight. Eugene Tobin was one of several who dived on yet more bandits. At around nineteen thousand feet he fired at a twin-engine Me-110. "[The German's] left motor stopped and he started down in a series of crazy turns and spins," recalled Tobin. "This time I followed, to give him another burst and finish him off."[12]

His airspeed topping 400 mph, Tobin chased the German in a tight turn. Then, suddenly, everything went blank and his Spitfire began to spin down. He had blacked out from lack of oxygen and too much g-force. Above, the other 609 pilots watched, sickened, as Tobin plunged toward the Channel, slumped forward in his harness, dreaming while unconscious. "Everything seemed fine, yet something seemed to say, 'You are in an airplane and you are fighting,'" recalled Tobin. "'You'd better come to: there may be someone on your tail.'"[13] Tobin opened his eyes and saw that, by some miracle, he was flying straight and level at just over a thousand feet. Close below were the cold gray waves of the English Channel.

Far above, Hans-Karl Mayer and the fighters from the Ace of Spades were still duking it out. "Most of my squadron was engaged in combat with the Hurricanes," recalled Mayer. "Suddenly, I saw a Hurricane diving . . . I followed him . . . The Hurricane opened fire at long range. Simultaneously I fired, also at long range, and the enemy aircraft broke away downwards . . . I followed the Hurricane in the dive, and closed to 50 metres. I fired, and the Hurricane went up in flames, the pilot bailing out at 500 metres."[14]

Meanwhile, Eugene Tobin had flown back toward Middle Wallop. The other pilots in 609 were delighted to see him: they had assumed the worst after seeing him fall toward the Channel. "I was sure you'd been hit, the way you broke off and went spinning down," one of them said. "I knew you hadn't bailed out, so I watched you as long as I could. The last I saw, you were still spinning and awfully close to the water."[15]

Squadron Leader Darley was also relieved to learn that Tobin had survived after they had combined so well to down one of Göring's Me-110s. "I blacked out colder than a clam," Tobin told him.[16]

Darley had just returned from the dispersal hut, where he had placed a call to RAF Warmwell. Thanks in part to 609 Squadron, only seven Ju-88s had managed to drop their loads on the base, damaging a couple of hangars and cutting telephone lines but failing to knock it out of action. "I could not resist the temptation to ring up the station commander," Darley recalled, "and say that I did not expect any thanks for saving the hangars, personnel and planes, not to mention the officers' mess and kitchen."[17]

On the other side of the English Channel, Hans-Karl Mayer landed back in Cherbourg, delighted that he could add another two white stripes to his tail fin and others in his squadron could add another five. The only sour note was the sacrifice of Mayer's wingman, Broker, on his second mission—he would be lost to a POW camp for almost seven years because he had been too busy watching Mayer's backside to see the enemy shooting at his.

Back in England, 609 no doubt lifted many a glass to their good fortune and happy hunting. "Tobin had brought over a whole suitcase full of jazz records," recalled a fellow pilot. "We [often] played them on a battered hotel phonograph. No matter what their nationality, everybody enjoyed the music. The favorite was 'Roll Out the Barrel.'"[18] The two Poles in 609 could not understand the lyrics but would hum along.[19]

In the space of twenty-four hours, both Tobin and Mamedoff had cheated death. Others had not been so lucky: eight RAF pilots had been killed or wounded that day alone.[20] Tobin's flight commander, Frank Howell, had only recently commented: "Our luck can't last at this pace." Now the joker from California surely must have known he was right. Indeed, flying "the sweetest ship" he had ever seen was no longer "a million laffs."

Later that night, before turning in, Tobin scribbled in his diary: "Today at 6 p.m. I had my first combat and I probably shot down 2 Messerschmitt 110s but I don't know for sure because I did not actually see them go in. I dove after one from 19,000 feet and blacked out and had a funny dream. I came to at 1,000 feet over Bournemouth doing better than 500 mph, and it was all I could do to keep the plane under control. It was one of the scariest days I have ever had in my life, but I learned plenty about combat."[21]

Berlin was again the target. On the night of August 28, Bomber Command hit civilian areas in the vicinity of the Görlitzer rail station. The following morning, Hitler ordered yet more reprisals. He also sent an urgent message to Hermann Göring. It was brutally simple: Either the Luftwaffe destroyed the RAF in the first weeks of September or the invasion of Britain would have to be postponed until the spring of 1941. The stakes were now set for the climax of the greatest air battle in history.

At Middle Wallop, meanwhile, the end of August was duly noted by 609's diarist, Johnny "Dogs" Dundas. "The squadron was becoming cosmopolitan," he wrote in his final entry for the month. "One might think that this heterogeneity would interfere with team-work or morale, but this was not so. Under Squadron Leader Darley's quietly firm and competent leadership the squadron gained steadily in skill and confidence, and remained a veritable 'Band of Brothers.'"[22]

The twenty-one brothers included three Americans, two Poles, and a Dominion pilot. As the squadron's official history records: "Between 8th and 18th August alone—the Phase Two period during which Fighter Command destroyed 367 enemy aircraft at a cost of 154 of its own pilots killed, missing or severely wounded— this 'Band' had been credited with thirty-four confirmed victor- ies plus ten 'probables' for the loss of a single pilot."[23] It was the best performance of any squadron, and because of it 609 bubbled with enthusiasm and radiated confidence.[24] "Whenever in the future the squadron went into action," recalled David Crook, "I think the only question in everybody's mind was not 'Shall we get any Huns today?' but rather, 'How many shall we get today?' There was never any doubt about it."[25]

Nor was there any doubt, as that summer waned, that 609 had been extraordinarily fortunate. For the rest of Fighter Command, that August had been a bloody, enervating month, the deadliest in its history. The endless round of fear, anxiety, heart-stopping excitement, and primal elation followed by loss or relief was gnawing at every pilot, no matter how experienced: several aces now tucked their feet under their rudder bars to stop their knees knocking. "You dragged yourself into the air more exhausted each morning," recalled one pilot, "and you came back at nightfall too keyed-up to rest. Long after you landed there was a roaring in your ears, so you shouted and drank, with your pals in the mess or at the local [pub] . . . At last you got back to your little room and crawled between the soft, white sheets . . . and you found you couldn't sleep because of the sudden silence, so you just lay there alone in the darkness and it was then your nerves began to tauten and twitch inside their casing of beaten, numbed flesh. It was then that you were forced to listen to your thoughts, to take a tally. Every day now, somebody you knew got the chop. Secretly, so secretly that you kept it from yourself most of the time, you'd faced the fact that your turn was bound to come soon. There was a noose around your neck—it was a question of time, you were just a number that would be wiped from the slate tomorrow. Or the day after tomorrow."[26]

Lord Beaverbrook's Ministry of Air Supply was churning out more and more planes, but Churchill's fear now was that they would stand idle for lack of pilots to fly them. The loss of experienced leaders in the air was even more worrying. There remained no more than a dozen squadron leaders who had been with their units since the battle began, and they had to fight, inspire, and try to teach replacement pilots such as the Americans how to stay alive.[27] It was a Herculean challenge given that the training period for new pilots had recently been slashed from a month to two weeks. Teenagers were being sent up with just a few hours in a Hurricane or a Spitfire, unable to work their reflector sights, told they would receive their "final polish" at their new squadrons. All too often, it was the Luftwaffe who polished them off instead. One mess steward recalled that pilots died before he had even had a chance to change their sheets.

Middle Wallop's 609 Squadron had indeed had a very good month. Elsewhere in Fighter Command, it was now common for ground crews to find pilots slumped in their cockpits, asleep, only a few moments after their planes had taxied to a halt. "After eight scrambles in a day, you came to write up your logbook," one pilot recalled, "and you couldn't remember beyond putting down the number of times you'd been up ... I had nightmares about blazing planes crashing all around me."[28] One airman remembered how "boys came back men after an eighty minute sortie . . . faces would be gray . . . there'd be yellow froth round their mouths."[29]

Alcohol had become the universal anodyne. Teetotalers such as Art Donahue, still recovering from his burns, were few and far between. According to one pilot: "People in squadrons who used to go to bed early and not go out and chase a few pints were far more likely to buy it than people who were a little on the wild side."[30] In many squadrons the race to the pub at stand-down was as earnest as any sprint during a scramble. No matter how many losses, or how hard the day's combat had been, getting to the local pub before closing time at 10:30, only an hour after sundown, was a must for many pilots. At the Square Club in Andover, where Tobin and the other 609 pilots sometimes drank, the cocktails were now so strong that pilots would be plastered after just one round.

Sometimes, pilots would stay in London's West End all night, getting back to their dispersal huts around 4 a.m. and napping in deck chairs, flying jackets draped over their beer-stained uniforms, until a greasy breakfast of bacon, eggs, and baked beans arrived just before dawn. A few strong whiffs of oxygen and gut-wrenching fear were remarkably effective cures for even the heaviest hang-over. By contrast, other pilots now lived on such taut nerves that they could no longer tolerate even a half pint, vomiting several times before every sortie.

On the German side, the tension was just as great, perhaps more so: pilots were not rotated and remained in combat until they were either promoted or became casualties. Twenty-four-year-old Captain Helmut Wick, the young star of JG 2 fast closing on Mölders's and Galland's scores, now survived on English cigar-ettes and black coffee, unable to keep solids down. "As long as I can shoot down the enemy," he declared, "adding to the honor of JG Richthofen and the success of the Fatherland, I am a happy man. I want to fight and die fighting, taking with me as many of the enemy as possible."[31]

Some German bomber crews were so drained that they were starting to turn back at the first sight of Spitfires, dropping their deadly loads into the Channel. In one Junkers 88 outfit, 25 percent of aircrews had mysteriously reported sick. Forced to escort these lumbering targets, much to their bitter frustration, even the Jagdwaffe's highest scoring units, such as Galland's JG 26 and Werner Mölders's JG 51, were starting to crack. Only foul weather was their friend, calling a time-out in a daily grind of often five sorties before sundown. "You could count on your fingers when your turn would come," recalled Adolf Galland. "The logic of the theory of probabilities showed us incontestably that one's number was up after a certain amount of sorties. For some it was sooner, for some later."[32] Protected by his two loyal wingmen, Galland hoped it would be the latter.

Superstition reigned all along the Normandy coast, from Mölders's base at Guines to the heavily camouflaged dispersal areas at Adolf Galland's base in Caffiers, where every morning now, it seemed, there was an empty chair at the breakfast table and extra hot rolls and coffee for the weary survivors. Some German pilots even refused to have their photograph taken, remembering that Baron von Richthofen in World War I had died only minutes after he'd been snapped. Among Mölders's former comrades in JG 53, it now seemed that their fate was to be attacked no matter how low they flew to avoid being detected by radar. "It often happened that some of us came home with bent propeller tips after having touched the water," recalled Erich Bodendiek of JG 53.[33]

"Red lamp!" screamed others in their nightmares, echoing the cry of many a Luftwaffe pilot halfway across the Channel, when his fuel gauge suddenly showed that his tank was almost empty. "Red lamp!"[34]

On both sides of the Channel, pilots knew they were in a desperate battle of attrition. From their inner resources, all but a very few found the will to keep flying, scramble after scramble, attack after attack. From his hospital bed, one badly wounded RAF pilot wrote to his parents late that summer: "I go forth into battle light of heart . . . I regard it as a privilege to fight for all those things that make life worth living—freedom, honour and fair play . . . Flying has meant the companionship of men . . . the intoxication of speed, the rush of air and pulsating beat of the motor awaken some answering chord deep down which is indescribable."[35]

Meanwhile, across the Atlantic, more and more Americans were following the battle, aware that their own destiny would perhaps be decided by its outcome. Given unprecedented access to RAF operations by Churchill's propaganda chiefs, CBS's Ed Murrow and *Collier's* Quentin Reynolds were thrilling millions of readers and huge radio audiences with vivid reports on mass dogfights above the White Cliffs of Dover. German propagandists in Washington spread stories that the RAF's claims of downed planes were vastly overstated, giving the false impression that Britain was not yet on the ropes. But these faded fast from the public consciousness thanks to the cinematic prose of eyewitnesses such as Ben Robertson from the New York daily, *P.M.* In Robertson's eyes, all Americans should know about a new frontier—the skies above Britain, where the RAF's knights of the air soared and dived with breathtaking elegance, "like the white birds you see in far off parts of the Pacific Ocean, like the white birds you see off Pitcairn."[36]

In Britain, every newspaper had adopted 609 and the RAF's other fighter boys as the men of the hour, the potential saviors of England and of far more, according to some editorial writers who echoed Churchill's rhetoric about civilization itself being on the line. Pilots seldom had to buy a drink in pubs. Young women, humming the hit of the summer, "A Nightingale Sang in Berkeley Square," flocked around them in nightclubs in Mayfair's Shepherd's Market, a popular stomping ground for off-duty pilots. With the popular press splashing each day's "score" across front pages, as if the battle were a celestial cricket match, the boys in blue batting for England became enormously attractive. Losing one's virginity in the back row of some Piccadilly cinema, shrouded by blue cigarette smoke, was almost as easy as losing one's life.

Art Donahue, fast recovering from his burns, wrote his folks in St. Charles, Minnesota: "My uniform has become the key to the best hospitality everywhere. These people almost worship the Royal Air Force pilots. Conductors on buses, policemen in the streets, just fall over themselves to help me find my way about. A number of times I've had just ordinary people say to me, 'Words can't express how we feel toward you boys!' 'You're wonderful.' 'You're the greatest heroes we've ever had.'"[37]

They meant every word. The British people felt intensely alive and proud. Memories of that late summer of 1940 would never wane. Rebecca West, one of the period's finest reporters, would write: "Under the unstained heaven of that perfect summer, curiously starred with the silver elephantines of the balloon barrage, the people sat on their seats among the roses [in London's Regent's Park] . . . their faces white. Some of them walked among the rose-beds, with a special earnestness looking down on the bright flowers and inhaling the scent, as if to say, 'That is what roses are like, that is how they smell. We must remember that, down in the darkness.' . . . Most of these people believed . . . that they were presently to be subjected to a form of attack more horrible than had ever been directed against the common man."[38]

They were right.

On September 3, Göring and his deputies—Field Marshals Albert Kesselring and Hugo Sperrle—met to discuss how best to finish off the British. Sperrle was all for continuing the offensive against the RAF's bases and communications—Fighter Command was now almost on its knees. In fact all but one of 11 Group's sector airfields had been badly hit. Several operations rooms had been put out of action. And although Göring had ordered a halt to the bombing of radar stations, arguing that they had little effect, such strikes had caused considerable chaos.

Kesselring was far from convinced. "We have no chance," he countered, "of destroying the British fighters on the ground. We must force their last reserve of Spitfires and Hurricanes into combat in the air."[39] Only by luring the RAF's remaining pilots into the crosshairs of Galland, Mölders, and their like could the battle be won. If Göring sent huge bomber fleets to flatten London, argued Kesselring, the British pilots would have no option but to defend their capital in large numbers, thereby exposing themselves to the Luftwaffe's best. Much to Sperrle's frustration, Göring agreed with Kesselring. And so the date for the first mass attack on the city was set—Saturday, September 7. The change in strategy would be code-named Target Switch. "For the second time in twenty-five years," 85 Squadron's Peter Townsend would later write, "the Germans were out to subdue the British with their own Teutonic invention, murder from the sky."[40]

The following day, September 4, Adolf Hitler made it chillingly clear what he now had in store for the buffoon Churchill and his deluded people. But first, before a vast audience in Berlin's Sports Stadium of mostly female nurses and social workers, Hitler addressed the question everyone was asking: When would Germany invade England?

The British are just as anxious to find out, Hitler quipped. They keep asking, "When is he coming?"

"Don't worry," Hitler shouted. "He's coming! He's coming! They should not be so curious!"

Laughter filled the stadium that had hosted the 1936 Olympic Games.

Hitler then got down to business.

The RAF's night bombing of Berlin—Churchill's "new invention"—would not go unavenged.

"We are answering, night for night, and in growing strength . . . We will eradicate their cities."

The women of Berlin were on their feet, the stadium thundering now with applause.

"The hour will come when one of us will go under," Hitler concluded, "and it will not be National Socialist Germany."

Again, the women leaped from their seats.

"Never!" they screamed. "Never!"[41]

In the meantime, Fighter Command continued to absorb blow after blow. On Saturday, August 31, it had suffered its worst losses of the battle to date: thirty-nine fighters shot down and fourteen pilots killed. Now, as Göring and his deputies conspired to obliterate London, some squadrons were shot to pieces. In nine days or less, 603 Squadron lost twelve pilots and sixteen Spitfires, 616 lost five pilots, and 253 lost nine pilots. The RAF was being bled dry with precious few reserves to fill ever more empty cockpits. By September 6, a fifth of the RAF's active duty fighter pilots had become casualties in just two weeks: 103 pilots killed and 128 severely wounded.

At Tangmere, 601 Squadron was also fast running out of luck.

On September 4, Carl Davis took down his tenth bandit, an Me-110 from ZG 76's II Group, over Worthing. The next day, the squadron learned it would be withdrawn from the battle in forty-eight hours. It was also scrambled and soon found itself pitted against fifty Messerschmitt 109s. In the ensuing dogfight, two 601 pilots were badly wounded but managed to bail out of stricken planes. A further three pilots only just nursed their Hurricanes home.

The following day, September 6, 601 again scrambled to inter-cept a large group of German bombers. Before it could do so, a far superior force of Me-109s bounced the Millionaires over Tunbridge Wells. In less than a minute, four Hurricanes were falling to the earth, belching smoke and flames. Two pilots bailed out. But Willie Rhodes-Moorehouse and his fellow ace Carl Davis went down with their planes, dying within a few miles and a few seconds of each other when they slammed into the ground at more than 500 mph.[42] Rhodes-Moorehouse, Billy Fiske's former flight commander, and Davis had both won the DFC and were the last of the squadron's stalwarts, having joined the Millionaires well before the war.[43] In the ensuing obituaries, it was noted that Willie Rhodes-Moorehouse's father had won the first Victoria Cross in the air during the First World War.

The loss of Davis and Rhodes-Moorehouse was a crushing blow to a squadron whose morale had been continually eroded since Billy Fiske's death. "The death of one experienced pilot was a bigger loss to a squadron in those days than ten Spitfires or Hurricanes, because however many fighters we lost or damaged, replacements always turned up immediately," recalled a fellow ace. "But experienced pilots could never be replaced. You could only train the new ones as best you could, keep them out of trouble as much as possible in the air, and hope they would live long enough to gain some experience. Sometimes they did."[44]

Yet again, 601's intelligence officer, Tom Waterlow, was sent out to find deceased comrades. A joyful and dedicated man, he loved most aspects of his work but not when it entailed "rushing around the countryside looking at crashed aircraft and identifying my friends by the numbers on their machine guns."[45]

The next day, a badly mauled 601 Squadron was pulled from the front line and sent to Exeter. None of Billy Fiske's old skiing friends remained.

The Millionaires were no more.[46]

The last days of summer were, by contrast, rather a bore for 609 Squadron. "No bombings today, no dog-fights," Tobin complained in his diary. "We just sat on our ass and told dirty jokes."[47] Assigned to factory and airfield protection patrols, the squadron was scrambled many times but did not encounter the enemy, and on the one day when a nearby factory was heavily bombed, it was ordered to patrol elsewhere. It seemed that the luck of the Irish was still with red-haired Tobin, his fellow Yanks, and their English mates. Miraculously, they still held the "Grim Reaper" at bay.

12. The Blitz

Within 50 feet of a large bomb its wind-blast will tear a man
to pieces and will shatter a solid brick wall. Further away,
the blast will deafen people by bursting their ear-drums,
and may kill them by paralysing their lungs.[1]

**"A Practical Guide for the Householder and
Air-Raid Warden," 1940**

For the first time since joining 609 Squadron, Pilot Officers
Eugene Tobin and Shorty were enjoying a break from the war
as they sauntered around London beneath clear blue skies. It was
Saturday, September 7, 1940. Early that morning, unknown to the
Americans, the Air Ministry had issued its first invasion alert—
attack imminent. The Germans were coming.

Across the English Channel, Hermann Göring sat in his personal
train, *Asia*, relaxing after being injected by a Luftwaffe flunky,
Herr Doktor Ondarza, who now joined Göring's ever-present
"needlewoman," Christa Gormanns, in keeping him smiling.
Dressed in a new, pale blue uniform, he toyed with his gold baton
as *Asia* pulled into a siding near the Pas de Calais, from where
he planned to watch his bombers pass over on their way to pound
London. Göring had come up with a suitably Wagnerian code
name for the day's attack—Loge, the god of fire.

Göring stepped out of *Asia* to be greeted by a sycophantic
Kesselring and lackeys carrying picnic baskets and crates of champagne. Before the big show began, Göring inspected a group of
LG 2 pilots, bantered with them, recalling some of his own exploits
as a First World War ace, and then tried to climb into the cockpit
of an Me-109 conveniently parked nearby. Fatty Göring, as every

Luftwaffe pilot already called him, had put on a hundred pounds since the Great War and failed to fit into the Messerschmitt's cockpit. Shrugging off his embarrassment, Göring grabbed a couple of bottles of the finest champagne and was soon settled down above the cliffs of the Pas de Calais beside a picnic basket to watch the progress of Loge through his binoculars. The white cliffs of Dover, just twenty-three miles away, were clearly visible in the bright afternoon sunlight.

From airfields across Normandy arose the largest air armada in history. It had only one objective: to carry out an enormous reprisal attack against the British. And today the navigators had only one route to mark on their maps.

Nach London!

It was 3:54 p.m. when a young WAAF at Fighter Command's HQ placed a counter indicating that many bandits were airborne. By 4 p.m., Göring was squinting into the sky, watching fleets of his bombers lumber toward their target. He had told some aides that today, finally, the battle would be won.

It was 4:30 p.m. at Middle Wallop when 609 was scrambled. Andy Mamedoff's flight commander, "Butch" MacArthur, recalled what happened next: "Whilst on patrol at 10,000 feet between Brooklands and Windsor, we saw about 200 enemy aircraft surrounded by [anti-aircraft] fire. We climbed toward them and I led the squadron into a quarter attack."[2] 609 faced daunting odds, being outnumbered at least ten to one. Twenty-five-year-old Flying Officer Keith Ogilvie, a Canadian who had joined 609 on August 20, recalled that there were so many 109s in the air that day that they seemed to be "zooming and dancing round us like masses of Ping-Pong balls."[3]

Meanwhile, Eugene Tobin and Shorty were seated in a posh hotel in London's West End, the Regent Palace, chatting with Colonel Charles Sweeny. It wasn't long before the American flyers and Sweeny got around to "the dough angle," as Tobin put it. When would they receive the money owed them from their time in France? Sweeny promised he would sort things out and get back to them soon.[4]

Across town, at an anti-aircraft installation in the East End, a searchlight operator, Lieutenant Alan Rook, was suddenly disturbed by his commanding officer.

"My, God, they've started!"

Rook ran out of his office and looked up into the clear skies. "It was a wonderful summer's day," he recalled. "Coming up the river in close order was the biggest fleet of aeroplanes I have ever seen. White against the blue sky, like cherry blossoms seen from below, in level rows of squadrons, hundreds strong, filling the air with a throbbing roar, they came very slowly, following the river toward London."[5]

It was around 5 p.m. when Eugene Tobin, Shorty, and millions of Londoners heard the sound of sirens. Then bombs began to whistle down. The Blitz had begun. There would be no respite for almost three months.

Within minutes, the sun looked as if it were setting in the east, a violent red tinge spreading across London's docklands.[6] Watching from St. Paul's Cathedral, the Reverend William Matthews heard a frightened worshipper mutter: "It's the end of the world."

"It's the end of *a* world," said another.[7]

It certainly felt that way in Poplar, at the heart of the Luftwaffe's target zone, where eighteen-year-old Len Jones was pulled and pushed by the "suction and compression from the high explosive blasts . . . you could actually feel your eyeballs being sucked out. I was holding my eyes to try and stop them from going . . . I thought, well, I must be dead . . . so I struck a match and tried to burn my finger. I kept doing this to see if I was alive."[8]

Back at Cap Griz Nez, Hermann Göring's wife was on the line. "Yes, it has been a wonderful day, Emmy," said the Reichsmarschall. "I've sent my bombers to London; London's in flames."[9]

Twenty-five thousand feet above the city, JG 26's Adolf Galland gazed down in awe as the flames leaped into the evening sky. According to his biographer, he felt "a pang of horror at the thought that such punishment could ever be meted out to a German city."[10]

Above the chalk cliffs of Cap Griz Nez, Göring could no longer control himself. The sight of his bombers crowding the skies had gone to his head. Suddenly, the Luftwaffe chief grabbed the microphone of a radio reporter standing nearby. "I have heard the roar of victorious German squadrons," Göring told his fellow Germans, "which have for the first time struck the enemy right to the heart!"[11]

Now the river Thames itself was on fire. Far above, the middle-aged pilot of Hurricane "OK 1" looked down on a vast column of smoke rising toward him and sighed with relief. "Now London is taking it," thought Sector 11's Air Vice-Marshal Keith Park, "we shall be saved." The Germans had switched targets, and not a moment too soon. Had they continued to attack Park's airfields, "the fighter defense of London would have been in a perilous state."[12] Now his Sector 11 might be able to recover from the previous weeks' hard pounding and repair its ravaged communications. Indeed, the Luftwaffe's new focus on the capital, then the largest city in the world, was bad news for the people of London but offered a much-needed respite for Fighter Command. Park hoped there would now be time to train more pilots, refresh others, and bring new planes into the front line. And while doing so, Park knew he would enjoy a critical advantage. Thanks to radar, he could more easily pinpoint the enemy flocks of bombers because his observers would know where they were all headed— toward London.

Below, the fires raged on and on, soon spreading for a continuous nine miles across the East End—designated Sector A by the Luftwaffe. Not since the Great Fire of London in 1666 had an inferno so engulfed the city. People coming out of a performance of *Faust* at Sadler's Wells looked into the sky and saw "a real hell reddening the sky to east."[13]

Later that evening, when the all-clear sirens had sounded, Tobin and Shorty returned to Middle Wallop. The officers' mess was strangely quiet: all of 609, including Andy Mamedoff, had gone to a cocktail party, organized by the British actor Gordon Harker, to raise money for the Spitfire Fund, which helped the families of killed and wounded pilots. The fund-raiser was no idle gesture: that day, nineteen more RAF pilots had been killed.[14]

Before turning in for the night, Tobin learned that 609 had had a very good day. "Our squadron got 10 confirmed and 10 probable, damn good, no loss to ourselves," Tobin noted in his diary. "But 234 lost its CO [commanding officer], that's bad."[15] In fact, 609 had claimed two Do-17s, three Me-110s, and one Me-109 destroyed, and five others damaged. Eleven of the squadron's twelve pilots in the air that day had fired on the enemy with MacArthur, Howell, and the squadron's sole sergeant pilot, Alan Feary, inflicting particularly heavy damage.[16]

The next day, September 8, 609 was ordered with all other 11 Group squadrons to concentrate its energies on the defense of the capital. Once more it would fly into the eye of the storm, now centered over London.

That morning, Winston Churchill toured the bombed-out areas of the East End where just hours before 430 Londoners had lost their lives—the bombing had continued through the night. Churchill was seated in the back of his staff car beside his brother Jack and Lord Ismay, his chief of staff. The car moved slowly, avoiding still-smoldering ruins and rubble, and then stopped at an air-raid shelter that had been hit. When Churchill learned that forty people had been killed, he could contain his emotions no more and began to cry. As he got out of the car, he was quickly surrounded by a crowd of onlookers.

"It was good of you to come, Winnie."

"We thought you'd come."

"We can take it. Give it 'em back."

"You see," said an old woman, "he really cares, he's crying."[17]

Churchill moved on, through smoke, past burned-out homes. To one teenage bystander, he looked "invincible . . . tough, bulldogged, piercing."[18]

Despite the devastation, Londoners were trying to get to work, to carry on as if as normal, bonded as never before by rage and dread.

Churchill's aides tried to get him to return to the car. Sirens sounded. Churchill would not be budged.

"Good old Winston!"

"Give 'em socks!"

Churchill cried out in his deep baritone: "Are we down-hearted?"

"No-o-o-o-o."[19]

As he finally returned to his car, Churchill turned to Ismay. "Did you hear them?" he said. "They cheered me as if I'd given them victory, instead of getting their houses bombed to bits."[20]

That night, the Luftwaffe returned and by dawn the next day another 412 Londoners would be dead—only 86 less than the total for RAF fighter pilot losses during the entire Battle of Britain.[21]

By September 11, more than a thousand civilians had perished. That day, Churchill made a radio broadcast that was heard by an estimated 70 percent of the nation as it gathered silently around radio sets in factories, pubs, and bomb-damaged homes: "The next week may be one of the most important in British history. It ranks with the days when the Spanish Armada was approaching the Channel and Drake was finishing his game of bowls; or when Nelson stood between us and Napoleon's Grand Army at Boulogne. We have read all about this in the history books; but what is happening now is on a far greater scale, and of far more consequence to the life of the world and its civilization than these brave old days of past . . .

"These cruel, wanton, indiscriminate bombings of London are, of course, a part of Hitler's invasion plans. He hopes, by killing large numbers of civilians, and women and children, that he will terrorise and cow the people of this mighty imperilled city, and make them a burden and anxiety to the Government and thus distract our attention unduly from the ferocious onslaught he is preparing. Little does he know the spirit of the British nation, or the tough fibre of Londoners . . . who have been bred to value freedom far above their lives.

"This wicked man, the repository and embodiment of many forms of soul-destroying hatreds, this monstrous product of former wrongs and shame, has now resolved to try to break our famous Island race by a process of indiscriminate slaughter and destruction. What he has done is to kindle a fire in British hearts, here and all over the world, which will glow long after the traces of the conflagration he has caused in London have been removed. He has lighted a fire which will burn with a steady and consuming flame until the last vestiges of Nazi tyranny have been burnt out of Europe, and until the Old World—and the New—can join hands to rebuild the temples of man's freedom and man's honour, upon foundations which will not soon or easily be overthrown."[22]

Among those profoundly moved by Churchill's defiant words was Eugene Tobin, now determined to "kick the living hell" out of the German bombers. "Today will be a day that will go down in history," he noted in his diary after hearing Churchill's speech. "Churchill gave a speech . . . he summoned everybody to do his part. Every night the Germans drop their damn bombs anywhere and run like cowards. There have been many casualties, mostly harmless civilians, but everybody is going on just as though nothing happened. We are bombing the Germans much more though. I wonder who will hold out the longest?"[23]

13. Their Finest Hour

You catch him right smack in the middle of your sights and give him a complete burst. The Brownings go to work, and, brother, when they are working they're not kidding! Eight guns, 1,400 rounds per minute. Figure it out for yourself.[1]

Eugene Tobin, 609 Squadron

Ground crews hooked starter batteries to 609 Squadron's Spitfires, standing silhouetted in the dawn light near the bungalow that doubled as the dispersal hut. A few hundred yards away, Eugene Tobin lay in deep slumber in his quarters.

"I say, old boy, better wake up."

Pilot Officer Johnny "Dogs" Dundas was trying to shake Tobin awake.

"I say, old boy, you really must pull yourself together."

Tobin opened his eyes.

Dundas yawned, still dressed in his bathrobe.

"What's the idea?" said Tobin groggily. "Why do I have to get up at this ungodly hour?"

"I'm not sure, old boy, but they say there's an invasion on, or something."

Tobin leaped out of bed. "We didn't know then that September 15, 1940, was going to go down as the biggest day in the history of the Royal Air Force," Tobin recalled, "[and] that never before had so many planes filled the sky in aerial combat; that more than 500 planes would be zooming and diving in the fighting over London."[2]

Tobin dressed quickly and then headed out to the airfield. For the next two hours, he and his fellow 609 pilots flew above London, seeing familiar landmarks and still-smoldering fires below but no action.

Meanwhile, Air Vice-Marshal Keith Park was seated opposite his wife, Dol, at the breakfast table in their home, a stone's throw from his office: the so-called bunker—Fighter Command's Sector 11 operations control room. It was not a good start to the day. Dol said something about it being her birthday. Park had forgotten. He apologized. Dol understood—he had been rather busy recently. Never mind. "A good bag of German aircraft would be an excellent present," she told him.[3]

By midmorning, 609 Squadron had returned to Middle Wallop. Yesterday had been stormy, with heavy thunder and cloud cover. But this Sunday morning, when Tobin should have been at Mass, the skies were an ominous blue. It was 57 degrees, warm enough to roll up shirtsleeves. A thin film of mist hung above the airfield, but the sun would soon burn it off.

At Chequers, Winston Churchill also noted the weather and decided to pay Air Vice-Marshal Park a visit. He was soon speeding toward Uxbridge, west of London, with his armed bodyguard; his private secretary, John Martin; and his wife, Clementine. The car's police bell clanged.

It was around 9:30 a.m. at Cormeilles-en-Vexin, the home base of Dornier bomber unit KG 76. Aircrews streamed out of a meeting room. Among them was a thirty-eight-year-old Bavarian, Alois Lindmayr, leader of the KG 76's III Group: a coolheaded veteran of devastating raids on RAF Kenley and Biggin Hill. He had just briefed his men on that day's mission. The news that KG 76 was to have the great honor of leading the Luftwaffe across the Channel had not been received with stamping feet and applause.

Earlier that morning, Field Marshal Kesselring had ordered Lindmayr to fly at the spearhead of the greatest strike force ever sent against a civilian target—more than 1,120 German aircraft. Although Lindmayr had few experienced pilots at hand, having lost eleven bombers out of thirty in the last fortnight, he had been able to cobble together the required number of planes by combining the remnants of his III Group with I Group, an even more heavily battered unit.

Lindmayr's men were soon clambering aboard their Dornier 17 bombers. Among them were Sergeant Rolf Heitsch and his crew of three. Each man had a pistol strapped to his belt. If he found himself trapped in his burning plane, unable to bail out, he could put the Mauser to his temple and pull the trigger.

The Dornier was nicknamed the "Flying Pencil" by RAF pilots, for whom its long slim body was easy prey. With no armor plating, underpowered, and capable of carrying at most 2,200 pounds of bombs, it was also called a "Flying Coffin" by some former crews now in British POW camps and French hospitals. It had started life, like so many of the Luftwaffe's medium-range bombers, disguised as a mail-carrier back in 1934, when every German aircraft was supposed have a nonmilitary function. By now, it was clearly obsolete and yet one out of every four bombers sent over Britain was a Dornier. The only two strengths Heitsch and his fellow pilots found in the lumbering albatross were its reliability and capacity to absorb large quantities of Tommy lead.

Radio operator Technical Sergeant Stephan Schmidt made his way to the rear of the plane. He had been chosen to operate a top-secret weapon when KG 76 inevitably clashed with the Hurricanes and Spitfires that now flocked to greet the fleet whenever it neared the English coastline. The new device was in fact a flamethrower that had been borrowed from the Wehrmacht and fitted to the rear fuselage. If it worked, it would be fitted to other bombers.[4]

Heitsch ran through his checks, and then the plane's two 1,000 hp, nine-cylinder, Bramo 323P air-cooled engines roared to life. With his left hand, Heitsch opened the throttles and the Dornier sprang forward, its wings rocking as it picked up speed on the uneven airfield. At 10:10 a.m. Heitsch felt the Dornier leave the ground and set course for Cap Gris Nez.[5] It was not an auspicious beginning to the mission: because of heavy cloud cover, ten minutes were lost trying to link up with I Group.

Back in England, it was around 10:30 a.m. when Keith Park learned that Churchill was about to arrive at the bunker: Fighter Command's Sector 11 operations control room. Sure enough, Churchill and his party soon filed in. Park greeted them and once again had to explain diplomatically that the prime minister could not smoke inside the bunker. Churchill grunted and then bit down on his unlit Cuban.

"I don't know whether anything will happen today, sir," said Park. "At present all is quiet."[6]

Churchill and his party took their seats in the gallery above a plotting table and several WAAFs.

Around 11 a.m., over the chalk cliffs of Cap Gris Nez, Technical Sergeant Heitsch spotted his escorts above: Me-109s from Hans-Karl Mayer's Ace of Spades and several squadrons from JG 3, who would stick as close as possible to the Dorniers.[7]

It was 11:04 a.m. in the bunker at Uxbridge. Radar reports indicated that KG 76 and its escorts were stacking up over Boulogne and Calais. Then a young WAAF put down her knitting and walked calmly over to the plotting table and placed a wooden block on it. The block indicated that at least thirty bandits were heading toward England. A few minutes later, two more blocks were on the plotting table.

"There appear to be many aircraft coming in," said Churchill.

Park looked calm. "There'll be someone there to meet them."

More blocks appeared on the plotting table.

"Northolt, Kenley, Debden," Park called out.[8]

Bulbs on panels covering a wall opposite the gallery began to light up, indicating each squadron's status: at readiness, scrambled, or engaged. More blocks appeared on the table. There was now a palpable sense of crisis in the sixty-foot square room, fifty feet below ground.

At 11:20 a.m., Park ordered the rest of his squadrons into the air and told 10 Group to alert Middle Wallop. A few minutes later, 609 Squadron was scrambled.

Eugene Tobin tucked maps into his boots and followed several other pilots out of the dispersal hut at Middle Wallop. Shorty Keough did the same, two cushions under his arm, and was soon being helped up onto the wing of his Spitfire by his ground crew. Andy Mamedoff climbed into his cockpit and was quickly strapped into his safety harness.

At 11:30 a.m., 609 reached twenty thousand feet, the best performance altitude for the Spitfire. Tobin checked that his oxygen supply was working. London was below, terraced housing stretching far into the distance, skirting the Thames. Barrage balloons hung like giant gray sausages over the charred East End.

"Climb to twenty-five thousand and maintain patrol."[9]

Back at the Uxbridge bunker, Winston Churchill looked with mounting concern at the wall of bulbs facing him. All but a few of the bulbs now glowed, indicating that most of Fighter Command was in the air or intercepting the enemy.

It was around midday when the Dorniers of KG 76, led by Alois Lindmayr, began a "flak waltz," zigzagging to avoid anti-aircraft fire, as they crossed over the southern outskirts of London. In a few minutes, they would begin their bombing runs. Then the flak stopped and Hurricanes and Spitfires began to attack. At the rear of the Dornier formation were Rolf Heitsch and his crew. In his headset, Heitsch suddenly heard the excited voice of Stephan Schmidt, who was manning the flamethrower. A Hurricane was fast closing in on them from astern. At four hundred yards, its pilot let rip. Bullets tore into the Dornier. Schmidt grabbed the flamethrower and sent a giant squirt of burning gasoline toward the Hurricane. The jet of flame fell far short, but Schmidt succeeded in spraying some unlit oil over the British fighter's windscreen, forcing its pilot to push its nose down, duck below the Dornier and pull away. Rolf Heitsch flew on, now straggling dangerously behind the rest of KG 76.[10]

Meanwhile, twenty thousand feet above central London, Pilot Officer Andy Mamedoff looked around and up, watching for bandits. Once again, he was weaving back and forth, the tail-end Charlie to 609's B Flight led by "Butch" MacArthur, who had been in a particularly gloomy mood of late and so depressed a week back that he could not eat. As Butch saw it, 609 and the rest of Fighter Command had failed miserably to protect the people of London from the "Grim Reaper" on September 7. Maybe today 609 would have some success in keeping him at bay.

Eugene Tobin was as usual weaving behind Johnny "Dogs" Dundas and his A Flight Leader, Frank Howell.

"Many, many bandits at four o'clock!" shouted Dundas.

Tobin looked up and saw more than fifty 109s from Hans-Karl Mayer's JG 53, around four thousand feet above.

"Okay, Charlie, come on in," Howell called to Tobin.

Tobin glanced over his shoulder. Three bandits were diving toward them.

"Danger, red section!" shouted Tobin. "Danger, danger, danger!"[11]

Howell heard him and broke fast to the right.

Tobin began a 360-degree turn, immediately feeling the g-force. Suddenly, he spotted 609's Pilot Officer Geoffrey Gaunt climbing to his left, followed by a furious Messerschmitt. Then Tobin was turning tighter and tighter, pulling the stick as far over as he dared without blacking out, holding the Spitfire in its life-saving arc. A Messerschmitt flashed past at more than 400 mph. Then he was easing out of the turn, head spinning as he searched the sky for bandits. And there they were—more Me-109s. Tobin set out after one of them. It was soon in his sights. He fired. Smoke streamed from the German's motor. But before he could fire again, the German disappeared in cloud cover. Tobin broke to his left and began to climb, opening the throttle, weaving back and forth violently behind Howell and Dundas at around 275 mph, not caring now whether he or his Spitfire could take the strain. He had no time "for pretty tricks. The main thing was to get where you could shoot . . . and then get where [they] couldn't shoot at you. A neat barrel roll looks nice from the ground and so does a wreath."[12]

Tobin suddenly saw a 609 Spitfire around two hundred yards away, out of control, cockpit ablaze. It began to spin down trailing black smoke. Then Tobin spotted Technical Sergeant Rolf Heitsch's Dornier diving toward clouds. Tobin thumbed his firing button. His tracers streaked through the sky and struck one of the bomber's engines.

Heitsch looked out of his cockpit. His left propeller had stopped spinning. Even if he could escape Tobin, could he then nurse the stricken bomber back across the dreaded Channel, or should he try to land? Now white smoke was billowing from his other engine. Tobin had hit the glycol tank or a radiator. 609's Johnny "Dogs" Dundas suddenly appeared as if from nowhere—he had climbed almost vertically below the bomber—and also let rip. More pieces flew off Heitsch's plane. Then both Tobin and Dundas were "pressing the tit," sending streams of bullets through the sky. Stephan Schmidt, manning the flame-thrower, was hit badly in the chest. He dropped the flamethrower and slumped to the floor.

Heitsch somehow flew on. He had trained as a doctor before the war and knew that to stand a chance of saving Schmidt from bleeding to death he would need to land as soon as possible. Meanwhile, Tobin was lining up for the kill. "I moved the ship over a bit so that his left wing was right in the bull's eye and sawed off his aileron," he recalled. "Part of the wing fluttered off and he disappeared into the cloud." A few seconds later, he re-appeared. Any moment now it would surely be all over, but seeing that Heitsch's plane was critically damaged Tobin and Dundas chose not to press on with their attack. "[Heitsch] came down after a while," recalled Tobin, "just from sheer weight of lead, but we didn't knock him apart."[13]

Heitsch spotted a field near the village of Shoreham and told his surviving crew to brace themselves for a forced landing. With great skill, he brought the stricken bomber down, narrowly avoiding power lines.[14] The Dornier crashed wheels up with an awful screech of metal and breaking propellers and skidded to a sudden halt, just missing several cows. Heitsch threw off his harness, stood up, and began to open an escape hatch.

A few hundred feet above, Tobin circled the crash site. He opened his cockpit and slid back the hood. He could see Heitsch and another of his crew climbing out of the Dornier, carefully pulling the badly wounded Schmidt after them. Tobin waved his handkerchief, signaling to a growing group of hop pickers to stay back from the German plane. "A mile away, a Spitfire and a Hurri-cane were down in the same field," he recalled. "But the white billowy folds of two parachutes nearby showed that their pilots were safe. Crashed planes were a dime a dozen. Wherever you looked between London and the coast, there were cracked-up airplanes."[15]

A white tracer flashed past Tobin. He pulled his stick back and climbed. Then he realized that the tracer had been meant not for him but for another Spitfire, dueling with an Me-109 two thousand feet above him. "It was quite a show," remembered Tobin. "Once in a while the German would loose off with the two cannons in his wings and they would blink like a couple of rabbit's eyes. Cute as can be until one of the shells screams past your cowling. Then you move out of the way fast, just as I did. By the time I climbed above the two fighting planes, the Spitfire had sent the German down in a long sickening spin and the air was clear of enemy planes."[16]

Tobin was suddenly alone. He checked his fuel gauge—just seven gallons left. It was around 12:20 p.m. After refueling at Biggin Hill, he flew back toward Middle Wallop. The airfield soon appeared below and he began his approach, but then a truck emerged from behind a hangar into his landing path. It was too late to climb. Tobin heard one of his wheels skim the vehicle and jolt back into the fuselage. "Now I couldn't even make a belly landing, which is the safest thing to do if your landing gear goes haywire. I circled the field a couple of times and then came in to land on the one wheel with the other wing up. It was a pretty tricky business, but my luck held. As the wheel touched the ground, the ship wobbled for an instant and then I felt the other wheel flop down from the impact. I eased the stick and she settled down nicely."[17]

After making out his combat report, Tobin was credited with shooting down Heitsch's Dornier. But then he learned that his plane needed to be serviced and there was no other available, which meant he was effectively grounded for the rest of the day. Disappointed and frustrated, Tobin joined his fellow pilots for lunch. They were particularly pleased that Fighter Command had scrambled them early enough and had then sent them high enough to avoid being bounced.[18]

Back in Shoreham, Kent, the local Home Guard was soon on the scene and arresting the crew of Tobin's downed Dornier. Technical Sergeant Sauter had been badly wounded in the ankle and was taken to Maidstone Hospital. Technical Sergeants Rolf Heitsch and Pfeiffer, the bomber's observer, were escorted to the nearest pub. Someone bought the two trembling German airmen a couple of brandies to calm their nerves. Then they were driven to Seven Oaks Police Station. Their other comrade, Technical Sergeant Stephan Schmidt, did not go with them. He was pronounced dead on arrival at Seven Oaks Hospital, his chest torn apart. According to one subsequent news report, the hospital also admitted a hop picker with a bullet wound in the leg. Allegedly, one of two circling Spitfires—either Dundas or Tobin— had opened fire on the grounded bomber and hit the man in the leg.[19]

Meanwhile, Heitsch's fellow KG 76 pilots struggled back across the unforgiving Channel. Just fifteen of Alois Lindmayr's Dorniers were still in formation. Ten were missing. It was a pitiful sight: the "flying pencils" limping across the dark waters, full of dead and wounded, cockpits holed and smeared with blood, engines coughing, props flailing, gashed fuselages letting in gushes of freezing salty air, white glycol smoke trailing several as if they were signaling surrender.

It was not supposed to turn out this way. Had Göring not claimed that the RAF had just fifty Spitfires left, that it would take just a few days in early September to finish the Lords off? The chilling truth was that the Lords were stronger than ever and better organized, attacking from higher than before, out of the sun. The change of targets from airfields to London had been a disastrous mistake, allowing them time to recover. They had been out for the count. Now they were surely ahead on points. Alois Lindmayr had only to glance out his cockpit to see how they had won this round.

Very soon, another round would begin. Kesselring had gath- ered another massive force for an afternoon attack on the capital: 150 bombers escorted by three times as many fighters. Once again, the bombers would simply be bait to draw up Park's squadrons so that the Luftwaffe could then tear them apart, thereby dealing Fighter Command the deathblow, or so Göring hoped. Among the flocks of Messerschmitts would be two of the most lethal Jagdwaffe units, JG 54 and JG 26, led by an increasingly ill-tempered Adolf Galland.

Just a few days ago, Galland had been forced to stand between his two main rivals, Mölders and Helmut Wick, and listen as Göring had yet again upbraided him over the Jagdwaffe's lack of aggression. "The bombers are more important than a fighter pilot's record of kills," Göring had complained. "Your job is to protect them and each time you fall down on it."[20] Galland had defended his men but Göring had dismissively ignored him. Then Göring had asked what the group commanders needed. Werner Mölders had said he would like as many Me-109E-4/N planes as possible. Their new engines would allow JG 51 to outperform the Spitfire. Göring had begun to walk away when he had suddenly turned around and looked at Galland. "And you?" Galland had looked straight into Göring's bright blue eyes. "I'd like some Spitfires."[21] Göring had sighed, his cheeks reddening with anger, and walked off.

It was now early afternoon on September 15 as Galland made his way toward his Messerschmitt at Caffiers. Yet again, he was suffering from "throat-ache." He knew that Werner Mölders would also be flying later this afternoon, also looking to add another stripe to the thirty-seven carefully painted onto his tail fin. Galland was now just five kills behind. But at the rate Mölders was taking down planes, it wouldn't take long for him to hit forty and then he, not Galland, would be off to have tea with the Führer at the Chancellery, his beaming, bony face splashed across the front pages, the Oak Leaves—added to his Knight's Cross—clear for everyone to see.

At 1:45 p.m., back in the bunker in Uxbridge, a young WAAF placed a marker on the plotting table. Several more soon followed. From the gallery, Winston Churchill again watched intently as Park once more marshaled his forces, scrambling several squadrons.

Gambling that the Germans were all headed toward London, just as on September 7, Park decided not to intercept until Kesselring's armada had reached its most vulnerable position: the big turn over London. By then, the German pilots would be getting nervous, glancing at their fuel gauges, able to fight for only a few minutes at the limit of the Me-109's range.

Luck was on Park's side. The German bombers were forced to circle over Maidstone because they missed their rendezvous with their escorts. From Maidstone, it was sixty miles to London: a heart-pounding journey now dubbed the "racecourse" by many a rattled German pilot. That afternoon, it took the bombers and their escorts thirty very long minutes, more than enough time for Park to direct his forces toward them.

It was 2:15 p.m. when the first two squadrons intercepted.

"Mitor and Gannic squadrons, tally-ho, tally-ho!"[22]

Twenty-seven British fighters dived out of the sun into Kesselring's armada of 450 planes.

"*Achtung, Spitfeuer!*"[23]

Churchill's few had the sun and height on their side, and some had learned how to fight like Galland's hunting packs—a screaming dive, with the target in sights and guns blazing, and then break away in a flash.

Minute by minute, more RAF squadrons followed. Soon, the bright blue sky was scarred by tracer bursts and the oily smoke of burning planes.

At Middle Wallop, the telephone rang. Shorty grabbed his two cushions and then ran with Andy Mamedoff and the rest of 609 toward Spitfires waiting close by, their engines warm.

Meanwhile, Göring's bombers lumbered on. But not for long: over the East End, thirteen more RAF squadrons pounced on them, ripping several into pieces as pilots lined up to wait their turn to open fire. The formations finally broke up and the German pilots then turned tail, dropped their loads over leafy suburbs, and began the desperate journey back to France. One in four would not make it home.

High over central London, meanwhile, JG 26's Adolf Galland

was on the hunt once again. He had only a few minutes of fuel left before he would have to turn back for France. Suddenly, he spotted 310 Hurricane Squadron, tightly bunched below, cockpits glinting in the sun. "I dove from about [2,500 feet] above them, approached at high speed," recalled Galland, "and fired at the far left aircraft in the rear flight, continuing fire until point-blank range. Finally, large pieces of metal flew off the Hurricane. As I shot past this aircraft, I found myself in the middle of the enemy squadron, which was flying in stepped formation. I immediately attacked the right-hand aircraft of the leading flight of three. Again, metal panels broke off; the aircraft nosed over and dove earthward, ablaze. The remaining English pilots were so startled that none as much as attempted to get on my tail; rather, the entire formation scattered and dove away. Two parachutes appeared about [1,600 feet] below our formation."[24]

In just ten seconds, Adolf Galland had added another two stripes to his tail fin. Now, if Mölders had not scored, he was only three behind. At this rate, with a little luck, he could make up the difference in just a few days. Never one to linger after a kill, Galland then dived away from the mêlée, ordering his squadron to follow him back to Caffiers before their red lights started to flicker. There was no need to remind them of what might happen if they dawdled for even a minute. Not long back, JG 26 had lost twelve planes on one sortie alone when their fuel ran out.

It was now 2:35 p.m. in the bunker in Uxbridge. Winston Churchill noticed that Park was standing stock still, unusually tense. The reason became clear when Churchill looked at the wall of bulbs. Every one was glowing red, indicating that all of Fighter Command was now engaged.

"What other reserves have we?" Churchill asked.

Park turned around. "We have none."

Churchill looked grave, and for good reason. "The odds were great," he recalled, "our margins small; the stakes infinite."[25]

But for 609, at least, the odds were for once very much on their side. To intercept the fleeing bombers, Squadron Leader Darley had led both A and B Flights away from London to the southeast. Suddenly, as 609 neared the coast, two battered formations of Dorniers were spotted. The bombers were a long way off and diving at maximum speed, their pilots trying to get as low as possible and then skim unnoticed across the choppy waves back to France. Only a few German fighters were flying escort. Darley ordered 609 to give chase. Throttles open, the West Riding Squadron gladly obliged, soon closing on two stragglers.

Shorty was flying as wingman to Green Section's leader, Pilot Officer Michael Appleby.

"Green Section, No. 1. Attack, go!" shouted Appleby.[26]

Shorty latched on to one of the stragglers, a Dornier from KG 2. "I followed Green 1 [Appleby] into attack on [the Dornier]," he reported, "and attacked from quarter and then astern."[27] Satisfied that the bomber was done for, he broke away and dived through the clouds. Emerging from them, he could not find Green Section and decided to return to Middle Wallop. The Dornier pilot somehow kept his plane in the air and turned back for England, where he crash-landed ten minutes later in a field at Eighteen Pounder Farm, near the historic town of Hastings, at 3:15 p.m. Hastings had been the scene of Britain's last defeat at the hands of an invader, almost a thousand years before, in 1066.[28]

Meanwhile, Andy Mamedoff and several other 609 pilots tore chunks out of the other straggler like a pack of ravenous wolves. "Everybody in B Flight was absolutely determined to have a squirt at the Hun," recalled 609's David Crook, "and as a result there was a mad scramble in which people cut across in front of each other and fired wildly . . . regardless of the fact that the air was full of Spitfires."[29] Mamedoff's flight leader, Frank Howell, saw two German crew members throw packets of marker dye into the Channel and then bail out. Mamedoff and another pilot had finished off the plane "with the concentrated fire of their sixteen machine guns. They actually sawed one of the Dornier's wings off before she crashed. Andy was particularly pleased about this because it meant that for a change he was giving something instead of taking it. His back was still sore from the cannon shell."[30]

The Canadian Keith Ogilvie had earlier that day shot a Heinkel in half, the tail end landing near a pub in Pimlico in London "to the great comfort and joy of the patrons."[31] Now he watched one of the Dornier's crew drift down in his parachute to the waters below. The German splashed down and "waved wildly," Ogilvie later reported, "figuring I was going to machine-gun him."[32]

Ogilvie did not. Instead, Johnny "Dogs" Dundas and Frank Howell "took different bearings [with their compasses] to enable the German to be rescued."[33]

It was now 3:25 p.m. in Park's bunker at Uxbridge. The bulbs on the wall facing Churchill began to change. Some now indicated that squadrons had landed and were refueling. One bulb showed that 213 at Tangmere, Billy Fiske's old base, was ready to be scrambled again. There was a reserve once more. The crisis had passed. Park and Churchill were visibly relieved.

"I am very glad, sir, you have seen this," Park told Churchill, "Of course, during the last twenty minutes we were so choked with information that we couldn't handle it. This shows you the limitation of our present resources. They have been strained far beyond their limits today."[34]

Churchill and his party thanked Park and left the bunker, bound for Chequers, where Churchill was soon taking an afternoon nap.

But it was not over yet. At Middle Wallop, 609 was scrambled yet again at around 5:40 p.m. It was Shorty's fourth sprint to his Spitfire that day. 609 joined six other squadrons above Southampton, but neither Fighter Command nor the Luftwaffe had any luck. Thirteen Me-110s, skimming above the Channel, missed their target, and Shorty and 609 were sent too high to intercept.

Finally, September 15, 1940, drew to a close. At Middle Wallop, the shadows cast by 609's Spitfires stretched long across the grass. Dusk settled and then darkness: the cue for the pilots to be released at last and head to the officers' mess for a bite to eat. At Chequers, Churchill woke from his nap. John Martin, his private secretary, had allowed him to sleep through the afternoon, knowing how emotionally drained he had been by the bunker experience. Now Martin quickly brought Churchill up to date on the day's developments. "This had gone wrong here," recalled Churchill, "that had been delayed there, an unsatisfactory answer had been received from so-and-so; there had been bad sinkings in the Atlantic." Martin paused. "However," he then said, "all is redeemed by the air. We have shot down 183 for the loss of under 40."[35]

It was the best news Churchill had received all year.[36]

Across the Channel, Field Marshal Albert Kesselring picked up the telephone in his headquarters and put a call through to the Reichsmarschall aboard the sumptuous *Asia*. Göring was not in the mood for bad news, having been served sedatives by his nurse Christa Gormanns.

"We cannot keep it up like this," said Kesselring, "we are falling below the standard of safety."[37]

The Luftwaffe was in fact bleeding to death, having now lost so many bombers that if Göring kept throwing them at Fighter Command in daylight attacks, there would soon be none left. Kesselring's two attacks that day had failed spectacularly. Fighter Command had not been wiped out. Instead it had decimated the best of the Luftwaffe's bomber force.

As the sirens began to wail in London, signaling the onset of yet another night of air raids, the presses on Fleet Street began to roll. Within twenty-four hours, the RAF's thrilling success on September 15 would be front-page news throughout the free world. In America, newspapers and radio would repeat the RAF's inflated claim of 183 downed German planes, prompting an outpouring of support and sympathy across the nation for the plucky British. A full-page advertisement in the *New York Times* would even call for immediate union with Britain: the first round in the propaganda campaign aimed at drawing America into the war had been won.[38]

For 609 Squadron, the night was still young. There was time to sink several pints before closing time in the officers' mess or at a nearby pub. "The squadron had shot down seven confirmed and five probables, which isn't bad for a couple of hours' work," recalled Tobin. "My friend Jeff [Gaunt] was the only one not there to share in the victory."[39]

David Crook was particularly troubled by Gaunt's disappearance.

"We had known each other all our lives and been at school together for about twelve years," he recalled. "Only a week or two before, I had said to him one evening that if anything were to happen to him, I should feel rather responsible because he was an only son, and I had persuaded him to join the RAF with me."[40]

Late that night, Tobin opened his diary. "Today was the toughest day—we were in a terrific battle over London," he jotted. "Geoffrey Gaunt, one of my best friends, is missing. I saw a Spitfire during the fight spinning down on fire. I sure hope it wasn't Jeff. If it was—well, from now on he'll be flying in clearer skies."[41]

The following day, Göring raged at a conference of his senior commanders about the Jagdwaffe's abysmal efforts yet again to protect his bombers.

"The fighters have failed!"[42]

This time, Göring's rant backfired. The Jagdwaffe's many brave pilots, prime among them JG 26's Adolf Galland, deeply resented his criticism. Göring was delusional, basing his assertions on hopelessly inaccurate intelligence. For the first time, there were mumblings on some airfields about the impossibility of winning not just the battle but the war.

On September 17, Grand Admiral Erich Raeder recorded in the official German War Diary: "The enemy air force is by no means defeated. On the contrary, it shows increasing activity." And then the all-important words: "The Führer therefore decides to postpone Operation Sea Lion indefinitely." Britain would not be invaded. Instead she would be brought to her knees through terror bombing at night and slow starvation by day. What was left of the Luftwaffe's bomber fleet and the Atlantic U-boat packs would sooner or later surely see to that. Besides, Hitler now nursed a greater design than the humiliation of Winston Churchill—the conquest of Soviet Russia. "I want colonies I can walk to without getting my feet wet," he would soon tell one of his confidants.[43]

Churchill's fighter boys did not yet know that they had fought off the greatest threat to Britain's survival in a millennium, and that they had done so by the narrowest of margins. Only with the passage of time would it become clear that on September 15,

1940—"the hardest day"—they had made possible a far greater victory. As an official RAF historian would write: "When the details of the fighting grow dim, and the names of its heroes are forgotten, men will still remember that civilisation was saved by a thousand British boys."[44]

And a few Americans.

PART FOUR
Last Flights

Sooner or later came the moment when we, the surviving
witnesses of this gay, sporting carnage, had had our fill;
and fatigue, with its by-products fear and revolt, blunted or
destroyed our natural (or should we say professional?) impulses.
And we became infected instead with a morbid terror of
dying, filled with the same of killing, saddened with the
endless departure of friends to their lone home, repulsed by
the futile, boasting claims of the wiping-out, the annihilation
of the enemy. Lauded as heroes, hung with medals, we only
longed
to withdraw into the mountains—or the marshes—
there to forget yesterday and tomorrow.[1]

Peter Townsend, 85 Squadron

14. Horrido!

One is not in London forty-eight hours before being
extremely conscious of the fact that one is living with a
people who are fighting for their lives—whether they fight
by sleeping uncomfortably in a shelter so that they may
work again tomorrow, or fight by putting out fires or by
sucking oxygen out of a mask so that they do not lose their
depth perception when aiming a machine gun at high
altitudes. And one feels there is a quality of indecency in the
eagerness of one's curiosity, an intrusion on something
personal and intimate of which one is not really a part.[1]

**Ralph Ingersoll, American visitor to London in
September 1940**

The Germans had taken a "good licking" on September 15 but
they were far from down for the count. There was still a great
deal of "hard pounding" left to do, as 609's David Crook put it.
But not for his American friends: just four days later, on September
19, 1940, they were posted to 71 Eagle Squadron, the first men to
join the first American unit in the RAF's history. Mamedoff, Tobin,
and Keough would be much missed by their fellow 609 pilots. The
entry in 609's Operational Record Book for September 19 reads:
"The three American pilots left us with evident reluctance and to
our great regret. Both in the air and on the ground they had
contributed colour, variety and vocabulary to the Squadron, and
their 'wise cracking' will be missed."[2] David Crook was particularly sad to see his American friends go: "Just as they were becoming
really good, they were posted away," he recalled. "We were very
sorry to lose them, because they were grand fellows."[3]

The Americans' new outfit, 71 Squadron, would not have existed had it not been for Colonel Charles Sweeny's nephew, confusingly also called Charles, who in April 1940 had contacted Lord Beaverbrook, the Minister of Aircraft Production, with the idea of an all-American squadron, whose shoulder patch would resemble the insignia of the eagle on his American passport. Beaverbrook, whose own son Max Aitken had at the time been 601's squadron leader, had liked the idea of such an Eagle Squadron and had recommended that Sweeny contact Brendan Bracken, personal assistant to Winston Churchill. Bracken was an old friend of the Sweeny family and had forwarded the idea to Churchill, who was supportive. The potential for positive propaganda was unrivalled. Here were America's finest young airmen, ready to lay their lives on the line for democracy while their own country slept—an all-American squadron flying in the RAF would powerfully and symbolically undermine the notion of American neutrality.[4]

Over the summer, other Americans had passed through the RAF's training schools, and some were now posted to other squadrons in the RAF because the newly formed Eagle Squadron could not take them all. One of these volunteers was nineteen-year-old John Kenneth Haviland, who was sent to RAF Digby, home to 151 Squadron, in time to fly in the Battle of Britain.[5] Haviland had been born in Mount Kisco, New York, the son of an American navy officer and an English mother. Unlike his fellow Americans now forming the Eagle Squadron, he had been largely educated in England, having attended Nottingham University, where he had learned to fly. He had joined the RAF Volunteer Reserve in July 1939, only weeks before the Germans had invaded Poland.

Haviland was just one of far too many woefully inexperienced flyers brought into decimated squadrons that September—pilots who had not even practiced deflection shooting and had less than twenty hours flying fighters. Raw and scared, many crashed their planes and died or were wounded in accidents rather than in combat. This was the case with Haviland, who collided with another Hurricane during formation practice the day after he joined 151 Squadron. Thankfully, he was able to bring his Hurricane down in a paddock; he would see no further significant action in the Battle of Britain.[6]

Another American pilot who joined the fray at this time was twenty-eight-year-old Pilot Officer Phillip Howard "Zeke" Leckrone, who had grown up in poverty on a farm outside Salem, Illinois. His marriage had fallen apart because of his decision to risk his life at a time when America was strictly neutral. In his wife's eyes, he had abandoned her and their two children back in Salem to join the RAF. From boyhood, Leckrone had been attracted to danger, driving motorcycles and cars too fast, as Andy Mamedoff had also done, before learning to fly.[7] He had arrived in Britain via Canada in July 1940, just as the Battle of Britain was starting in earnest, and in early September had been posted to 616 Squadron, which had lost six pilots in just a few hours on August 26, 1940.

The RAF's need for new blood was now so great that Leckrone was rushed into operational duties only a few days after joining 616. On September 16, radar detected a German bomber heading to attack a convoy, code-named Pilot, in the North Sea. Scrambled early, Leckrone and his flight leader, Colin MacFie, were able to close fast, despite the thick cloud cover over the North Sea, and destroy the German Ju-88A. The bomber ditched several minutes later. It was Leckrone's sole combat during the Battle of Britain. On October 12, he would leave 616 Squadron to join Mamedoff, Tobin, and Keough in the newly formed 71 Eagle Squadron.

The last of the Americans who flew in the Battle of Britain was Pilot Officer Hugh William Reilley, who had been born in Detroit, Michigan, but had spent most of his life in Canada. Like Eugene Tobin, Reilley had lost his mother at an early age. He had made his way to England in May 1939, convinced that war was imminent. It was assumed that he was Canadian because he had traveled on a Canadian passport and kept his true nationality secret from even his fellow pilots in 66 Squadron: "a truly motley throng," according to one veteran, "consisting of young men from every walk of life. Regular air force officers, sergeant-pilots who had been in peacetime dockhands, clerks, motor-mechanics; there was even an ex-dirt-track motorcycle expert with us."[8]

On September 17, 1940, Reilley took his first operational flight. The following day, he was paired with twenty-one-year-old Flight Leader Bobby Oxspring, the son of a decorated 1914–18 fighter ace. "A tallish, good-looking, fair-headed bloke," noted one contemporary, "[Oxspring had] a typical schoolboy complexion, liable to blush every now and then . . . he can take his beer like a man, comes from the north and has a typical Yorkshire outlook."[9]

For 66 Squadron and others that late September, there was no respite from fatigue and fear, just as there had been none the previous month for the RAF's front-line pilots. The fight between the RAF and the Luftwaffe to control airspace over the English Channel would last many more weeks, and now, as temperatures dropped and the leaves began to fall, they had a new enemy to contend with—the weather. Although increased cloud cover provided some protection, colder temperatures made flying several scrambles each day even more taxing. The Hurricane and Spitfire's cockpits were unheated and now vapor trails formed at lower altitudes, making it easier for the higher-flying Messerschmitts to spot their prey. Above twenty-five thousand feet, neophytes such as Reilley, who jumped into their planes with dew-sodden boots, could suddenly find their feet frozen stiff to the pedals.

On September 24, Hugh Reilley and Oxspring were on standby at dawn. There was a fruitless patrol just before midday. Then at 4:35 p.m., Oxspring led B Flight up on yet another scramble. Around 5 p.m., Oxspring spotted a German bomber, a Heinkel from KG 126, a few miles off the coast of Gravesend. "As I closed in to range with my Number 2, Pilot Officer Hugh Reilley, the Heinkel made off in a shallow dive," recalled Oxspring. "We fired in turn at the engines which both emitted smoke. Shortly afterwards it disappeared into the haze and we claimed it as a probable. Something disastrous must have occurred aboard because later we heard it had been confirmed as having crashed between

Maidstone and Gravesend. All the crew was killed."[10] Oxspring
was now an ace, with five confirmed victories.

Across the Channel that evening, at JG 26's base in Audembert,
a jubilant Adolf Galland and his fellow pilots polished off several
cases of champagne. That morning, Galland had bounced a
17 Squadron Hurricane and thirty seconds later had watched his
fortieth victim turn upside down and then bail out. He was now
neck and neck with his rival, Werner Mölders.[11] There was indeed
much to celebrate: his name was back in the headlines and he
had earned the highly coveted Oak Leaves to the Knight's Cross
of the Iron Cross. Tomorrow, he would fly to Berlin to meet with
none less than the Führer himself.

It was late the following afternoon when Galland entered the
Chancellery in Berlin, proudly wearing his polished Oak Leaves.
He was soon seated alone with the Führer for the first time and
being asked what he thought of the RAF's pilots. "I expressed
my great admiration for our enemy across the water," recalled
Galland. "I was embittered by several insidious and false repre-
sentations and commentaries by the press and on the radio, which
had referred to the RAF in a condescending and presumptuous
tone." To Galland's surprise, the Führer did not interrupt him.
Instead, he nodded his agreement. "He too had the greatest respect
for the Anglo-Saxon race . . . He called [the Battle of Britain] a
world historical tragedy . . . If we won the war, a vacuum would
be created by the destruction of Great Britain, which it would
be impossible to fill." Like so many others, Galland had been
quickly charmed by Hitler and left the Chancellery "no longer
[feeling] bitter" about the Luftwaffe's inept leadership.

The Third Reich's most glamorous ace was then whisked away
to see Göring at the Reich Hunting Lodge in East Prussia, a far
less ostentatious retreat than Karinhall but just as renowned for
its fine hunting. At the entrance, Galland met an irritated and
impatient Werner Mölders. Göring and Hitler had kept him away
from JG 51 for three days, and he was eager to get back into the
air and increase his score. The Oak Leaves had not cured his

"throat-ache," quite the opposite. "The obligation to defend your title as the most successful fighter pilot in the world was taken very seriously," recalled Galland.

Mölders hurried toward a waiting car and then called back to Galland: "The Fat One promised me he would detain you as long as he did me. And by the way, good luck with the stag I missed."

Galland walked on toward the Reich Hunting Lodge and then Göring strode out of the building to greet him, dressed in a "green suede hunting jacket over a silk blouse with long puffed sleeves, high hunting boots, and in his belt a hunting knife in the shape of an old Germanic sword." Göring was in high spirits. The dismal failures of Eagle Day and September 15 appeared to be forgotten, as well as cutting remarks from Hitler about Göring's failure to wipe out the RAF as he had promised during the summer. Galland could hear huge stags rutting in the distance as Göring congratulated him on his forty kills and said he had a suitably special gift for his outspoken ace with the expensive cigars, film-star friends, and brand-new silver Mercedes: Galland would be given the high honor of hunting one of the stags reserved for Göring, a Reichsjägermeister Hirsch—a royal stag. "I promised Mölders to keep you here at least three days, so you've got plenty of time."[12]

The next morning, September 27, Galland soon had the stag of a lifetime in his sight. He squeezed the trigger. The stag fell. Now he could leave and get back to the real hunt above England. But Göring was having none of it and made Galland stay on at the lodge.

Back in England that morning, 66 Squadron and the RAF's other front-line units braced themselves for yet another hard day's fighting. It was now so cold at higher altitudes that some of Hugh Reilley's fellow pilots cut up potatoes and smeared the juice over their cockpits to prevent them from icing up; others wore their cricket sweaters under their flying jackets to add a layer of warmth.

On the other side of the Channel, the pilots of JG 53—the Ace of Spades—attended briefings at their bases in Normandy. Today, they were to escort Ju-88 and Me-110 attacks on aircraft factories. The Ace of Spades was now led by Captain Hans-Karl Mayer, the burly pilot who had nearly killed Andy Mamedoff on August 24. Mayer was at his zenith. On September 5 he had been awarded the Knight's Cross for twenty kills, and soon after he had been promoted to group commander. As JG 53's new leader, he had rapidly increased his tally. Below the swastika on his tail fin, there were now twenty-nine white stripes.

It was around 5 p.m., with the light fading, when Fighter Command scrambled 66 Squadron and several others to meet the incoming bombers and JG 53. Twenty minutes later, 66 Squadron's pilots spotted the bandits near Ashford in Kent. One was flown by Lieutenant Erich Bodendiek of II Group from JG 53. "We [had] received orders for the entire Group to once again carry out a fighter sweep over England," he recalled. "A total of 18 machines were still serviceable, the rest had bullet holes and other damage that needed repair . . . We had crossed the English coast, when Spitfires—obviously under radar control—suddenly emerged from a cloud bank below us and to the right."[13] The Spitfires were 66 Squadron.

Bodendiek and the Ace of Spades attacked—cannon and machine guns blazing—and then scattered toward the clouds. After taking evasive action by pulling into steep turns, 66 Squadron gave chase, but the Messerschmitts were faster. Only one of the Germans failed to escape back across the Channel—Lieutenant Bodendiek. "My aircraft plodded forward," he recalled, "gaining scarcely any height and even less speed. I felt totally helpless—for I could only hope to slowly reach the cloud deck, knowing the Spitfire was not as good as the [Messerschmitt] in a shallow climb." Unfortunately for Bodendiek, he had been spotted by Hugh Reilley's flight leader, Bobby Oxspring, who was soon on his tail and then opened fire. Oxspring was on target with a beautiful deflection shot: Bodendiek flew straight into a hail of bullets. "Oxspring's chance was one in a thousand, but it worked," recalled Bodendiek. "He hit my tank, which was unprotected from below, and my aircraft caught fire. I had to get out—and I did."[14]

★

Back at the Reich Hunting Lodge in East Prussia, Adolf Galland had been enjoying the peace and quiet of the wilderness, its heather-scented air and autumn colors. Late that afternoon, he joined Göring as reports from Luftwaffe commanders on the day's actions were delivered. There had been very high losses: fifty-four aircraft destroyed and thirteen damaged. "Göring was shattered," recalled Galland. "He simply could not explain how the increasingly painful losses of bombers came about."[15]

Galland asked whether he could return to his base on the Channel coast. A morose Göring agreed. On the way back to France, mechanical failure forced Galland to land at the nearest airfield and he had to continue his journey by train. His fellow passengers were nauseated and astonished: Galland had brought his royal stag with him, eager to show his men the bounty he had collected—Oak Leaves and a truly massive set of antlers.

September drew to a close. For the Luftwaffe's bomber units, it had been a disastrous month, with a quarter of the force destroyed. For the fighter wings, it ended just as badly. On the final day of that month, they lost twenty-eight Me-109s, the highest number in one day so far. It was clearly time for a change of strategy, and in early October Göring ordered that a third of the Jagdwaffe be adapted to carry bombs so that they could perform hit-and-run sorties while the remainder of the fighter units carried out Jagd-freie, or free hunts. No longer would he send over massive daylight raids escorted by every fighter Kesselring could muster. The losses involved were unsustainable.

Göring's new plan of attack delighted his finest pilots. Free hunts were what they had wanted all along, and JG 2's Helmut Wick, JG 26's Adolf Galland, JG 51's Werner Mölders, and JG 53's Hans-Karl Mayer were now all competing to end the year as the Luftwaffe's leading ace. On October 5, Wick had shot down no fewer than five RAF fighters in two sorties, ripping apart three Hurricanes from 607 Squadron in just a few ferocious seconds, and bringing his total to forty-two. Now the handsome JG Richthofen's young star also had the Oak Leaves, and Mölders and Galland were in danger of being quickly overtaken.

By the second week in October 1940, the skies above the Channel and southern England were more dangerous than ever for Hugh Reilley and the RAF's hundreds of other newly minted fighter pilots. "The marauding German fighter squadrons were operating as hunting packs," recalled 66 Squadron's Bobby Oxspring, "and their numbers varied from half a dozen or so to formations of 200 plus . . . Freed from our 'backs to the wall' role against the bomber menace, we were hunting too . . . We were living under considerable tension. Each of us wondered when it would be our turn to stop a pack of lead."[16]

On October 17, around 2:30 p.m., 66 Squadron was vectored to intercept Me-109s flying as Jabos—fighter bombers—each carrying a single 250 kg bomb. The temperature plunged as Hugh Reilley and 66 Squadron soared higher and higher, vapor trails stretching ominously behind them.

Meanwhile, JG 51's Werner Mölders flew ahead of his wingman, his latest model Messerschmitt 109F-0 easily coping with the thin air because of its powerful fuel-injection engine. Mölders may have had the sun on his side, flying out of the south, when suddenly he spotted 66 Squadron and then pounced on Hugh Reilley at thirty thousand feet. Reilley was in a less responsive plane above its optimum height. At 3:25 p.m., the twenty-two-year-old became the second American to die in the Battle of Britain. His body was later discovered in his Spitfire, which crashed and burned at Crockham Hill, west of Seven Oaks in Kent.

JG 53, with whom Werner Mölders had first flown in the Battle of Britain, was also involved in fierce fighting that afternoon. Back at the German unit's base, its leader, Hans-Karl Mayer, listened to the radio in alarm as his two most senior pilots were shot up. Five days before, on October 12, he had scored his thirty-first kill—the five hundredth for JG 53. Determined to help his surviving pilots get back across the Channel safely, Mayer now jumped into the nearest available plane, a new Me-109-E7, and was soon heading toward England. Unfortunately, the Messerschmitt had not been fitted with a working radio or a life raft, and its gun breeches were empty. Mayer did not meet up with his hard-pressed pilots. Ten days later, his body washed up on the beach at Littlestone in Kent.[17] Mayer's Ace of Spades pilots were grief-stricken at the loss of their leader: a father figure and inspiration to so many of them. Mayer had come to personify the now legendary JG 53, and after his death the unit would never be quite as successful or as confident again.

Back at RAF Kenley, Flight Leader Bobby Oxspring and 66 Squadron were deeply affected by Hugh Reilley's death. He had been a popular, unassuming man whose single but great misfortune had been to be surprised by the greatest German fighter pilot of his generation, Werner Mölders. Oxspring recalled that when Reilley was buried, the families of dockers in Gravesend lined the streets and the town's graveyard "in large numbers to pay their respects as the cortege went by."[18] Only now was it revealed that Reilley had been an American, and his name was eventually added to the RAF's list of U.S. citizens who fought for England in the greatest aerial conflict in history.

On October 31, 1940, just two weeks after Mölders had killed Reilley, the Battle of Britain finally ended. Its highest scoring pilots were both German: Adolf Galland and Mölders, tied with fifty kills each.

15. The Eagles

Somehow I nursed her across the Channel, past the golf
courses of Sandwich Bay and down to the longest runway in
England at Manston. There wasn't much left of the fabric or
the tailplane. Before they took me off to the hospital,
I hobbled over and patted what was left of the fuselage.
"Thanks, old girl! You were a real lady!"[1]

James A. Goodson, Eagle Pilot

The Battle of Britain was over. Now began the hard slog of
taking the war to the enemy by hitting targets across the
Channel in northern France. But doing so posed an ever-greater
challenge as winter set in—even for the pilots who could fly blind
in bad weather. Not surprisingly, only the very best of "the few"
were now able to increase their scores. Meanwhile, the newly
formed American Eagle Squadron, arguably the least experienced
and most ill-disciplined unit in the RAF, struggled to get airborne
let alone launch hit-and-run raids on German defenses.

It was clear early on that the first Eagles needed skillful leadership, so a decorated Battle of Britain veteran, thirty-three-year-old
Walter Churchill, was posted to RAF Church Fenton to command
the fledgling unit. "They're a mad bunch of Wild Westerners,"
Colonel Charles Sweeny warned him. "They need licking into
shape and it's no use being easy with them just because they are
Americans. You must be tough from the word go, but you can
justify your toughness by your record. Remember, you've fought
in the Battle of Britain, you've seen action . . . Just let that message
sink in."[2]

Churchill had his work cut out for him. The Eagles did not

lack the courage and "moral fiber to get the job done" recalled Royce Wilkinson, a British flight commander posted to Church Fenton with Churchill. But they were indeed a wild bunch. In the eyes of the old RAF hands at the base, they acted like "saboteurs of military tradition." Most had no idea about discipline or RAF customs and it showed. They drank heavily, shocked mess sergeants with their table manners, played intense games of craps on the wool carpet in the officers' mess, and were described even by other Americans as "a bunch of renegades."[3]

Churchill did his best to rein in the more undisciplined among the first Eagles, but he knew full well that only when they were back in the air and undergoing difficult and dangerous combat training would they start to truly gel as a squadron.[4] Fortunately, the challenge of turning the Americans into a first-class unit became a little easier with the arrival at Church Fenton of a new intelligence officer, thirty-three-year-old J. Roland "Robbie" Robinson, who would later become Lord Martonmere, governor and commander-in-chief of Bermuda.

It was none other than Robinson who had helped Tobin, Keough, and Mamedoff gain acceptance into the RAF earlier that year. Now he rapidly set about smoothing away some of the Eagles' rough edges and soon became an avuncular figure who invited his American "pals" to his country home and even lent them money when they ran short. "The Eagle pilots settled down quickly," he recalled. "Their only real difficulty was probably that they were always broke owing to the inadequacies of the Royal Air Force pay which was at a lower standard than American pay."[5]

Another frustration was dealing with an endless stream of reporters, who now beat a path to Church Fenton, intent on glorifying the Eagles before they had even become operational. Fawning portraits began to appear in Britain and America, where isolationist sentiment had weakened in large part because of the RAF's success in fending off invasion, contrary to the dire predictions of aviation legend Charles Lindbergh and Ambassador Joseph Kennedy.

A few weeks after his arrival at Church Fenton, Eugene Tobin was interviewed by a British radio journalist who described him in language typical of most of the propagandist material churned out about the young American pioneers of 71 Squadron: "[He] has hair like a torch so his friends call him Red. His walk is loose-limbed. He is tall and absolutely without fear. Talking to him is rather like watching one of those old-time jugglers of the music halls, keeping six dazzling jeweled Indian clubs in the air at the same time. Red Tobin talks like that. He couldn't be dull if he tried. His slang sets fire to everything. It is amusing to hear him talk of his parachute as his jump sack, to hear him ask for bang water when he wants petrol; most amusing to hear him ask for the band stand when he wants the cruet on the mess table."

Why was Tobin fighting for Britain?

"Well," replied Tobin, "at first I just felt I wanted to fly some of these powerful machines, so I just came over . . . I guess one's views change a little once one is over here. The British are a swell people. This is a nice little country and I don't mind fighting for it a bit."[6]

But Tobin wasn't fighting for it. And this soon began to grate on him and others who had tasted combat that summer. Indeed, 71 Squadron's first recruits were not a happy crowd. In his diary, Tobin complained day after day about being bored, sitting on his "ass" in dreary Yorkshire. Church Fenton was a far cry from Middle Wallop and the intensity of late August.

News of his friends in 609 Squadron only made Tobin more frustrated and impatient to return to combat. Sergeant Alan Feary had been shot down and killed on October 7, but the rest of 609 were still battling with exceptional results, Johnny "Dogs" Dundas adding another five kills and David Crook at least three confirmed since the Americans had left Middle Wallop with heavy hearts.

It took another of the Eagle Squadron's first recruits, Pilot Officer Art Donahue, only a few days to get fed up with Church Fenton. After taking one look at his fellow Eagles and discovering that they had yet to be provided with planes, he demanded a transfer back to 64 Squadron. Colonel Charles Sweeny, now appointed the honorary commander of the Eagles, tried to prevent Donahue's departure. "I hated to see him go," he recalled. "He was a mean little guy, with more poetry than meanness in his make-up. I saw in him the makings of an excellent squadron leader. I tried to stop his transfer, kicked like a base steer, but it did me no good."[7]

Donahue packed his bags and on October 26, 1940, returned to RAF Kenley, where a delighted Squadron Leader Aeneas MacDonell welcomed him back to the fold. "I hope you won't think I'm foolish because I didn't want to be in the Eagle Squadron," Donahue wrote his parents a few days later. "I am considerably ahead by being in my old squadron. This in spite of the fact that [the Eagles] will no doubt soon be covered in glory while the newspapers are not liable to get any more news concerning me unless I really earn it by accomplishing something."[8]

Donahue certainly wasn't missing anything. Six weeks after arriving at Church Fenton, the Eagles were still without planes. Finally, on November 7, 85 Squadron's Peter Townsend and eight of his pilots landed at Church Fenton in nine battered Hurricanes that had seen extensive action in the Battle of Britain. Here, at last, were the Eagles' first mounts. "Everything good happened today," it was noted in the squadron's official diary. "Nine Hurricanes arrived, delivered by 85 Squadron. The commanding officer, Squadron Leader Townsend, most attractive fellow, stationed at Gravesend, was leading his squadron into battle daily despite one foot in a plaster cast, having had several toes taken off by a cannon shell."[9]

Not long after the Eagles finally received their banged-up "kites," Eugene Tobin suddenly collapsed. It was thought that he was perhaps suffering from delayed shock and exhaustion after such a strenuous year. But then Tobin was found to have lupus, an often fatal affliction resulting from a failure of the immune system.[10] For the rest of his time in the RAF, it would wear down his stamina and sap his spirits. He would eventually be so tired that as soon as he was released from duties each evening, he would go to bed and fall into a deep sleep. He kept the illness a secret, rightly fearing that if discovered it would quickly put an end to his flying career.[11]

It was around two o'clock on November 28—Thanksgiving Day in America—when twenty-five-year-old Helmut Wick lifted himself from the cockpit of his Messerschmitt. His ground crew quickly gathered around. Wick beamed with pride. Near the Isle of Wight, he had just seen his fifty-fifth victim fall to the waters below.

The competition to be the Luftwaffe's highest scoring pilot of 1940 was reaching its climax. On October 29, Werner Mölders had downed his fifty-fourth plane. Incredibly, on November 5 and 6, Wick had then shot down eight RAF pilots and drawn level with Mölders. Never one to be outdone for long, on November 17 Adolf Galland had surpassed both aces, destroying three RAF fighters to take his total to fifty-five, which had put him ahead of his two rivals by just one kill.

Now Wick had drawn level again.

With the onset of winter and rumors that the entire Jagdwaffe would soon be pulled back to Germany to be refitted, the pressure was more intense than ever. Only a few hours of hunting remained. Wick was ruthlessly committed to flying as many missions as he could squeeze into the shortening days, ever more obsessed with becoming the Second World War's Red Baron, the unrivaled heir to his unit's namesake—Richthofen. He appeared to be as dynamic as ever, but in fact he was dog tired, operating on his last reserves of nervous energy. Still, it was worth it. That morning, he had not only added another white stripe to his tail fin but also seen his grinning face on the cover of the latest issue of the *Berliner Illustrierte,* surely a good omen. If he could only keep killing at his current rate, he would end the year as the Luftwaffe's unchallenged star.

It was around 3:20 p.m. when the phone rang in JG 2 headquarters. An officer from JG 26 was on the line. He had bad news: Major Adolf Galland had just bagged a Hurricane and again pulled ahead. Wick turned to his ground crews and ordered them to refuel and rearm his squadron. There was still time for a last prowl over the white cliffs of the Isle of Wight's jagged southern coast-line, called the Needles. Around half an hour later, JG Richthofen's commander went through his checks and then led his flight into the air, headed for his second free hunt of the day, hell-bent on catching up with Galland.

It was a clear afternoon. Wick and his wingmen scanned the horizon. Meanwhile, back at base, an order came through from Berlin: Wick was not to fly again. He was now too important a Nazi propaganda figure to be allowed to die in combat.

Across the Channel, Fighter Command's radar stations detected Wick and his squadron as they flew toward the Isle of Wight. Not long after, the telephone shrilled in 609 Squadron's dispersal hut at Middle Wallop. Squadron Leader Michael Robinson and 609 were soon airborne and then vectored toward the Isle of Wight.

It was 4:10 p.m. when Helmut Wick and one of his most trusted wingmen, Rudi Pflanz, spotted Spitfires climbing fast southwest of the Needles. Wick picked out 609's Paul Baillon and ordered Pflanz to follow him in a diving attack. Baillon was soon in his sights and Wick opened fire. Smoke streamed from Baillon's Spitfire. Wick pressed on with his attack, sending another volley into Baillon's stricken plane. To his delight, his fifty-sixth victim bailed out and parachuted down into the Solent. He had done it. He had drawn level with Galland once more. It must have been a glorious moment for the young pilot.

Wick then pulled out of his dive and banked steeply, passing through the reflector gunsight of Johnny "Dogs" Dundas, now 609's highest scoring ace with sixteen kills. Dundas "pressed the tit" and bullets ripped into Wick's plane, disabling it. Then Dundas saw Wick's canopy fly away.

"I've finished a 109, whoopee!"

"Good show, John!" replied Squadron Leader Robinson.[12]

Helmut Wick pulled himself up from his cockpit and bailed out. Meanwhile, his wingman, Rudi Pflanz, had latched on to Dundas and opened fire. A few seconds later, Dundas's Spitfire went screaming down into the Solent.

Helmut Wick and his nemesis, Johnny "Dogs" Dundas, two of the most talented fighter pilots of the Battle of Britain, would never be seen again.

A week later, on December 5, 1940, the race to be number one was finally decided. During an early afternoon encounter with three RAF squadrons, Adolf Galland shot down his fifty-seventh victim and became the highest scoring German fighter pilot of the war so far. Mölders lagged three behind as JG 51, JG 26, and many other front-line units were then pulled back to Germany from their bases in Normandy and the fierce fighting over the Channel and southern England came to an end.

It seemed that the Eagles would never go operational. By the time Galland and his fellow aces were withdrawn from France, the first recruits to the Eagle Squadron—Eugene Tobin, Andy Mamedoff, and Shorty Keough—had been out of action for almost three months. And to their utter frustration, there was little prospect of returning to combat before the New Year: their fellow Americans in 71 Squadron needed a lot more time in the air if they were going to stand a chance in a dogfight.

After moving the squadron to RAF Kirton Lindsey, ten miles from Scunthorpe on a windswept Lincolnshire plain, Squadron Leader Churchill began a grueling schedule of formation flying and gunnery exercises. Cameras mounted on their Hurricanes recorded pilots' first efforts at deflection shots. The results were not impressive—most of the Americans had never used a reflector gunsight let alone fired at a moving target while flying at more than 300 mph.[13]

Even the most gifted found the training tough going. The simplest mistake could be fatal. On October 28, after losing control in a power dive from ten thousand feet, Phillip "Zeke" Leckrone, the Illinois pilot who had fought in the Battle of Britain, blacked out but then came to in time to crash-land, sustaining minor back injuries and severe shock.[14] "Zeke and I were flying in formation," Eugene Tobin recorded in his diary. "We came in for a landing and Zeke overshot and dumped the thing on its back. I jumped out of my plane and ran over and helped get him out. He was out colder than a clam, and when he came to he didn't remember anything."[15]

As Christmas approached, the Eagles were full of thoughts of home.[16] Eugene Tobin wondered what his "little honey"—Anne Haring—was doing back in Los Angeles. It was his first Christmas away from his family and he vowed he would be with "Pa and sisters and all [his] friends" in America for the next. His fellow Eagles were happy despite the foggy and damp weather. "Merry Christmas everybody," Tobin wrote in his diary on Christmas Eve, "except for Hitler—the bastard."[17] At the end of his diary for 1940, Tobin listed all the places he had visited, and in its cash ledger he entered the names of six friends who had been killed in as many months. On New Year's Eve, Tobin danced the night away until six the following morning at the Trocadero club in London. "I hope this goddamn war is over this time next year," he wrote in the first entry to a new diary for 1941. "I have made a lot of friends but . . . some of my pals are here no more. They're flying in clearer skies—great guys, every damn one of them. So, boys, till we meet again."[18]

Finally, on January 4, 1941, the Eagles officially became operational. The following day, they took off from Kirton Lindsey, flying together for the first time as a fully fledged RAF squadron. Morale was high. At twenty thousand feet, they split into four sections to practice tight formation flying. One of the sections comprised Shorty, Pilot Officer Edwin "Bud" Orbison, and Phillip Leckrone. Seated on his two customary cushions, Shorty watched, aghast, as the wing tip of Bud Orbison's Hurricane suddenly collided with Leckrone's plane, chopping off its tail. Orbison was able to return to Kirton Lindsey and land without injury, but Leckrone went into a tailspin and plunged toward the ground.

Shorty followed Leckrone down, shouting at him over the radio transmitter. "Bail out! Bail out!"

Leckrone did not reply and made no attempt to bail out. He died instantly on impact, the first Eagle to lose his life, and the third fatality among the Americans who had flown in the Battle of Britain. He had received his private pilot's license less than a year before in Salem, Illinois, where the local airport today bears his name.

The operations book for 71 Squadron reported: "Zeke [Leckrone] was quiet and reserved . . . His death will help this unit for, if nothing else, it will tend to impress on the other pilots the attention they must pay to detail in these practice flights. It is true of this squadron, as of most others in the RAF, that they are inclined to treat all this practice flying as a bit of a bore."[19] Leckrone had joined the RAF "for the highest of motives—not for the glamour, if any, or the thrills, but to defend our way of life."[20]

Eager to escape the dreary confines of Kirton Lindsey, especially after Leckrone's death, the Eagles were soon seizing every opportunity to visit London. In the capital, they now enjoyed celebrity status among their fellow expatriates and were often the star guests of boisterous parties hosted by journalists such as Quentin Reynolds of *Collier's* and Robert Casey of the *New York Herald Tribune*, who both got on particularly well with Eugene Tobin.

When the Eagles ventured into villages near their airfield, they were made to feel just as welcome. Most British people had only seen Americans in a movie. Meeting a Yank in real life was a rare occurrence. The sight of Tobin and his pals in RAF blue, with eagle patches on their shoulders, was at the very least intriguing and more often than not worth toasting—it was common knowledge that they had broken their country's strict neutrality laws to come to Britain's aid. "Very often," recalled twenty-one-year-old Eagle pilot Bill Geiger, "a bartender would say 'you don't pay for drinks here, Yank.' While other fighter pilots often got the same kind of treatment, the Americans got it more often."[21]

They also didn't lack for girlfriends, and it wasn't long before several had fallen for numerous English "roses." One night, Andy Mamedoff met a young aristocrat named Penny Craven, who had a cut-glass accent and an infectious laugh. One of the most eligible young women in England, she was due to inherit millions from her family, which had made a fortune in the cigarette business—quite a catch for the swashbuckling but penniless White Russian émigré. Soon, Mamedoff and Craven were planning to get married and to visit his parents back in Connecticut as soon as he was granted some extended leave. Penny would then get to enjoy true Cossack hospitality, dance with Andy to gypsy music at the Russian Bear restaurant his parents owned, and taste his mother's home cooking: beef stroganoff, mocha rum cake, and borscht fit for a czar.

In late January, the Eagles began patrolling over the treacherous North Sea as convoy escorts. There was little danger of being bounced by Messerschmitts—most of the time they were beyond the German fighters' range. The thick blanket of cloud just above the swells worried most of the Americans far more. In such conditions, even the best pilots were prone to vertigo—losing track of altitude and direction—with often deadly results.

The first to fall victim was twenty-two-year-old Californian Bud Orbison, who had been involved in the fatal accident with Phillip Leckrone. On February 9, 1941, he crashed as he tried to orient himself at four thousand feet. Yet again, Eugene Tobin and his fellow Americans mourned the loss of a popular pilot, killed like Leckrone on a Sunday. "I don't know of a better day to go," jotted Tobin in his diary that night. "So to my great pals Phil and Bud, 'Happy Landings' in your new 'Hunting Grounds.'"[22]

The next Eagle fell just a week later on February 15, 1941. "A section of Hurricanes was scrambled to fly protection over a convoy just off the east coast," recalled Jim Goodson, a twenty-two-year-old New Yorker who had been trained in Canada before joining the Eagles. "Pilot Officer Nat Maranz and Shorty [dived] into cloud. . . . For some reason Shorty stayed in the dive and must have come out of the cloud too low to recover and went into the sea. Coast guards heard the sound of a crash."[23]

Some of the Eagles thought vertigo had also caused Shorty to hit the waves at over 500 mph. According to twenty-one-year-old Chesley Peterson, however, there was a more mundane reason: "[Shorty] forgot to turn on his oxygen and blacked out [during the dive] simply for lack of air."[24] A couple days after Shorty crashed, a Coast Guard unit found a pair of size five flying boots floating amid wreckage. "Nobody but little Shorty could wear such small boots," it was noted in 71 Squadron's operations record book. "There can be little doubt that Shorty's plane dived into the sea at great speed and that he was killed instantly."[25]

The women in the local pub Shorty had frequented were deeply saddened at the news of his death. They had told a visiting journalist a while back that "they'd like to keep him on their mantel shelf forever."[26] Shorty's two closest pals, Eugene Tobin and Andy Mamedoff, were stunned. Shorty had become as close as a brother. Never again would he sprint at their side during a scramble, his two cushions tucked under one arm. "The fates are being most unkind," noted Robbie Robinson in the squadron diary.[27]

A much-needed visit from Charles Sweeny lifted the Eagles' spirits for a few days, but soon they were even more downcast: it was rumored that because of the flying accidents the squadron was to be disbanded and the Eagles sent back to America. No less than the head of Fighter Command, Sholto Douglas, had called them a "bunch of prima donnas."[28] Immediately, the Eagles chose Chesley Peterson, one of the most able of the squadron's pilots, to make their case before Air Marshal Hugh Sanders, the commander of 12 Group. Peterson asked that the Eagles be moved south to 11 Group where there was a much greater likelihood of engaging the enemy. "If we were to be prima donnas, the squadron resolved to be the best prima donnas in the entire RAF," recalled Peterson.[29] Before Peterson's request was passed on to Sholto Douglas, however, it was decided in any case to move the Eagles into the front line in 11 Group. At last, 71 Squadron would see combat. After all the setbacks, the Eagles finally had something to celebrate.

Also based at Kirton Lindsey that spring was 616 Squadron's Johnnie Johnson, destined to become World War II's highest scoring British fighter pilot. He recalled a particularly raucous party, even by the RAF's standards, before the Eagles moved south: "The champagne corks were popping, and along the length of one corridor the defeat of Cornwallis at Yorktown was being reenacted with some spirit. Numerous fire extinguishers were deployed by the Americans, whilst the inferior British fire was restricted to soda siphons from behind a defensive screen of potted palms. Once again, as in 1776, the Americans had the upper hand and both the palms and the British were decidedly the worse for wear."[30]

On April 9, 1941, the Eagles arrived at Martlesham Heath in Suffolk. They did not have to wait long to sight the enemy, chasing a Ju-88 on April 13, shooting at a Dornier 17 a few days later, and finally getting into their first real dogfight with Me-109s on May 15 without loss. By July, they were being scrambled almost daily and claiming their fair share of kills. A congratulatory telegram from 11 Group headquarters came toward the end of the month: the American prima donnas were finally earning the RAF top brass's admiration and respect. Soon, the high and mighty were turning up in person to shake their hands: Air Minister Sir Archibald Sinclair; the actor Noël Coward; Air Marshal Sir Sholto Douglas, head of Fighter Command; and even the American ambassador, John Winant, who had replaced Joe Kennedy earlier that year.

Kennedy had not been missed. Badly shaken by the Blitz, he had fled London the previous October but not before telling his mistress, Clare Boothe Luce: "There is a popular song called 'There'll Always Be an England.' There always will be, but you'll hardly recognize it; and I know damn well I'll not be around to be in it!"[31] Not long after Kennedy's arrival back in America, on November 5, President Roosevelt had been reelected to an unprecedented third term. The next day, Kennedy had met with Roosevelt for five minutes at the White House. According to Kennedy, Roosevelt had said he would not accept his resignation until he had found a replacement. Roosevelt's second son, Elliott, later claimed just the opposite: his father had asked Kennedy to resign.[32] Roosevelt had finally had enough of his anti-Semitic and defeatist ambassador. He would soon introduce several wide-ranging measures, most famously Lend Lease, to provide Britain with all possible support short of declaring war on Germany.

★

They formed a solemn line as they entered the cathedral in their dark blue uniforms and then took their seats to pay respects to the first of them to fall. Eugene Tobin and Andy Mamedoff were both among the dozens of pilots soon sitting in pews that Independence Day afternoon of 1941. Indeed, many of 71 Squadron's pilots had been given leave to attend the memorial service for Billy Fiske at St. Paul's in London. The service was a propaganda coup: the perfect opportunity, on the perfect date, to remind Americans that some of its citizens were already dying for freedom—that the isolationist course was inevitably doomed. The new American ambassador, John Winant, attended, as did Air Minister Sir Archibald Sinclair, who had met with Fiske the previous summer and asked him to go to America to recruit pilots.

As cameras from NBC rolled, Sinclair eulogized Fiske, the first American airman to die in the Battle of Britain:[33] "Here was a young man for whom life held much. Under no kind of compulsion he came to fight for Britain. He came and he fought, and he died."[34] Many more Americans in the RAF would soon follow Fiske to the grave. But none would have a plaque bearing their name placed in St. Paul's crypt only a few yards from a statue of America's first president, George Washington.[35]

The following month, August 1941, brought big changes to 71 Eagle Squadron. So many American volunteers were now in Britain that several stalwarts were posted away to form the nucleus of a new Eagle squadron, 133 Squadron. Andy Mamedoff was selected to lead one of its flights, thereby becoming the first American to be so honored by the RAF. The promotion surprised some of his fellow Eagles. Twenty-one-year-old Californian Bill Geiger would later vividly recall Mamedoff during this period: "He was a damn good pilot. But you couldn't have said to Andy Mamedoff, 'Look, you're supposed to address the squadron leader as sir and salute him the first time you see him in the morning.' Mamedoff would have said 'ha, ha, ha' and 'forget that.'"[36]

Shortly before leaving 71 Squadron in late August 1941 for his new assignment with 133, Andy Mamedoff also became the first of the American "few" to take a war bride: Penny Craven, the fun-loving aristocrat who stood to inherit a vast fortune. The wedding reception was too tempting a target for some of his fellow Eagles to pass up. "The day Mamedoff got married we were due to have gunnery training," recalled Bill Geiger. "But just as the rest of the squadron was due to head off for training, another Eagle pilot called Ed Bateman and I were ordered to make a convoy patrol. The patrol was uneventful. As we returned, Bateman said: 'Let's see what's going on at Mamedoff's wedding.' So we flew toward Epping. We knew where the reception was. Sure enough, when we came in low, we saw the wedding party in a back garden. So we buzzed it. I'm pretty sure we actually went in so low that Andy ducked down. To make matters worse, when the rest of the squadron returned from gunnery practice, they buzzed the town itself. There was all hell to pay because of all the complaints. The mayor of Epping finally said: 'Look, these people are risking their lives for us. If they want to celebrate a comrade's wedding then so they should.' "[37]

On September 7, not long after Mamedoff's wedding, Eugene Tobin joined eight other pilots for 71 Squadron's first mission over enemy territory. "The idea was to fly over in poor weather in sections of two or perhaps four, and shoot up anything that looked German," recalled Eagle pilot Jim Goodson. "If they got into trouble, they could nip into cloud and head for home. That was the theory anyway. The main problem however was that one generally had to fly low and if caught by ground fire one was often too low to do much but hit the deck."[38]

Setting out for northern France, three planes in 71 Squadron soon had mechanical problems and were forced to return home. Tobin and others flew on. Around seventy-five miles inland, radar announced bandits to their rear, between them and the Channel. The bandits turned out to be 75 Messerschmitts from none other than JG 26, still let by Major Adolf Galland with 82 kills now to his credit. Squadron Leader Stanley Meares, who had joined the Eagles only a few weeks before, suddenly called out over the radio: "Every man for himself now chaps!"[39]

From twenty-nine thousand feet, Galland and his fellow JG 26 aces screamed down at more than 400 mph, bouncing several Eagles, flashing past others, spitting tracer and cannon. According to one account, a German plane was soon tumbling down in flames; pieces flew off another. 71 Squadron's Pilot Officer Bill Geiger watched as Eugene Tobin broke formation and set off after yet another.[40] At some point, a recently married young pilot called Hilard Fenlaw was killed and Pilot Officer Bill Nichols was shot up badly, forced to crash-land, and soon captured.

It is thought that around 5:20 p.m. Tobin tangled near Montreuil with the formidable twenty-two-year-old Joachim Müncheberg, who had 52 white stripes on his tail-fin and was nicknamed the "Spitfire hunter" by his fellow Jagdwaffe veterans. There was an unconfirmed report that Tobin survived the encounter and was seen to give the thumbs-up, indicating that he was unharmed, as he took his badly damaged plane in for a forced landing. But it was far more likely that he was shot down and killed, his Spitfire being one of six claimed by Müncheberg, Galland, and four other JG 26 pilots that day.

Back in England, ground crew waited in vain for Tobin to return. Never again would they hear him call out: "Saddle her up! The great lover and adventurer is gonna ride high again today."[41] It is not known how Andy Mamedoff reacted to the disappearance of the man with whom he had gamboled so often through the high cirrus above California's Sierra Nevada. But he must at times have wondered how much longer his luck could last now that his two closest friends had fallen.

Over sixty years later, Eugene Tobin's sister, Helen Maher, vividly recalled hearing that her brother was missing. She was visiting her in-laws in Denver when she received a call from her uncle, who owned a local radio station. He had seen a wire report stating that Tobin had been shot down over enemy territory.

"Helen, have you heard from your father?"

"No. Why?"

"Well . . . evidently you haven't heard the news. I hate to be the first to tell you but I don't want you to hear it on the news . . . Gene is reported missing."

Twenty-five-year-old Maher broke into tears and fled to her bedroom. The next day, she drove around Denver alone for hour after hour, full of memories of a lanky, wisecracking teenager at Hollywood High—the "first latchkey kid in Los Angeles," who had once stolen a neighbor's flowers so that he could give them to his dying mother.

"Damn it," she sobbed, "he never got a break—not one."[42]

Tobin was soon confirmed as missing. But had he been killed? A telegram sent by the journalist Quentin Reynolds left the Tobin family hoping that he had survived the German bounce and been taken prisoner: "[Tobin] listed as killed but I talked with two pilots with him on sweep and both sure he landed safely, not losing control of airplane. You know how I like that kid. He stayed with me night before he got it. If I get definite word he [is] alive, taken prisoner, will get location prison camp."[43] Tobin's father told a Los Angeles newspaper the following day that he was sure Eugene was "all right." Meanwhile, twenty-four-year-old Anne Haring, Tobin's girlfriend in Los Angeles, contacted the International Red Cross, writing to the agency the day she learned the love of her life had gone missing.

For the Eagles, September 7, 1941, was the blackest day in their history: three pilots lost in a matter of minutes. Tobin's disappearance was particularly hard to accept. He had been the most experienced fighter pilot with the unit and immensely popular, lifting the young Americans' spirits through the dark days the previous winter just as he had done with the British pilots in 609 Squadron during the Battle of Britain. He would be dearly missed by fellow Eagle pilots such as Jim Goodson, who had befriended Tobin that summer. Goodson would later recall how his grief over the loss of more and more of his friends finally overwhelmed him one night: "I was eating dinner and I looked down at my plate and saw water on it. I looked up at the ceiling to see where the leak was but didn't see one. Then suddenly I realized that I was crying. I guess it was just the desire to release my feelings because I don't recall crying another time during the war. You were just so busy and you identified with the guy who got shot down and realized it could have been you."[44]

It was late October 1941 when Tobin's girlfriend, Anne Haring, received a reply from the International Red Cross: "It is with the deepest regret that we have to inform you that F/O Tobin was killed in action. We have received the following information from the Official Bureau for Prisoners of War, Berlin: F/O Tobin 81622, killed 7.9.1941. Buried 9.9.1941, at Boulogne, East Cemetery."[45] When RAF personnel went through Tobin's belongings in his quarters, they found just one shilling and three pence, worth twenty-eight cents. "The fortune of a hero," reported an American newspaper, "who died in a foreign plane, riding foreign skies above a foreign land."[46]

Andy Mamedoff had joined 133 Eagle Squadron at RAF Duxford by the time Tobin flew his last mission. The newly formed unit's emblem was an American eagle at the center of a circle filled with stars; its motto was "Let us to the battle." The mood of the squadron itself, however, was far from gung ho.

At its first meeting, 133's Squadron Leader George A. Brown, a Battle of Britain veteran, was brutally frank: "Gentlemen, no Englishman is more appreciative than I to see you American volunteers over here to assist us in our fight. It is going to get a lot tougher as time goes by—so, take a good look around this room, because a year from now most of you will be dead."[47]

There was a long silence.

Mamedoff watched as the pilots in his flight "glanced around at one another, all with the same thought in mind—'You poor ignorant bastards, you've had it.'"[48]

There followed intensive practice in formation flying at Duxford, with Mamedoff putting his flight of eight pilots through their paces. The youngest included William White, Hugh McCall and Roy Stout, who had just arrived from a training unit and needed all the guidance they could get. By late September, Mamedoff was leading them on their first mission, a low-level sweep of the Dutch coastline in search of German torpedo boats. It was then decided to transfer 133 Squadron to RAF Eglington in Northern Ireland, from where it would fly vital convoy patrols over the North Atlantic.

On October 8, 1941, Andy Mamedoff and fifteen of 133's pilots left RAF Fowlmere in Cambridgeshire for their new posting. They were scheduled to refuel twice on their way to Northern Ireland. All went well on the first leg of the journey. Mamedoff led 133's Hurricane MK 11Bs to the first refueling stop at RAF Sealand, near Chester, in less than an hour. But as Mamedoff and his pilots prepared for the next leg, they saw the sky starting to darken as bad weather drifted in from the Irish Sea to the west. Undeterred, the Americans took off, headed into storm-laden skies toward the next refueling stop: RAF Andreas on the Isle of Man.

The weather got worse, forcing the Americans to rely on their instruments. Soon, visibility was almost zero degrees. Vertigo began to affect several pilots. Two wisely decided to return to Sealand. Three others soon put down at other airfields. Six more were lucky enough to find a break in the cloud cover and were able to land, much relieved, on the Isle of Man at Andreas, having missed several hilltops by only a few feet.

Mamedoff and his three youngest pilots found no break in the clouds. Not far from the village of Maughold, southeast of Ramsey, local farmers heard the roar of four Rolls-Royce Merlin engines. The sound was louder than usual, indicating that the planes were flying dangerously low. Suddenly, there was a massive explosion followed by the crackle of machine-gun bullets spitting in several directions. The farmers sprinted into a nearby field, where they discovered Hurricane Z3781 ablaze. Twenty-eight-year-old Flight Commander Andy Mamedoff, the first Jewish American pilot to fight against the Nazis in World War II, had been killed instantly on impact, his plane falling suddenly from the air.[49]

On October 14, 1941, Mamedoff's parents, Lev and Natasha, were busy as usual managing their Russian Bear restaurant, filled with vacationers touring Connecticut to peak at the fall leaves, when they learned that their only son had died. He would soon be buried in Brookwood Military cemetery in Woking, England, in a special plot reserved for American volunteers in the RAF. Devastated by his nephew's loss, the Nazi supporter Count Anastase told a Norwich *Bulletin* reporter the following day that Mamedoff's death was "unnecessary." The thoughtless remark would not be forgotten or forgiven in Thompson, and from that moment on he was quickly isolated within the community.[50] Mamedoff's parents would soon leave Connecticut and try to start over in St. Petersburg, Florida.

16. Dawn Patrol

I had a rather bad night of it, as I usually do when I have a particular operation planned for the morning, because I can't keep it out of the back of my mind, and so I got to sleep thinking about it. Then after I've been asleep awhile, at the time when one's normal defenses are way down and nerves and feelings all bared and sensitive, the dread sets in and all the dangers seem vivid and terrifying.[1]

Art Donahue, 258 Squadron

After recuperating from his burns, Art Donahue spent the winter of 1940–41 flying Channel patrols with 64 Squadron, skimming above swells before landing and then looking up to see his vapor trail still etched in the sky. "*Please* don't ever waste any sympathy on me," he wrote to his family back in St. Charles, Minnesota. "I'm having the time of my life, happier than I've ever been. You can't imagine the joy I've got out of the few meetings I've had with those barbarians, and the joy I get out of patrolling and hunting for them. I have yet to meet up with one of them whom I couldn't easily out fly."[2]

As spring beckoned and the days grew longer, Art Donahue was posted to 91 Squadron on the south coast. In late March 1941, he took a much deserved break from the war, making a brief visit to Minnesota, where he was greeted as a returning hero at St. Charles's train station by his weeping mother and hundreds of proud Minnesotans. Thankfully, the FBI was not waiting to arrest him for breaking neutrality laws. The U.S. State Department had decided not to prosecute Americans who now fought with the RAF.[3]

Donahue barely had a moment to relax in his hometown of St. Charles, such was his newfound celebrity. "I had more invitations than I could possibly accept to speak at various gatherings and over the radio," he recalled. "The Commercial Club of St. Charles gave a banquet in my honor and presented me with a wonderful gold wrist watch and my mother with a bouquet of flowers . . . Most of the week I was in a daze, every one was so good to me."[4]

It was bizarre to be in a country so far removed from the war. He had been away for just eight months but had changed so much in that time that he felt as if he had been absent for far longer. Donahue was bewildered by the bright lights (there was no black-out); upset that he could not wear his uniform because of America's official position as a neutral country; and outraged by striking aircraft workers, earning more than the finest RAF fighter pilots, and now "jeopardizing England's chances."[5]

Donahue arrived back in London one morning in April. The previous night, the Luftwaffe had launched the "greatest bombardment" the city had yet suffered. "The sun was a red ball glowing feebly through the haze of brown smoke that covered the city," he recalled. "It was a painful though dramatic contrast [with America]." When he got back to his base at Hawkinge on the south coast, even worse news awaited. Two pilots he had flown with the previous summer had been killed. And his former squadron leader, Aeneas MacDonell, whom Donahue idolized and who had made his trip home possible, was now a prisoner of war. On March 13, he had been shot down by no less than Werner Mölders, becoming the German ace's sixty-second victim.[6] MacDonell had bailed out above the Channel and had eventually been picked up by a German motorboat.

For the next six months, Donahue flew sweeps across the Channel as the RAF stepped up its offensive over northern France. Then, in October 1941, at the invitation of Squadron Leader Jock Thomson, Donahue joined 258 Squadron, which was being posted abroad. He could not tell his family where he was going, even if he had known, because of censorship. But he did explain why he wanted to leave England: "While I may be a little farther away from you in miles I expect to be closer to home in time, because one of the attractions of this posting [is] that I'll have a better chance to work a trip back to the States . . . another reason [for going abroad] is the thought of getting away from the lousy English winter fogs and other flying hazards."[7]

Unfortunately, Donahue was forced to wait in Gibraltar en route to his foreign posting because of the sinking of the British aircraft carrier *Ark Royal*, which had been scheduled to transport 258 Squadron to warmer climes. Twenty-year-old John A. "Red" Campbell, a fellow American, recalled one evening in Gibraltar when Donahue joined him and other pilots in a bar popular with British servicemen: "I remember Donahue standing at the bar . . . with one hand tucked into his tunic. Some people thought it was a war hero pose, but it wasn't. He had to hold his hand that way because of his Battle of Britain injuries. Art was an idealist—one of the few real ones in the squadron . . . It was the first chance he had for a lot of time to think about what the war meant to the parents of fighter pilots on both sides. He said he felt like weeping for the mothers of the German airmen he had killed. Art wrote a series of articles about air combat for a magazine—I think it was the *Saturday Evening Post*. Someone suggested he do a book. I was with him when he bought a typewriter."[8]

Donahue turned out to be as talented a writer as he was an aviator, one of that rare breed who can elegantly evoke in pristine prose the high-octane mix of emotions that pilots experience in combat. According to the highly literate British fighter pilot, Peter Townsend: "The best airmen are mostly simple people, who have been so overwhelmed by their love for flying that it has driven some of them to drink, others to silence, as great love often does. But occasionally there arises one, a poet, a philosopher, who succeeds in lending coherent reason to their love."[9] Such was Arthur Gerald Donahue. His book, titled *Tally-ho! Yankee in a Spitfire*, would be published in the spring of 1942 to favorable reviews and brisk sales. It recounted his experiences with 64 Squadron during the Battle of Britain but made no reference to his brief stay with the by now famous 71 Eagle Squadron. According to Red Campbell, Donahue had been far from impressed by the first Eagles, describing the unit to Campbell as "a motley crew that would never amount to anything."[10] For once, Donahue had been wrong: that October and November of 1941, 71 Squadron downed more aircraft than any other in Fighter Command.

The youngest Inspector of Fighters in the Luftwaffe's history took his seat in a Heinkel 111 of KG 27 and waited for Lieutenant Georg Kolbe, a fellow Condor Legion veteran, to taxi along the rough landing strip. It was early on November 22, 1941, and twenty-eight-year-old Werner Mölders was on his way back to Berlin to attend the funeral of General Ernst Udet, the man many obituaries were now describing as the father of the Luftwaffe.

The Heinkel lumbered into the air. In Berlin Mölders would get to see his wife, Louise, the widow of one of his many fallen comrades. They had married on September 13, shortly after Göring had grounded him. Like Helmut Wick before his death, Mölders was now far too important a figure in Nazi Germany to be risked in combat. He had won every laurel, beating Adolf Galland to the ultimate cure to "throat-ache"—the Diamonds to the Knight's Cross. By the time Göring had forbidden him to fly in combat, the tail fin on his Messerschmitt had been covered from one end to the other with 101 white stripes.

Through the cockpit of the Heinkel, Mölders could see that the weather was starting to deteriorate. He watched as Kolbe put down at Lemberg to refuel. Before long the Heinkel's two 1,100 hp Daimler-Benz engines were roaring to life once more and they were lifting off the ground again. The weather got worse. Near Breslau, the port engine failed. Kolbe brought the Heinkel down through thick cloud cover. Then disaster struck. It was 11:30 a.m. when the second engine failed and the Heinkel fell to the ground like a stone, killing all aboard.

News of Mölders's death plunged the entire Third Reich, it seemed, into mourning. JG 51 was quickly named *Jagdgeschwader Mölders* in his honor. His funeral brought Berlin to a standstill as countless admirers pressed against barriers to watch a gun carriage, bearing Mölders's coffin, pass on its way to the Invalidenfreidhof, the last resting place of Baron Manfred von Richthofen, the greatest ace of the last war. Among the mourners was Mölders's great rival Adolf Galland, now his replacement as Inspector of Fighters. Although he had not achieved Mölders's mythical status, fate would deal him a far kinder hand: he would go on to fly the Luftwaffe's first jet fighter, bring down his last bandits only days before the end of the war, and die an old man.

Finally, the gun carriage drew to a halt before the cemetery. The massive crowds fell silent, arms outstretched in the Nazi salute. A few yards from the swastika-draped coffin stood Hermann Göring. He too had come to pay his final respects to the finest fighter pilot he and Germany had ever known.

The Mediterranean flashed below the Hurricanes, whitecaps sparkling in the winter light. It was a relief to be back in a cockpit rather than in some dingy Gibraltar bar trying to kill time playing darts. The smell of oil, burnished metal, and leather always made Art Donahue feel better. It had been his balm since his first solo flight above the Minnesota town of Winona, nestled on the banks of the Mississippi River—from the air an endless, shining artery through the Midwest's rolling hills, bluffs, and patchwork of cornfields and dairy farms.

Although he was still waiting to ship out to the Far East, Donahue was able that December to keep his flying skills honed through low-level patrols along the Spanish coast. And there was always the off chance that he might run into easy prey: German Focke-Wulf Condors flying out of Cadiz to attack Allied convoys in the Atlantic.

On December 7, 1941, Donahue returned to his billet after watching a movie. Before turning in for the night, he switched on his radio. At 11 p.m., he heard his first news report on the bombing of Pearl Harbor. Many of his fellow Americans serving in the RAF were deeply shocked, but they also celebrated the news of the Japanese attack until the early hours because it signaled the end of American neutrality. Donahue described his reaction in a letter to his parents: "For the first few hours after I heard the news of the attack on Hawaii I seemed to take it quite casually. Then when it really began to sink home I found myself more really and truly mad at the Japs than I have ever been able to be toward the Germans—with all their crimes. Somehow, the fact that it's your own people who have been attacked seems to make a tremendous difference."[11]

Donahue was in fact so enraged that he decided to apply for a posting to the Far East, but before he could do so he and 258 Squadron received orders to fly part of the way to their new posting, which was still a secret. Just before Christmas they set out on a long journey across North Africa. In Nigeria, early in the New Year, Donahue learned of his final destination—Singapore, then under attack by the Japanese. Donahue could not have been more pleased: now he would have a chance to strike back at the Japanese. On January 29, 1942, 258 Squadron finally arrived in the British colonial outpost, finishing its marathon journey aboard a transport ship. There was no time for rest. Within forty-eight hours, 258 Squadron was in action, defending the island from Japanese dive-bombers. The squadron faced overwhelming odds and had to operate in terrible humidity without adequate fuel supplies, spare parts, or reserves of ammunition.

By February 16, barely a fortnight later, 258 Squadron had been reduced to a few bone-tired pilots and battered planes. Early that morning, Donahue led a search for Japanese invasion barges that had been spotted heading toward the mainland of Singapore. Flying as Donahue's Number 2—his wingman—was British pilot Terrence Kelly. "You know what I need?" Donahue had asked Kelly just a few days before. "Just a nick. Just something that'll get me home to an American squadron now we're in the war."[12]

Donahue, Kelly, and four other pilots from 258 flew north toward the port of Pladjoe. Oil wells nearby had been set alight to prevent the Japanese from exploiting them. "The smoke rose for several thousand feet before, catching some air current, it spread away like a sign-post, a huge black swathe across the sky pointing to the target and we flew under it as cover," recalled Kelly. "It was a strange atmosphere—above the queer black cloud, below the darkened jungle broken only by the turgid brown swathes of many rivers which made the Moesi delta."[13]

Donahue and Kelly spotted a small group of boats and attacked. But then they learned that their victims were not part of the invasion armada that had been reported. "I kept close to Donahue and he was puzzled too, looking this way and that," recalled Kelly, "and then we came upon the barges."[14] Donahue had never seen so many enemy troops so vulnerable to attack. "Often I had machine-gunned German soldiers, sailors, or airmen on the ground or in ships, but always where they either had a little shelter or concealment, or at least could scatter and throw themselves flat," he explained. "These fellows had no shelter or concealment except the thin sides of their boats, no better than paper for stopping our bullets, and they were jammed in so tight that they couldn't scatter or throw themselves flat or do anything except just sit up and take it."[15]

Donahue came in low, around a hundred feet above the water. He made a last check for Japanese fighters—Navy Zeros. The barges loomed larger in the amber glow of his reflector sight. He moved his thumb over to his firing button, wanting to send his first bullets a little high, knowing they would dip. Then he opened fire: "There was an abrupt shattering roar from the guns in my wings and then eighty ghostly white tracers snaking out ahead eagerly, toward the boat and its helpless passengers. They would know nothing more."[16]

Donahue's wingman, Terrence Kelly, had the perfect view of the ensuing slaughter: "I probably saw the effect of Donahue's attack much better than any of my own because I had fallen astern behind him waiting my turn and with nothing to do and not much to think about but watch. I really don't believe Donahue missed a barge, his guns raking the convoy from head to stern. The bullets made an unforgettable pattern. There was a pincushion of water ahead of the nearest barge which moved along so that as the bullets raked through a barge what one saw was the pinpoints of light in the barge itself."[17]

Donahue had lost too much altitude, so he pulled the stick back and corrected, aiming at a barge farther in the distance. His aim was again perfect, its effect devastating. Tracers tore into the bodies of twenty tightly packed Japanese soldiers. He could see their faces as they died. Then he began to bank and turn away to attack another barge.

"Wham!"

A 20 mm anti-aircraft shell hit Donahue in the calf of his left leg. He looked down in shock at two holes. "One [was] small and round," he recalled. "The other [was] a gaping sort of thing an inch wide by a couple inches long, with raw red and blue flesh and muscle laid open, before the blood welled up and started streaming out." Donahue turned away sharply from the anti-aircraft fire toward an endless green carpet of jungle. The shock began to abate and his instinct for survival kicked in. He was almost a hundred miles from his base. He had a tendency to black out when he began to bleed. Could he stay conscious long enough to get home?

A few minutes later, Donahue began to feel light-headed. He grabbed his trouser leg above the wound and tried to twist it to form a tourniquet. But still his ruptured veins spurted and blood collected in a bright red pool in his heel rest, a metal trough underneath his rudder pedal. He looked at his altimeter, spattered with pieces of his flesh, and knew that if he faded away for even a couple of seconds he would crash. He gritted his teeth, his ears ringing, dots filling his vision. He couldn't even summon the strength to close his jaw.

"I mustn't faint, I mustn't faint!" Donahue said to himself.

His vision blurred.

Donahue began to panic.

"I *am* fainting—I mustn't faint—I *am* fainting!"

The seconds passed slowly. He realized he was still awake. He could hear the Rolls-Royce engine purring. He wondered whether he should crash-land, and whether to shut down the engine before he did so. Then he had a smart idea: he would keep himself awake with extra oxygen. He let go of the stick, reached to his instrument panel, and increased his oxygen supply. Although flying just a few hundred feet above the jungle's canopy, he was soon breathing enough oxygen to stay wide awake at forty thousand feet.

Donahue still grabbed his torn trousers with one hand. He opened his throttle, letting go of the stick again for a second or two, and then checked his wound. He was still losing blood. There was only one thing for it. "It seemed easy," he later recalled. "I let go [of] the hold I had of my trouser leg above the wound, grabbed up the torn cloth right over it, twisted it, and then jammed my gloved fist, knuckles first, as deep as I could into the large hole, and held it that way."

Donahue almost blacked out. He tried to breathe more slowly so he could stay conscious. His oil and temperature gauges showed normal. They had not been hit. His reserve fuel tank was still full. Constantly, he turned his head, looking out for Japanese Navy Zeros, flying as low as he could above the trees. Finally, the jungle gave way to rice fields and waterways—he was getting close to his home base. He looked down at his wound and saw that it had stopped bleeding: "The red rivulets down my leg and shoe seemed to be stationary, and the puddle of blood in the heel rest was no longer bright but dark, which meant that there couldn't be any fresh blood on it. The pain, which never had been agonizing, had settled into a heavy ache as from a badly bruised muscle. My hopes of making it really soared."

Donahue flew south, unable to recognize landmarks because they were obscured by smoke from bombings and many fires. If only he could spot a familiar railway line to lead him home. The weather had now closed in and he had to concentrate hard to avoid several rainstorms. Suddenly, there were the blessed rail tracks. Donahue banked slightly and followed them. And then there it was—his airfield. Now he would have to land with one hand: he dared not pull his gloved one out of the hole in his leg. Donahue came in low, slowly wagging his wings to show that he was hurt. He let go of the stick for a second to lower his wheels for landing and then he eased off the throttle. Still too much speed. He used his left elbow to throttle back even more. Then the wheels hit the ground and he bounced violently for a hundred yards. "The feeling of triumph at having made it safely made the bad landing seem inconsequential! I felt almost boisterous as I taxied up to the watch office."

The surviving pilots and ground crew of 258 Squadron ran out to Donahue's plane and helped him out of the cockpit. A fellow officer dressed his wound, and he was rushed to the nearest aid station. Donahue suddenly feared that if he was hospitalized he would inevitably become a prisoner of the Japanese, who in a matter of hours would seize all of Singapore. To his relief, after a quick call was put through to his squadron, he was carried to an ambulance and driven back to his base. "A Lockheed bomber bound for Java was held up waiting for me at Squadron Leader Thomson's intercession," recalled Donahue. "Two hours later I was safely in bed, three hundred miles from the fighting zone, in the Dutch Military Hospital of Bandoeng, a beautiful city in the mountains of west central Java. I had all that I promised myself— a bed to sleep in, with clean sheets, and the prospect of break-fast in bed in the morning! In addition I had a very pretty nurse to look after me."[18]

For his extraordinary courage in attacking the Japanese invaders and then managing to bring his plane back, Arthur Gerald Donahue was awarded the DFC, the RAF's second highest award for gallantry.[19]

After recuperating for several weeks, Donahue returned to England and resumed combat with 91 Squadron as a flight commander, flying sweeps across the Channel once more, the words MESSAGE FROM MINNESOTA now painted on his Spitfire's nose. By August 1942 he had become 91's acting commanding officer, the first and only American in the RAF's history to lead an all-British squadron. By all accounts, he was a natural leader in the air.

On most sorties, Donahue's wingman was Flight Lieutenant A. C. Young, with whom he had flown the previous year before accepting Jock Thomson's invitation to join 258 Squadron. On Saturday, August 29, Young recorded that day's mission: "Went to Dieppe on the dawn recco again and weather foul. Stooged around at 28,000 with Art Donahue and jumped two Spits who were returning from France. We attacked them just for the fun of it and they didn't even see us." On the evening of September 10, Young wrote: "I'm on dawn [patrol] tomorrow and Art is going to Ostend and I to Dieppe. He is going to lay [in wait] for a Ju-88 that our listening post service warned us was shadowing me yesterday. Hope he gets it and if not, he promised me the next crack at it."[20]

Young's entry the next day read: "Boy, what a tough luck day. Art went to the Ostend recco as arranged and I went to Dieppe. Art hadn't returned when I landed . . . The whole story goes, he found that Ju-88 that was shadowing me yesterday morning. He attacked it and set it on fire and our listening-post service picked up the German crew broadcast saying their rear gunner was dead, the port engine was on fire and they were trying to make [a nearby aerodrome]. Evidently, Art got a bullet from return fire and it hit his radiator making the motor cease. I refuelled and Pilot Officer Eddy and I went to search the area. It was a terribly hazy day, one of the worst we've seen and the sun made it almost impossible to see, let alone fly. We searched for an hour and ten minutes and all I found was some wreckage . . . parts of a Whirl-wind, as Spit's parts don't float. The rest of the guys searched in turn until noon when flying was cancelled due to the weather."[21]

Donahue had managed to report by radio that he had destroyed the Junkers 88.[22] He had indeed been hit. His last communication had been that his engine was overheating. He was too low to bail out, so he was going to ditch in the Channel eight miles north of Gravelines. Then his radio had gone silent.

Art Donahue's body was never found.

As with Eugene Tobin's disappearance, for some time Donahue's family and friends held out hope that he might have survived. But by 1943 they had all come to accept that he had died. On November 16 that year, a tribute from Donahue's intelligence officer in 64 Squadron, A. W. Fagan, appeared in the London *Times*. "[Art] had joined the RAF in spite of considerable difficul-ties, personal and otherwise, not from any wish for adventure or personal advancement, but rather in the spirit of a crusader who had no illusions about what lay before him, and had counted the cost. He had vision and he had courage in abundant measure. Modest and reserved by nature, he came to live among strangers in a strange land, whose outlook and habits were in many ways widely different from his own. Nevertheless, he quickly made friends, and was at once accepted, and I know, regarded himself as 'one of us.' I hope and believe that his short life among us was happy. He was a good friend and a very gallant gentleman."[23]

Epilogue—They Shall Not Grow Old

Lord, hold them in thy mighty hand
Above the ocean and the land
Like wings of Eagles mounting high
Along the pathways of the sky.[1]

Anonymous

Two hundred forty-four United States citizens eventually flew with the RAF Eagle Squadrons. By 1945, they were widely recognized as the "progenitors of the finest fighter wing in the U.S. Air Force."[2] But according to RAF rosters in 1940, just seven Americans belonged to "the few"—those who fought for Britain's survival during the greatest air battle in history.[3]

More than sixty years later, in July 2002, the only one of the American few to survive the war—John Kenneth Haviland—died peacefully at his home in Virginia. After flying Mosquitos and Blenheims, Haviland had returned to Spitfires in late 1944 and had been awarded the DFC as a flight lieutenant with 141 Squadron on February 16, 1945. After returning to America at war's end, he had gone to college on the GI Bill and had never left, retiring as a distinguished Professor of Aeronautics at the University of Virginia in the 1980s.[4]

In 2005 there were seventeen surviving Eagle pilots according to eighty-seven-year-old Bill Edwards, a former 133 Squadron pilot, the current President of the Eagle Squadron Association, and the only surviving Eagle who still flies. On a bright May afternoon, he banked his Cessna over Colorado Springs, where he has lived since leaving the U.S. Air Force, and as we then soared above the Rockies he reminisced about the happiest and saddest period in his seventy years of flying: his time as an Eagle pilot. He has maintained a profound affection for Britain and the RAF. Some might call it love. Whenever he gets the chance, he returns to England to look up old chums.[5]

Perhaps the most moving of his visits occurred in 1976, when he attended a reunion in London for the Eagle squadrons. Edwards and his fellow Eagles were given the red carpet treatment wherever they went and were fêted as prodigal sons who had returned to the country they had helped save. On September 15 that year, they attended a Battle of Britain memorial service at Westminster Abbey, taking their seats beside Winston Churchill's widow. They also sent Queen Elizabeth their best wishes and the following message: "We flew with pride under the flag of England in your superb Hurricanes and Spitfires. We shared in battle the defeats, the victories, and the glory of the Royal Air Force. The Eagle Squadrons were a result of the force that motivates men who believe in freedom, to join in the fight for it regardless of when and where it is threatened. Let those who would challenge our way of life be warned that this force is enduring, and will characterize the relationship of Great Britain and the United States for all time."[6]

One of Edwards's friends, 71 Squadron's Bert Stewart, recalled leaving a final gathering of the Eagles in London that year before returning to America: "As I was getting on the bus . . . the escort officer called me [over] to a little lady standing there. She was in her eighties, he told me. He said, 'Stu, here is a little lady who has walked twelve miles just to say thank you to an Eagle.' It grabbed me by the throat and still does. I said, 'Ma'am, you don't have to thank us, we thank you for holding the line.' She was so small I could have held out my arm and she could have walked under it. She said, 'No, we thank you because you came when we needed you.' I had her come on the bus and tell everyone what she had told me. She came up and made a few statements and there was not a dry eye on that bus, not one."[7]

Today, fewer and fewer of "the few" remain. As a result, perhaps, the significance of the greatest air battle in history has been downplayed. Many Americans do not realize that had it not been for "the few," the Second World War would have had a very different outcome. And to this day, even in England, the role played by foreign-born pilots tends to be overlooked. Indeed, it is generally assumed that the British fought alone during the summer of 1940. But in Boulogne's East Cemetery, on the RAF's Runnymede Memorial, and in many other corners of England, there are tragic reminders that this was not the case. A fifth of "the few" came from foreign shores. Of these 510 pilots, more than a quarter never returned home.

On July 4 of most years, in a corner of Boxgrove graveyard in Sussex, fresh flowers lie on the grave of one of these foreigners: Pilot Officer Billy Fiske, the first American to die in the Battle of Britain. The King of Speed lies between two British soldiers, a sapper in the Royal Engineers and a corporal in the East Lancashire Regiment. A small Stars and Stripes flag sometimes snaps in the wind above his final resting place. On his headstone, the following words are inscribed for all to see:

AN AMERICAN CITIZEN WHO DIED THAT ENGLAND MIGHT LIVE

The "Few"

Pilot Officer Arthur Gerald Donahue, 64 Squadron, killed September 11, 1942

Pilot Officer John Kenneth Haviland, 151 Squadron, survived the war

Pilot Officer Vernon Charles Keough, 609 Squadron, killed February 15, 1941

Pilot Officer Phillip Howard Leckrone, 616 Squadron, killed January 5, 1941

Pilot Officer William Meade Lindsley Fiske, 601 Squadron, died August 17, 1940

Pilot Officer Andrew Mamedoff, 609 Squadron, killed October 8, 1941

Pilot Officer Hugh William Reilley, 66 Squadron, killed October 17, 1940 [listed as Canadian in the 1940 RAF roster]

Pilot Officer Eugene Quimby Tobin, 609 Squadron, killed September 7, 1941

Note: According to RAF rosters in 1940, there were seven Americans who flew in the Battle of Britain. Hugh Reilley, though American, was listed as Canadian.

Battle of Britain

BRITISH AIRCRAFT

SPITFIRE
Max. speed: 353 mph
Range: 370 miles
Weapons: eight Browning machine guns

HURRICANE
Max. speed: 320–330 mph
Range: 560–620 miles
Weapons: eight Browning machine guns

DEFIANT
Max. speed: 298 mph
Range: 590 miles
Weapons: hydraulic tower with four
Browning machine guns

GERMAN FIGHTER AIRCRAFT

MESSERSCHMITT 109 E
Max. speed: 350 mph
Range: 400 miles
Weapons: two machine guns and
two 20 mm cannons

MESSERSCHMITT 110 ZERSTORER
Max. speed: 335 mph
Range: 600–745 miles
Weapons: five machine guns and
two 20 mm cannons

GERMAN BOMBER AIRCRAFT

JUNKERS 87 B STUKA
Max. speed: 230 mph
Range: 500–800 miles
Weapons: three machine guns
Bomb load: one 1,100-lb. bomb under
the fuselage or a 550-lb. bomb in the same
place plus four 110-lb. bombs

JUNKERS 88
Max. speed: 280 mph
Range: 1,426 miles
Weapons: three machine guns
Bomb load: approx. 5,000 lbs of bombs

DORNIER 17
Max. speed: 263 mph
Range: 680–1,740 miles
Weapons: six 7.9 mm machine guns,
plus two machine guns and
one 20 mm cannon
Bomb load: 1,100 to 2,200 lbs of bombs

HEINKEL 111
Max. speed: 254 mph
Range: 680–1,420 miles
Weapons: five 7.9 mm machine guns and
one 20 mm cannon
Bomb load: 2,200 to 4,400 lbs of bombs

Notes

Most of the dates, times of combat and names of those involved, as well as pilots' claims of downed or damaged aircraft, are drawn from individual combat reports, official squadron records and logbooks available from the National Archives in Britain. The author has also relied heavily on two definitive studies of the Battle of Britain, which have become bibles for all researchers: *Men of the Battle of Britain* by Kenneth Wynn (Second edition, CCB Associates: Surrey, England, 1999) and *The Battle of Britain: Then and Now* by Winston G. Ramsey (After the Battle: London, 1980).

PART ONE

Chapter One

1. Quentin Reynolds, foreword to "Eagle Squadron," courtesy of Helen Maher.
2. Norman Moss, *Nineteen Weeks* (Boston: Houghton Mifflin, 2003), p. 91.
3. Hector Bolitho, "Yanks over England," *Denver Post*, March 2, 1941.
4. Ibid.
5. "Soldier of Fortune," *New Yorker,* December 21, 1940.
6. Donald McCormick, *One Man's Wars: The Story of Charles Sweeny, Soldier of Fortune* (London: Arthur Barker, 1972), p. 173.
7. Ibid., p. 174.
8. Eugene Tobin, "Yankee Eagle over London," *Liberty* magazine, March 29, 1941.
9. Ibid.
10. Ibid.
11. Ibid.
12. Eugene Tobin, diary entry, May 10, 1940. On May 9, Tobin had written, by way of introduction to one of the most detailed and

vivid accounts of the Battle of Britain: "Memoirs of a Soldier of Fortune and a great lover."

13. Joe Iamartino, Thompson Historical Society, correspondence with author, May 10, 2004.

14. Norman Moss, *Nineteen Weeks* (Boston: Houghton Mifflin, 2003), p. 103.

15. Eugene Tobin, "Yankee Eagle over London," *Liberty* magazine, March 29, 1941.

16. Eugene Tobin, private correspondence to father, Quimby Tobin, May 15, 1940.

17. Helen Maher, interview with author.

18. Biographical information on Vernon Keough, Air Ministry archives, provided courtesy of Mark Crame.

19. Eugene Tobin, "Yankee Eagle over London," *Liberty* magazine, March 29, 1941.

20. Byron Kennerly, *The Eagles Roar* (New York: Harper and Brothers, 1942), p. 230.

21. Hector Bolitho, "Yanks over England," *Denver Post*, March 2, 1941.

22. Eugene Tobin, "Yankee Eagle over London," *Liberty* magazine, March 29, 1941.

23. Norman Moss, *Nineteen Weeks* (Boston: Houghton Mifflin, 2003), p. 103.

24. Ibid., p.104.

25. Eugene Tobin, diary entry, May 14, 1940.

26. Eugene Tobin, "Yankee Eagle over London," *Liberty* magazine, March 29, 1941.

27. Ibid.

28. Peter Townsend, *Duel of Eagles* (London: Orion Publishing, 2000), p. 217.

29. Winston Churchill, *The Second World War*, volume 2 (London: Cassell, 1949), p. 38.

30. Norman Moss, *Nineteen Weeks* (Boston: Houghton Mifflin, 2003), p. 105.

31. Ibid., p. 106.

32. Winston Churchill, *The Second World War*, volume 2 (London: Cassell, 1949), p. 40.

33. It was common knowledge that hundreds of French fighters stood idle in airfields, their ammunition and replacement parts held in centralized depots.

34. Sir Hugh Dowding, Cabinet War Papers (40) 159, Public Records Office.

35. German Luftwaffe unit designations are abbreviated as follows: JG—*Jagdgeschwader* (fighter wing); KG—*Kampfgeschwader* (bomber wing); StG—*Stukageschwader* (dive-bomber wing); and ZG—*Zerstoer-ergeschwader* (heavy fighter wing). A *Geschwader* (wing) consisted of slightly more than 100 planes. During the Battle of Britain, each *Geschwader* had three *Gruppen* (groups), denoted by the Roman numerals I, II, and III. A *Gruppe* consisted of three or four *Staffeln* (squadrons), each consisting of twelve to sixteen planes.

36. If one man's incompetence ever helped to save a nation and doom another, it was Beppo Schmid's. Over the next several weeks he would provide wildly inaccurate information on the RAF, severely hampering Göring's mission to bring Britain to its knees.

37. Peter Townsend, *Duel of Eagles* (London: Orion Publishing, 2000), p. 143.

38. Ibid., p. 225.

39. Eugene Tobin, diary entry, May 20, 1940.

40. A fortnight after Tobin's arrival, more than three thousand British troops and civilians would drown in the port, victims of a Luftwaffe attack on the liner *Lancastria*. Churchill banned all mention of Britain's worst maritime loss, fearing it would depress public morale.

Chapter Two

1. Jochen Prien, *Jagdgeschwader 53* (Atglen, Pennsylvania: Schiffer Military History, 1997), p. 118.

2. John Weal, *Bf 109D/E Aces, 1939–41* (Oxford: Osprey Aerospace, 1996), p. 51. The account of Mölders being shot down is based on Mölders's recollections in *Mölders und Seine Manner*, first published in 1941.

3. Jochen Prien, *Jagdgeschwader 53* (Atglen, Pennsylvania: Schiffer Military History, 1997), p. 118.

4. Ibid., p. 119.

5. Ibid., p. 120.

Chapter Three

1. Larry Forrester, *Fly for Your Life* (London: Panther Books, 1969), p. 51.

2. Eugene Tobin, diary entry, May 31, 1940.

3. CAB65/13, minute 14, National Archives (UK).

4. Hugh Dalton, *The Fateful Years: Memoirs 1931–45* (London: Frederick Muller, 1953), p. 335.

5. Martin Gilbert, *Churchill: A Life* (New York: Henry Holt and Company, 1991), p. 651.

6. Norman Moss, *Nineteen Weeks* (Boston: Houghton Mifflin, 2003), p. 136.

7. Peter Townsend, *Duel of Eagles* (London: Orion Publishing, 2000), p. 229. The Catholic Temme, one of ten children, had joined the Luftwaffe as it was being revitalized in the late thirties by Göring. Banned under dictates of the 1919 Versailles Treaty, the German air force had existed throughout the twenties as a shadow force of just a few hundred pilots. A keen glider pilot, Temme had rejoiced at the news that Hitler had declared Wehrfreiheit [military freedom] on March 13, 1935, brazenly ignoring the Versailles Treaty and throwing down the gauntlet to Germany's conquerors. By 1938, Temme belonged to arguably the most prestigious Luftwaffe squadron, named after Baron Manfred von Richthofen. The famous Red Baron had shot down eighty Allied planes, killing more than a hundred airmen, before he was shot down and killed by a single bullet through the heart on April 21, 1918, the victim of Captain Roy Brown, who was flying a British Sopwith. So revered was the Baron, so different was the sense of fair play back then, that the Baron went to his grave in a French cemetery borne on the shoulders of six saddened RAF officers.

8. Philip Kaplan and Richard Collier, *The Few, Summer 1940, The Battle of Britain* (London: Cassell and Co., 1990), p. 39.

9. Ibid., p. 41.

10. Flight Lieutenant Frank J. Howell, private correspondence, June 6, 1940.

11. Martin Gilbert, *Churchill: A Life* (New York: Henry Holt, 1991), p. 654.

12. Ibid.

13. Cleaver had skied for Britain and joined 601 in 1937 as a weekend flyer. On May 27, he had destroyed two Bf-110s over Dunkirk.

14. Tom Moulson, *The Flying Sword: The Story of 601 Squadron* (London: MacDonald, 1964), p. 75.

15. Peter Townsend, *Duel of Eagles* (London: Orion Publishing, 2000), p. 225.

16. Norman Moss, *Nineteen Weeks* (Boston: Houghton Mifflin, 2003), p. 152.

17. Jon Meacham, *Franklin and Winston* (New York: Random House, 2003), p. 51.

18. *New York Times*, June 4, 1940.

19. Martin Gilbert, *Churchill: A Life* (New York: Henry Holt and Company, 1991), p. 656.

20. Eugene Tobin, "Yankee Eagle over London," *Liberty* magazine, March 29, 1941.

21. Ibid.

22. Ibid.

23. Eugene Tobin, diary entry, June 4, 1940.

24. Eugene Tobin, "Yankee Eagle over London," *Liberty* magazine, March 29, 1943.

25. Eugene Tobin, diary entry, June 6, 1940.

26. Ibid. June 8, 1940.

27. Eugene Tobin, "Yankee Eagle over London," *Liberty* magazine, March 29, 1943.

28. For the young émigré, whose earliest memories were of bloody revolution, senseless violence, and lonely refuge in Siberia and then Harbin, China, the Russian Bear offered something deeply soothing—a home away from home. It was an exotic, laughter-filled place for Andy, who loved the dancing waitresses in peasant costumes, the joyous gypsy music, the long afternoon games of bridge, and his mother's exceptional cooking.

29. Eugene Tobin, "Yankee Eagle over London," *Liberty* magazine, March 29, 1941.

30. "Soldier of Fortune," *New Yorker,* December 21, 1940.

31. James A. Goodson and Norman Franks, *Over-paid, Over-sexed and Over Here* (Kent: Wingham Press, 1991), p. 17.

32. Donald McCormick, *One Man's Wars: The Story of Charles Sweeny, Soldier of Fortune* (London: Arthur Baker Limited, 1972), p. 180.

33. Eugene Tobin, "Yankee Eagle over London," *Liberty* magazine, March 29, 1941.

34. Ibid.

35. Eugene Tobin, diary entry, June 11, 1940.

36. Ibid.

37. Eugene Tobin, "Yankee Eagle over London," *Liberty* magazine, March 29, 1941.

38. Harry Watts, untitled press clipping, courtesy of Mark Crame.

39. Eugene Tobin, "Yankee Eagle over London," *Liberty* magazine, March 29, 1941.

40. Ibid.

41. Ibid.

42. Ibid.

43. Martin Gilbert, *Churchill: A Life* (New York: Henry Holt and Company, 1991), p. 659.

44. Ibid., p. 660.

45. Ibid.

46. The French surrendered before this promise could be kept. "Those German pilots all became available for the Battle of Britain," Churchill recalled, "and we had to shoot them down a second time."

47. Martin Gilbert, *Churchill: A Life* (New York: Henry Holt and Company, 1991), p. 661.

48. Ibid.

49. Eugene Tobin, "Yankee Eagle over London," *Liberty* magazine, March 29, 1941.

50. Ibid.

51. Ibid.

52. Ibid.

53. Harry Watts, untitled press clipping, courtesy of Mark Crame.

54. Martin Gilbert, *Churchill: A Life* (New York: Henry Holt and Company, 1991), p. 663.

55. Tom Moulson, *The Flying Sword: The Story of 601 Squadron* (London: MacDonald, 1964), p. 79.

56. Eugene Tobin, "Yankee Eagle over London," *Liberty* magazine, March 29, 1941.

57. Ibid.

58. Eugene Tobin, diary entry, June 19, 1940.

59. Ibid. June 20, 1940.

60. Harry Watts, untitled press clipping, courtesy of Mark Crame.

PART TWO

1. Eugene Tobin, "Yankee Eagle over London," *Liberty* magazine, March 29, 1941.

Chapter Four

1. *Parade* magazine, August 12, 1990.

2. Eugene Tobin, "Yankee Eagle over London," *Liberty* magazine, March 29, 1941.

3. Eugene Tobin, "Yankee Eagle over London," *Liberty* magazine, April 5, 1941.

4. Harry Watts, untitled clipping, courtesy of Mark Crame.

5. Helen Maher, interview with author.

6. Peter Fleming, *Operation Sea Lion* (New York: Simon and Schuster, 1957), pp. 90–91.

7. Eugene Tobin, "Yankee Eagle over London," *Liberty* magazine, April 5, 1941.

8. Stephen Bungay, *The Most Dangerous Enemy* (London: Aurum Press, 2000), p. 107. No great battle in history, before or since, has been decided by so few participants. At Waterloo, the Duke of Wellington had 67,000 men under his command.

9. Eugene Tobin, "Yankee Eagle over London," *Liberty* magazine, April 5, 1941.

10. Ibid.

11. Harry Watts, unpublished memoir, courtesy of Mark Crame.

12. Helen Maher, interview with author. The figure of 540 is given on Tobin's RAF record, AM Form 1406, Number 81622, Air Force Academy Eagle archives, Colorado Springs. Mamedoff had 720 hours of solo flying.

13. *New York Herald Tribune*, March 2, 1941.

14. The Americans' rapid acceptance into the RAF had been facilitated by fifty-nine-year-old Colonel Sweeny, who had lobbied the RAF and other senior officials on behalf of his recruits. Sweeny had done so after receiving a telegram from a contact in London, possibly his nephew, informing him—much to his relief—that several of his recruits had managed to escape France and reach England. Sweeny had first approached Embassy officials but was treated pretty much the same as his recruits. "[They] were embarrassed by his enthusiasm," recalled biographer Donald McCormick, "and when he persisted in urging them to 'cut the cant about neutrality,' they practically ordered him to return home and threatened to withdraw his passport." So Sweeny washed his hands of Kennedy and his bureaucrats and turned instead to his family and friends in England, who shared his determination to help Britain. When Sweeny then broached the concept of forming an all-American Eagle Squadron within the RAF, many prominent Americans in London, including the heiress Barbara Hutton, were happy to hand over large sums to fund the project. Others began to lobby MPs such as Robinson, powerful air ministry officials, and others close to Winston Churchill. Within weeks, Sweeny's idea found favor at 10 Downing Street and by late September it became a reality. Source of quoted material: Donald McCormick, *One Man's Wars: The Story of Charles Sweeny, Soldier of Fortune* (London: Arthur Barker, 1972), p. 181.

15. Philip D. Caine, *American Pilots in the RAF* (Dulles, Virginia: Brassey's, 1998), p. 42.

   Several American pilots who swore loyalty to Britain before joining the Eagle Squadrons did not regain their citizenship until the 1970s, after the Supreme Court ruled that they could not be stripped of their nationality because they had joined the military service of a foreign power.

16. Peter Townsend, *Duel of Eagles* (London: Orion Publishing, 2000), p. 139.

17. Eugene Tobin, "Yankee Eagle over London," *Liberty* magazine, April 5, 1941.

18. Philip Caine, *American Pilots in the RAF* (Dulles, Virginia: Brassey's, 1998), p. 70.

19. Harry Watts, untitled press clipping, courtesy of Mark Crame.

20. Eugene Tobin, "Yankee Eagle over London," *Liberty* magazine, April 5, 1941.

21. According to Fiske authority and American researcher Alex Blanton: "Both the German sleds crashed in spectacular fashion in practice just before the games started (they flew off the track and into the woods), including the sled piloted by Billy's friend from winter sports days in St. Moritz and future Luftwaffe pilot, Captain Werner Zahn, whose sled had won the 1931 world championship. Zahn suffered a broken arm and could not compete . . . Billy loaned the German teams parts to repair their sleds and helped recruit German-speaking Americans to fill in for the four German team members who were in hospital. The Zahn sled, piloted by the German 2-man sled driver and winner of the 1931 world championship in the 2-man bobsled, Hanns Kilian, went on to win the bronze medal. [Kilian would also become a Luftwaffe pilot.]" Source: Alex Blanton, letter to author.

22. Charles Higham and Roy Moseley, *Cary Grant: The Lonely Heart* (New York: Harcourt Brace, 1989). Grant would marry and later divorce Cherrill.

23. Tony Holmes, "The Saga of Billy Fiske," *Air Classics*, December, 2003. Rather than ride to further Olympic glory, Fiske tried a new sport that winter—an extremely dangerous relative of bobsledding called skeleton, in which riders mount small sleds and slide down ice-runs at breakneck speeds. The adrenaline-soaked sport was all the rage among Europe's young aristocrats. Only members of the St. Moritz Tobogganing Club, described as "a kind of combination of an International Who's Who, a Social Register, and the Lost Battalion," could officially compete. By the late thirties, Jack and Joe Kennedy—the two eldest sons of Joseph Kennedy, the American ambassador to London—would also be skeleton enthusiasts as well as veterans of the Cresta Run. During his many months spent in St. Moritz, Fiske undoubtedly would have become acquainted with the future American president and his brother.

24. Michael Seth-Smith, *The Cresta Run: History of the St. Moritz Tobogganing Club* (London: Foulsham, 1976), p. 164.

   Fiske was a perennial favorite with the ladies in St. Moritz, where he often partied the nights away, one morning even going down the Cresta still wearing his tuxedo. A good friend, Andrea Badrutt, whose father owned the Palace Hotel, recalled Fiske asking her: "Why can't you put some cupboards in the bedroom passages?"

"What for?" she asked.

"For me to put my clothes in."

"But there are plenty of cupboards in your very nice bedroom."

"I guess that's right, but so far I have not spent a single night there and it's a damn waste of money."

Source: Ibid.

25. Derek Tangye, editor, *Went the Day Well* (London: George G. Harrap and Co. Ltd., 1942), p. 122.

26. Tony Holmes, "The Saga of Billy Fiske," *Air Classics,* December 2003.

27. Billy Fiske, diary entry, undated, courtesy of Pat Zabalaga.

28. Ibid.

29. Fiske expanded: "I believe I can lay claim to being the first US citizen to join the RAF in England after the outbreak of war. I don't say this with any particular pride, except perhaps in so far as my conscience is clear, but only because it probably has some bearing on the course of my career. My reasons for joining the fray are my own." Source: Billy Fiske, diary entry, October 29, 1939, courtesy Pat Zabalaga.

30. One of twelve New Zealanders on the course, Millar had been sponsored by the Royal New Zealand Air Force to join the RAF on a four-year short service commission. "There was no sense of we're here to save the country or we're here because we love the British and we hate the Germans," recalled Millar. "I can honestly say that most of us had no feelings like that at all. We went over for the excitement and the adventure and the chance of skiing holidays in Austria. It was about seeing the other side of the world." Source: Hugh Millar, interview with author.

31. Tony Holmes, "The Saga of Billy Fiske," *Air Classics,* December 2003.

32. Ibid.

33. Hugh Millar, interview with author.

34. James A. Goodson and Norman Franks, *Over-Paid, Over-Sexed and Over Here* (Kent: Wingham Press, 1991), pp. 7–8.

35. *Winona Republican-Herald*, March 15, 1941.

36. Ibid.

37. Robert Donahue, summary of Flight Lieutenant Arthur Gerald Donahue's career. Donahue family files.

38. Ibid.

39. Ibid.

40. Ibid., pp. 9–10.

41. Archibald Henry Macdonald Sinclair was Churchill's longest lasting political ally from a different party. The fourth baronet and first Viscount Thurso of Ulster was born in London on October 22, 1890. Educated at Eton, he attended the elite military academy, Sandhurst, and served on the Western Front throughout the First World War. Sinclair's relationship with Churchill began in January 1916 when he became the future Prime Minister's second-in-command with the 6th Royal Scots Fusiliers. He was Churchill's personal military secretary at the War Office from 1919–21, and was then his private secretary at the Colonial Office until 1922. Sinclair would remain Secretary of State for Air until his electoral defeat in 1945.

42. Derek Tangye, editor, *Went the Day Well* (London: George G. Harrap and Co. Ltd., 1942), p. 124.

43. Tom Moulson, *The Flying Sword: The Story of 601 Squadron* (London: MacDonald, 1964), p. 83.

44. Jack Riddle, interview with author.

45. *Los Angeles Times*, March 29, 1935.

46. Roger Bushell, a former member of the Cambridge University ski team, gifted actor, athlete, and expert defense lawyer, had left 601 in October 1939 to become squadron leader of 92 Squadron. On May 23, 1940, while leading a patrol to Dunkirk, Bushell was shot down and taken prisoner. For almost four years he would be the brains behind repeated escape attempts. He was murdered with fifty other escapees in March 1944 on the orders of Adolf Hitler. Bushell had been the principal organizer of the mass escape immortalized by the movie *The Great Escape*.

47. Tom Moulson, *The Flying Sword: The Story of 601 Squadron* (London: MacDonald, 1964), p. 83.

48. Unlike the Luftwaffe, the RAF had an appalling search and rescue

service. Once a pilot was downed in the Channel, he was pretty much done for. Even in high summer, the waters were so cold that most pilots would die of hypothermia after two hours. Only the very lucky were saved by a fishing vessel or lifeboat. Some pilots drowned within a mile of land. The Luftwaffe, by contrast, went to extraordinary lengths to fish its downed aces out of the "shit," even providing floating rescue-stations, buoyed throughout the Channel.

49. Billy Fiske, flight logbook, August 8, 1940.

50. Derek Tangye, editor, *Went the Day Well* (London: George G. Harrap and Co. Ltd., 1942), p. 125.

51. Only five percent of pilots mastered the art of aerial combat and became aces.

52. Norman Gelb, *Scramble, A Narrative History of the Battle of Britain* (London: Michael Joseph, 1986), p. 172.

53. Kenneth Bailey, interview with author.

54. Unlike their ground crew, 601 did not have to cycle to the pub. They drove. Indeed, high tides were far more likely to cramp their style than the strict fuel rationing that caused most Britons to use their cars only when absolutely necessary. The previous autumn, Fiske's skiing friend, Willie Rhodes-Moorehouse, had been appointed "petrol officer" and dispatched to secure enough fuel to keep the Million-aires' Bentleys and Morgans running. Rhodes-Moorehouse returned the following day. "Well," he was asked, "how much have you got?"

"Almost enough to last the war."

"What have you done?"

"I've bought a garage."

Rhodes-Moorehouse had driven to a nearby filling station, called over the owner, and simply pulled out his checkbook. Unfortunately, it was soon discovered that the station's fuel tanks were far from full. The Millionaires held a crisis meeting. Various means of stockpiling fuel were discussed.

"I'm not sure," one of the pilots finally said, "but I think I'm a director of Shell."

"What do you mean, you think you are? Telephone your secre-tary and find out." A few days later, just before rationing began, Willie Rhodes-Moorehouse's filling station was full. Source: Tom Moulson,

The Flying Sword: The Story of 601 Squadron (London: MacDonald, 1964), p. 60.

55. Jack Riddle, interview with author. "Billy was charming and very sociable," added Riddle. "He wanted to know exactly what everybody else around him was feeling. I remember my wife also saying one evening in the Ship: 'Watch how Billy behaves.' Somebody would come into the pub looking a little bit lost, particularly the new replacement pilots. He would find out who they were looking for or waiting for and have a drink with them while they were waiting." Fiske had none of the snobbery of some of his 601 peers. On the base, he was also popular with his ground crew, treating them as colleagues and not as servants as some did. He was genuinely interested in the men who kept his plane flying, who packed his parachute, and who armed his guns, and often worked around the clock to keep his Hurricane in the air. "His manners were rather old fashioned," recalled Jack Riddle. "He was absolutely charming and completely natural. There was nothing forced or fake about him. That's what endeared him to the whole squadron—pilots and ground crew—in the most extraordinary way."

56. The average life span for a pilot in the Battle of Britain was just 87 hours in the air.

57. Hugh "Stuffy" Dowding, head of Fighter Command, had persuaded the Air Ministry to fit the Hurricane and the Spitfire with bulletproof Perspex hoods, and the pilots' backs were protected by armor-plating, though at closer than 200 yards the enemy's fire could still easily penetrate. Dowding had told an Air Ministry conference: "If Chicago gangsters can have bulletproof glass in their cars I can't see any reason why my pilots cannot have the same." Source: Len Deighton, *Fighter* (New Jersey: Castle Books, 2000), p. 42.

58. Lothian to Sir Archibald Sinclair, July 18, 1940. National Archives, FO371/24230.

59. Norman Moss, *Nineteen Weeks* (Boston: Houghton Mifflin, 2003), p. 143.

Chapter Five

1. "Battle of Britain," *Daily Telegraph* Editorial Supplement, Part 1, June 16, 1990, p. 20.

2. Ernst Udet (1896–1941) was a legendary First World War ace who notched up 62 kills on the Western Front. He was finally forced to retire from combat in September 1918 because of injuries. At the time, he was second only to Manfred von Richtofen—the Red Baron. His exploits were truly extraordinary: he was one of the first pilots to use a parachute and to destroy a tank from the air. After the war, he worked as a stunt pilot in several films. In the thirties, he befriended Herman Göring and played a key role in resuscitating the Luftwaffe. Appointed Director General of Equipment and then Head of the Office of Air Armament in February 1939, he made a key strategic mistake in emphasizing the development of dive-bombers and fighters, thereby leaving the Luftwaffe without effective heavy bombers such as the British Lancaster and American Flying Fortress. Udet was unfairly blamed for the Luftwaffe's failures during the Battle of Britain. Increasingly critical of the Nazis, Udet committed suicide in 1941.

3. John Weal, *Bf109D/E Aces, 1939–41* (Oxford: Osprey Aerospace, 1996), p. 67.

4. Larry Forrester, *Fly for Your Life* (Bristol: Cerberus Publishing, 2005), p. 74.

5. Malan had famously compiled a list of the basic principles of fighter combat: "Fire short bursts of 1–2 seconds and only when your sights are definitely ON. Whilst shooting think of nothing else; brace the whole of the body, have both hands on the stick; concentrate on your ring sight. Always keep a sharp lookout. Keep your finger out. Height always gives *you* the advantage. Always turn and face the attack. Make your decisions promptly. It is better to act quickly even though your tactics are not the best. Never fly straight and level for more than 30 seconds in the combat area. When diving to attack always have a proportion of your formation above to act as top guard. Initiative, aggression, air discipline and team work are words that mean something in Air Fighting. Go in quickly, punch hard and get out!" Source: Adolphus G. "Sailor" Malan, "Ten of My Rules for Air Fighting," quoted, *The Few: Summer 1940, The Battle of Britain*, Philip Kaplan and Richard Collier (London: Cassell and Co., 2000), p. 116.

6. Eric Mombeek, *Jagdwaffe, Battle of Britain: Phase One, July–August 1940* (East Sussex: Classic Publications, 2001), p. 40.

7. Ibid.

8. Ibid.

9. Ibid.

10. Accounts of what happened that day vary. For a detailed discussion, see Stephen Bungay, *The Most Dangerous Enemy* (London: Aurum Press, 2001), p. 159. This account is based on the recollections of Mölders and his wingman as well as Len Deighton's report in his book *Fighter* (New Jersey: Castle Books, 2000), p. 140. Many sources credit Malan with wounding Mölders. Others make a strong case for Flight Lieutenant J. T. Webster of 41 Squadron, which also tangled with JG 51 that day.

11. Eric Mombeek, *Jagdwaffe, Battle of Britain: Phase One, July–August 1940* (East Sussex: Classic Publications, 2001), p. 15.

12. Ibid., p. 40.

13. Armand van Ishoven, *The Luftwaffe in the Battle of Britain* (London: Ian Allan, 1998), p. 26.

14. "After a very few days," explained Donahue's brother Robert, "Art saw the desperate need for pilots and volunteered for the RAF provided he would be assigned to a front-line squadron to meet the expected invasion. He wrote that he thought it better to fight Germany over Britain than over the US which would be necessary if Britain fell." Source: Biographical sketch of Art Donahue by Robert Donahue, Donahue family files.

15. All the American pilots at Hawarden that July were surprised when they first fired the Spitfire's guns. "I expected a hell of a noise, and expected the plane to shake," recalled Andy Mamedoff. "But it wasn't like that; you see tracers, but you hear practically nothing." Source: Hector Bolitho, "Yanks over England," *Denver Post*, March 2, 1941.

16. Arthur Gerald Donahue, *Tally-ho! Yankee in a Spitfire* (New York: Macmillan, 1943), p. 16.

17. Pilot Officer H. G. Niven, 601 and 602 Squadrons. Source: http://www.battleofbritain.net/0011.html.

18. Arthur Gerald Donahue, *Tally-ho! Yankee in a Spitfire* (New York: Macmillan, 1943), p. 16.

19. Ibid., p. 18. In a letter to his parents, Donahue explained that on his first flight in a Spitfire, he had been struck by the fact that the plane had eight machine guns. "The one I flew had a little guard over the firing trigger. The guard had the words 'Guns Loaded' written on it! These ships are never allowed to fly without the guns being loaded, in case of sudden attack. I didn't 'open up' the engine, but I did let the ship drop in a mild dive until the indicator read slightly more than 310 miles per hour! It is certainly a beautiful flying ship." Art Donahue, private correspondence to parents, July 24, 1940.

20. Eugene Tobin, "Yankee Eagle over London," *Liberty* magazine, April 5, 1941.

21. Ibid.

22. Ibid. "I almost died," Tobin later confessed to journalist Quentin Reynolds. "I didn't know how to handle such speed. I remembered what one of the boys had said about the Spitfire. He told me: 'As soon as you get off pull that hood over you and from then don't let the airplane get in front of you.' You never pull your hood over you until you take off. That business about not letting the airplane get in front of you means you should keep remembering you are going like a bat out of hell and don't kick the airplane all over the sky. When you're going that fast you can't kick your airplane around much. So I took off with a prayer and by golly everything was all right. Once we were up there it was easy. All you gotta do is remember that you're going fast. Try to bank when you're going like that and you'll black yourself right out. I landed it all right. They gave me a few weeks of training, and there I was right over the Channel having a scramble." Source: Quentin Reynolds, *A London Diary* (New York: Random House, 1962), p. 46.

23. *Denver Post*, March 2, 1941.

24. Eugene Tobin, "Yankee Eagle over London," *Liberty* magazine, April 5, 1941.

25. Perhaps the greatest contribution from foreigners in the Battle of Britain was made by the Poles. 303 Squadron, comprised of Poles, was the most successful unit in Fighter Command. The Poles' hatred for the Germans was matched only by their impatience to meet the

Hun in combat. By the end of the summer, the Poles had distinguished themselves as uncannily lethal pilots, having shot down more German planes than any other RAF squadron. Other pilots whose countries had been occupied by the Nazis also performed superbly, no doubt driven by all-consuming vengeance. Of the thirteen Frenchmen who fought with the RAF after their country had capitulated, for example, several lost their lives and those who survived went on to become the most outstanding French pilots of the war.

26. One additional American, Hugh Reilley, was listed as Canadian but later discovered to have been born in America.

27. Arthur Gerald Donahue, *Tally-ho! Yankee in a Spitfire* (New York: Macmillan, 1943), p. 19.

28. Ibid., pp. 21–22.

29. Eugene Tobin, "Yankee Eagle over London," *Liberty* magazine, April 5, 1941.

30. Arthur Donahue, RAF personnel file, Air Force Academy archives, Colorado Springs.

31. Raymond Lee, diary entry, July 31, 1940.

32. Norman Moss, *Nineteen Weeks* (New York: Houghton Mifflin, 2003), p. 261.

Chapter Six

1. Stephen Bungay, *The Most Dangerous Enemy* (London: Aurum Press, 2000), p. 202.

2. Arthur Gerald Donahue, *Tally-ho! Yankee in a Spitfire*, (New York: Macmillan, 1943), p. 53.

3. Kenneth G. Wynn, *Men of the Battle of Britain*, CCB Associates, Surrey, England, 1999, p. 321.

4. In the case of Pilot Officer Peter Brown, it took four sorties before he tuned in. "The first mission I went on seemed uneventful," he recalled. "When we got back and had a debriefing, I learned that some of the pilots had seen 109s in the distance and some others had seen something else. I had seen absolutely nothing. The next time up, I happened to see a little bit of something. But it took me about four trips to get tuned in, to see what was going on. A lot of people were hit in their first flights . . . If you look out the small

window of a passenger aircraft today, you see there's a lot of space out there to look for an airplane. If you open up the whole area above and below you, there's an enormous amount of space for an aircraft to be in." Source: Norman Gelb, *Scramble, A Narrative History of the Battle of Britain* (New York: Harcourt Brace, Jovanovich, 1985), p. 184.

5. Eugene Tobin, "Yankee Eagle over London," *Liberty* magazine, March 29, 1941.

6. Both were superb pilots and would survive the war. Nowierski had flown since 1930 with the Polish air force. He would return to Poland after the war. Osti would settle in Britain and change his name to Raymond.

7. David Crook, *Spitfire Pilot* (London: Faber and Faber, 1942), p. 54.

8. Ibid., pp. 57–59.

9. Flight Lieutenant Dudley Persse-Joynt, the son of a wealthy Yorkshire industrialist, disappeared along with John Gilbert, nicknamed the "Pink Boozer," on May 31. Desmond Ayre, who had worked in a coal mine as an engineer, crashed and was killed on June 1, the same day that his good friend Joe Dawson was shot down and also killed.

10. Patrick Bishop, *Fighter Boys* (New York: Viking, 2003), p. 223.

11. Harry Watts, untitled press clipping, courtesy of Mark Crame.

12. Darley was detested by some of the old-timers in the squadron at first but quickly won over his men through his tactics in the air. "The only way to overcome German superiority in numbers was to have superiority in tactics," he recalled. "Our tactics were awful to start with. The basic prescribed formation was a V shape of three aircraft. They had taught us that you fly astern of the bombers and open fire—bang, bang, bang. The curious omission was that they told you nothing about the enemy fighters who might be on your tail. That is where a lot of early losses occurred. You went in at the bombers, looking forward, nobody looking behind, and you were picked off. I adopted a more flexible formation. I made all our aircraft fly in line astern in formations of three, each of us protecting the other's tail . . . We had too many of our people killed in the beginning, with nothing to show for it. We had to kill a sight more

Germans than we had men shot down ourselves if we were going to get anything done. The tactics had to be changed. When they did change, our kill-loss ratio went up and up and up." Source: Norman Gelb, *Scramble, A Narrative History of the Battle of Britain* (New York: Harcourt Brace Jovanovich, 1985), p. 108.

13. Quentin Reynolds, "A Spitfire and a Boy," *Collier's*, September 21, 1940.

14. Ibid.

15. Arthur Gerald Donahue, *Tally-ho! Yankee in a Spitfire* (New York: Macmillan, 1943), p. 35.

16. Art Donahue, private correspondence to parents, August 24, 1940.

17. JG 54's I Group was led by Major Martin Mettig, and this group of planes was commanded by Captain Hubertus von Bonin. It flew from the French base of Guines.

18. Arthur Gerald Donahue, *Tally-ho! Yankee in a Spitfire* (New York: Macmillan, 1943), p. 40.

19. G-stirrups, which a pilot used to minimize G-force, were footrests placed higher than the foot controls.

20. Arthur Gerald Donahue, *Tally-ho! Yankee in a Spitfire* (New York: Macmillan, 1943), p. 43.

21. Quentin Reynolds, "A Spitfire and a Boy," *Collier's*, September 21, 1940.

22. Arthur Gerald Donahue, *Tally-ho! Yankee in a Spitfire* (New York: Macmillan, 1943), p. 47.

Chapter Seven

1. Norman Gelb, *Scramble, A Narrative History of the Battle of Britain* (London: Michael Joseph, 1986), p. 196.

2. Arthur Gerald Donahue, *Tally-ho! Yankee in a Spitfire* (New York: Macmillan, 1943), p. 54. The scene reminded Donahue of a sequence in a popular Hollywood movie, the 1938 classic *Dawn Patrol*, starring Errol Flynn and the urbane British actor David Niven, a frequent visitor to Tangmere that summer of 1940.

3. There was considerable difference between senior German generals regarding how long it would take to defeat Britain. After a conference in the Hague on August 6, during which he ordered

preparations for Eagle Day to be completed, Göring spoke with his Chief of Air Staff, Hans Jeschonnek, a forty-two-year-old, ardent, handsome, and loathsome Nazi who would soon urge the targeting of civilian areas to maximize the effect of terror bombing. Even Hitler blanched at such a blatantly murderous strategy. Jeschonnek was the archetypal Nazi sociopath, so arrogant that he was widely reviled by both his seniors and juniors and yet remained secure in his position so long as he remained Göring's obsequious pet. On August 6, 1940, he was certain that within six weeks the planned invasion would have succeeded and the British would be under Hitler's heel. Göring was not so sure. He had fought against the British in World War I and knew how tenacious they could be in combat. They were always at their best when attacked. "You must understand," Göring advised, "[that] a German will fight on even if Berlin was totally destroyed, and an Englishman is not to be any easier than a German. No . . . he will fight on, even if London is destroyed. The British [are] not like the French who, when we marched into Paris and occupied their capital, simply gave up the struggle to fight for their country. An Englishman is like a wounded bull, he is most dangerous when he is injured." Source: Battle of Britain Historical Society website, Diary of Battle of Britain, August 1–10, 1940, http://www.battleofbritain.net/0023.html.

4. Eric Mombeek, *Jagdwaffe, Battle of Britain: Phase One, July–August 1940* (East Sussex: Classic Publications, 2001), p. 16.

5. Philip Kaplan and Richard Collier, *The Few: Summer 1940, The Battle of Britain* (London: Seven Dials, 2000), p. 48.

6. Ibid.

7. According to Adolf Galland, the famous Luftwaffe ace: "From the very beginning the English had an extraordinary advantage which we could never overcome throughout the entire war: radar and fighter control. For us and our command this was a surprise and a very bitter one . . . The British fighter was guided all the way from take-off to his correct position for attack on the German formations." Source: Adolf Galland, *The First and the Last* (New York: Ballantine Books, 1953), p. 20.

8. Ibid., p. 21.

9. Arthur Gerald Donahue, *Tally-ho! Yankee in a Spitfire* (New York: Macmillan, 1943), p. 54.

10. Ibid., p. 55.

11. Pilots dealt with fear in their own way. "Some people were very quiet," recalled Richard Jones. "If anybody told you they didn't have fear you just didn't believe them because they were bloody liars. The time you didn't feel fear was when it was shit or bust—the adrenaline takes over. People didn't talk a lot about combat to one another afterwards." Source: Richard Jones, interview with author.

12. Arthur Gerald Donahue, *Tally-ho! Yankee in a Spitfire* (New York: Macmillan, 1943), p. 54.

13. Adolf Galland, *The First and the Last* (New York: Ballantine Books, 1953), p. 14.

    Galland was undoubtedly the most colorful and charismatic German fighter pilot in the Battle of Britain. He would survive the war and then establish Juan Perón's Air Force in the 1950s before prospering with his own aviation consulting company. Several of his former enemies with whom he had tangled would become good friends, notably 54 Squadron's Al Deere. Galland would end the war with 104 victories, his last coming at the controls of the revolutionary Me-262 jet on April 26, 1945. Holder of the Knight's Cross with Oak Leaves, Swords, and Diamonds, he died aged eighty-three in 1996.

14. Patrick Bishop, *Fighter Boys* (New York: Viking, 2003), p. 257.

15. Mike Spick, Luftwaffe *Fighter Aces* (London: Greenhill Books, 1996), p. 73.

16. Eric Mombeek, *Jagdwaffe, Battle of Britain: Phase Two, August–September 1940* (East Sussex: Classic Publications Ltd., 2001), p. 161.

17. Galland believed that "only the spirit of attack borne in a brave heart will bring success." Source: Adolf Galland, *The First and the Last* (New York: Ballantine Books, 1953), p. 14.

18. Arthur Gerald Donahue, *Tally-ho! Yankee in a Spitfire* (New York: Macmillan, 1943), p. 54.

19. Pilot Officer Richard Leoline Jones, interview with author.

20. Arthur Gerald Donahue, *Tally-ho! Yankee in a Spitfire* (New York: Macmillan, 1943), p. 58.

21. Ibid.

22. The Spitfire and its pilot survived but only after gravity-defying aerobatics to throw off Grzymalla.

23. Arthur Gerald Donahue, *Tally-ho! Yankee in a Spitfire* (New York: Macmillan, 1943), p. 22.

24. Ibid., p. 58.

25. David Baker, *Adolf Galland* (London: Windrow and Greene, 1996), p. 102.

26. MacDonell would eventually have nine confirmed kills before being shot down by Werner Mölders in March 1941 and ending the war in a POW camp. Mann would also become an ace with five confirmed kills. Both were truly remarkable characters. In 1989, after a long career as a commercial airline pilot, Mann was taken hostage in Beirut and survived more than two years in captivity. He died in November 1995.

27. Philip Kaplan and Richard Collier, *The Few: Summer 1940, The Battle of Britain* (London: Seven Dials, 2000), p. 184.

28. Battle of Britain Historical Society website. Diary for August 1–8, 1940. http://www.battleofbritain.net/0023.html.

29. Kenneth Wynn, *Men of the Battle of Britain* (South Croydon: CCB Associates, 1999), p. 277.

30. Arthur Gerald Donahue, *Tally-ho! Yankee in a Spitfire* (New York: MacMillan, 1943), p. 59.

31. A Royal Navy officer had told the boats' captains the day before: "We don't give a damn for your coal. We'd send you through empty if we had to. It's a matter of prestige." Source: Len Deighton, *Fighter* (New Jersey: Castle Books, 2000), p. 148.

32. Battle of Britain Historical Society website. Diary for August 1–8, 1940. http://www.battleofbritain.net/0023.html.

33. Arthur Gerald Donahue, *Tally-ho! Yankee in a Spitfire* (New York: Macmillan, 1943), pp. 61–62.

34. Ibid., p. 63.

35. Ibid.

36. Ibid., p. 64.

37. Ibid., p. 68.

38. Eric Mombeek, *Jagdwaffe, Battle of Britain: Phase One, July–August 1940* (East Sussex: Classic Publications Ltd., 2001), p. 66.

39. According to perhaps the most authoritative account of that day's fighting: "Nos. 145, 238, 152, 601, 213, 609 and 287 Squadrons were scrambled to intercept. They found some 150 aircraft, Ju-88s and He-111s escorted by Me-109s and Me-110s. Fierce dogfights developed as the bombers pressed home their high-level and dive-bomber attacks against docks, oil-tanks, barracks and gasworks at Weymouth and Portland. A resident of one of the houses attacked described the formations as being 'like a swarm of bees in the sky. I counted up to fifty and then stopped.'" Source: Derek Wood with Derek Dempster, *The Narrow Margin* (Yorkshire: Pen and Sword Military Classics, 2003), p. 157.

40. Peter Townsend, *Duel of Eagles* (London: Phoenix Press, 2000), pp. 361–362.

41. Winston G. Ramsey, editor, *The Battle of Britain, Then and Now* (London: Battle of Britain Prints International Limited, 1980), August 11, 1940 summary of 601 Squadron casualties.

42. Quoted, Memorial Souvenir Brochure, Tangmere Royal Air Force Station, September 23, 2002. See also Billy Fiske's logbook, August 11, 1940. National Archives (UK).

43. "Billy Fiske and 601 Operations at Tangmere," research summary compiled by Simon Lillywhite, based on National Archives (UK) research for author.

44. Derek Wood and Derek Dempster, *The Narrow Margin* (Yorkshire: Pen and Sword Military Classics, 2003), p. 157.

45. Larry Forrester, *Fly for Your Life* (London: Panther Books, 1969), p. 108.

46. Arthur Gerald Donahue, *Tally-ho! Yankee in a Spitfire* (New York: Macmillan, 1943), p. 69.

47. Ebeling's victories that day made Galland's III Group of fighter pilots the highest scoring unit in the Geschwader. In November, the highly decorated Ebeling would be shot down and become a POW with eighteen kills to his credit.

48. *Saturday Evening Post*, May 3, 1941.

49. *Winona Republican-Herald*, March 15, 1941.

50. Arthur Gerald Donahue, *Tally-ho! Yankee in a Spitfire* (New York: Macmillan, 1943), pp. 72–73.

51. *Winona Republican-Herald*, March 15, 1941.
52. Ibid.
53. *Saturday Evening Post*, May 3, 1941.
54. Arthur Gerald Donahue, *Tally-ho! Yankee in a Spitfire*, (New York: Macmillan, 1943), p. 74.
55. Ibid.
56. Ibid., p. 75.
57. Ibid.
58. Ibid.

Chapter Eight

1. Paul Richey, *Fighter Pilot* (London: Cassell, 2004), p. 96.
2. Patricia Ward, in Derek Tangye, editor, *Went the Day Well* (London: George G. Harrap and Co. Ltd., 1942), p. 126.
3. David Alan Johnson, *The Battle of Britain* (Conshocken, PA: Combined Publishing, 1998), p. 119.
4. Philip Kaplan and Richard Collier, *The Few: Summer 1940, The Battle of Britain* (London: Seven Dials, 2000), p. 145.
5. James A. Goodson and Norman Franks, *Over-Paid, Over-Sexed And Over Here* (Kent: Wingham Press, 1991), p. 9.
6. Billy Fiske, logbook, August 13, 1940. National Archives (UK).
7. Stephen Bungay, *The Most Dangerous Enemy* (London: Aurum Press, 2000), p. 258.
8. James A. Goodson and Norman Franks, *Over-Paid, Over-Sexed and Over Here* (Kent: Wingham Press, 1991), p. 9.
9. Billy Fiske, logbook, August 13, 1940. National Archives (UK).
10. Werner Mölders had test-flown the Me-110 before the war and concluded that only a true superman could pull the control stick with the strength required to compete with the Hurricane or Spitfire. In a mock dogfight with his brother Viktor, who flew an Me-109, and later with ZG 1, Mölders could not even stay on his younger sibling's tail. But as a fighter bomber, the Me-110 was a formidable threat, and its greatest successes during the battle came when it was used as such, in particular during raids on radar stations.
11. Arthur Gerald Donahue, *Tally-ho! Yankee in a Spitfire* (New York: Macmillan, 1943), p. 47.

12. Billy Fiske, private correspondence to family in America, April 14, 1940, quoted courtesy of Pat Zabalaga.

13. Ibid.

14. Derek Tangye, editor, *Went the Day Well* (London: George G. Harrap and Co. Ltd., 1942), p. 125.

15. Quoted, Philip Kaplan and Richard Collier, *The Few: Summer 1940, The Battle of Britain* (London: Seven Dials Press, 1989), p. 97.

16. The two Poles were, according to Squadron Leader Darley, "pretty bloodthirsty." Darley often entertained 609 at parties in his cottage near the airfield. One night, a fellow pilot tried to barrel roll over a piece of furniture and banged his head badly. "That was the first time they ever laughed." Source: Ibid., p. 180.

17. Richard Collier, *Eagle Day* (New York: Avon Books, 1966), p. 71.

18. Chris Goss, *Brothers in Arms* (London: Crecy Books, 1994), p. 40.

19. Frank Ziegler, *The Story of 609 Squadron* (London: MacDonald, 1971), p. 122.

20. Ostaszewski had shown a remarkable tenacity, following the Me-110 of Josef Birndorfer through the cables mooring Southampton's barrage balloons, then down to only a few feet off the ground and across the coast until he had Birndorfer in his sights at just 100 yards, and then across the Solent before finally destroying the German's plane with machine-gun bullets. The Me-110 crashed in flames on a road at Ashley Down on the Isle of Wight.

21. Frank Ziegler, *The Story of 609 Squadron* (London: MacDonald, 1971), p. 122.

22. Both their victims were fished out and became POWs: Sergeant Pfannschmidt was shot down by Nowierski at 4 p.m. Noncommissioned Officer Hohenfeldt crashed at the same time, shot down by Crook. They both belonged to 5/JG 53. Source: Chris Goss's research for the 609 Squadron website.

23. The Women's Auxiliary Air Force numbered fewer than 2,000 at the outbreak of war. By 1943, it would have 182,000 women in its ranks. Many men were opposed to these badly paid and mostly unrecognized women, who filled the role of men in working as drivers, cooks, clerks, and plotters. The WAAFs in operations rooms and at radar stations were of particular concern to the sexist old-timers.

As it turned out, they were as steady under fire as their male colleagues, notably so during savage attacks on radar stations in August 1940, when they stayed at their positions even as they plotted Me-110 fighter bombers right above their heads. Six military medals were awarded to WAAFs for gallantry in the face of the enemy. Not surprisingly, perhaps, many fighter boys fell for the young women, most of them their own age, wearing the same dark blue tunics. The WAAFs responded in kind. Perhaps the most moving story of a fighter pilot and his WAAF fiancée concerns Pilot Officer Denis Wissler and Assistant Section Officer Edith Heap. Wissler kept one of the finest fighter pilot diaries of 1940. He was killed in action on November 11, a few weeks after the Battle of Britain officially ended. His fiancée ended the war as an intelligence officer debriefing bomber command crews.

24. Frank Ziegler, *The Story of 609 Squadron* (London: MacDonald, 1971), p. 124.

25. http://www.battleofbritain.net/0026.html.

26. According to a subsequent Battle of Britain Historical Society report: "The crew, W. Heinrici, H. W. Stark and F. Ahrens were all killed instantly except for Ahrens who suffered severe injuries and died the following day." Source: http://www.battleofbritain.net/0026.html. David Crook and 609 scrambled immediately. A few minutes later, Crook flew over the crash site. He later recalled that he "had never seen an aeroplane so thoroughly wrecked; it was an awful mess." Source: Barry M. Marsden, *Derbyshire Fighter Aces* (Stroud: Tempus Publishing, England, 2004), p. 70.

27. David Crook, *Spitfire Pilot* (London: Faber and Faber, 1942), pp. 57–59.

28. Ibid.

29. That day, August 13, von Richthofen, commander of all the Stuka wings, was at a conference of senior Luftwaffe Officers held by Göring. It was decided to withdraw the Ju-87—the Stuka—from the battle. "The campaign is to proceed energetically but differently," he noted acidly in his diary. Source: Len Deighton, *Fighter* (New Jersey: Castle Books, 2000), p. 180.

30. According to 609's unofficial diarist, Johnny "Dogs" Dundas, 609 may

have delivered the decisive blow to the Stuka menace: "Thirteen Spitfires left Warmwell for a memorable teatime party over Lyme Bay and an unlucky day for the species of Ju-87 in which no less than fourteen suffered destruction or damage in a record Squadron bag, which also included five of the escorting Messerschmitts. The enemy's formation, consisting of about forty dive-bombers in four vic formation, with about as many Me-110s and 109s stepped up above them, heading northwards from the Channel, was surprised by 609 Squadron's downsun attack. All thirteen of our pilots fired their guns." Source: Edward Bishop, *Their Finest Hour* (New York: Ballantine Books, 1968), p. 64.

31. http://www.battleofbritain.net/0026.html.

Chapter Nine

1. J. E. Johnson, *Wing Leader* (Manchester: Crecy Publishing, 2004), p. 98.
2. Tony Holmes, *American Eagles: American Volunteers in the RAF 1937–43* (East Sussex: Classic Publications, 2001), p. 45.
3. Philip Kaplan and Richard Collier, *The Few: Summer 1940, The Battle of Britain* (London: Seven Dials Press, 1989), p. 115.
4. The Luftwaffe lost seventy-five planes. The RAF lost thirty-four. Seventeen pilots were killed and sixteen wounded. Source: Derek Wood and Derek Dempster, *The Narrow Margin* (Yorkshire: Pen and Sword Military Classics, 2003), pp. 168–169. Such losses prompted a disastrous change in tactics: Göring ordered that the fighters were to stay close to the bombers from now on, thereby fatally handicapping his aces, who became chained to the slow-moving bombers and were often easy targets as a result.
5. Jack Riddle, interview with author.
6. "After I had started the engine, the rigger would disconnect the battery truck, duck under the wing and turn on the oxygen supply and replace the panel. Meanwhile, the pilot [Sir Archibald Hope] had put on his parachute and climbed onto the plane. I would leave the cockpit and on the starboard side [Hope] would climb in." William Higgs, letter to Ray Campion's column, published in *Scramble*, March 2005, Issue 105.

7. "We were with them in sound and spirit," recalled Anne Turley-George. "We heard their shouts of 'Tally-ho!' . . . There was one boy who always burst into song as soon as he caught sight of the enemy and swung into the attack. We only heard these private war cries when they forgot to switch off their transmitters in the heat of battle, an awful yet uplifting experience. But that feeling of lead in the stomach when they failed to return was all too familiar . . . There were so many . . . The gay and gallant . . . so young and so well endowed, and such a wicked, wicked waste." Source: Norman Gelb, *Scramble: A Narrative History of the Battle of Britain* (London: Harcourt Brace Jovanovich, 1985), p. 171.

8. Nicolson would later disappear in 1945 on a routine flight in the Far East. Source: http://www.battleofbritain.net/0027.html.

9. Derek Tangye, editor, *Went the Day Well* (London: George G. Harrap and Co. Ltd., 1942), p. 125.

10. Tom Moulson, *The Flying Sword: The Story of 601 Squadron* (London: MacDonald, 1964), p. 87.

11. Norman Gelb, *Scramble: A Narrative History of the Battle of Britain* (London: Harcourt Brace Jovanovich, 1985), p. 152.

12. Ibid.

13. Ibid.

14. Ibid., p. 171.

15. Richard Hough and Dennis Richards, *The Battle of Britain* (London: W.W. Norton & Co., Ltd., 2005), p. 193.

According to Tangmere's 601 airman William Higgs: "Our only defenses were machine guns and Bedford lorries. These were filled with ballast and had one machine gun operated by a soldier of the Monmouthshire Regiment. We ground crew on the dispersal sites had rifles locked in the dispersal hut. These were to be used in the case of paratroopers or gliders landing. We each had 12 rounds of ammunition. When this was used we were to fix bayonets and charge." Source: William Higgs, letter to Ray Campion's column, published in *Scramble*, March 2005, Issue 105.

16. Dr. Courtney Willey, interview with author.

17. Tom Moulson, *The Flying Sword: The Story of 601 Squadron* (London: MacDonald, 1964), p. 89.

18. William Higgs, letter to Ray Campion's column, published in *Scramble*, March 2005, Issue 105.

19. Derek Tangye, editor, *Went the Day Well* (London: George G. Harrap and Co. Ltd., 1942), p. 125.

20. Jack Riddle, interview with author.

21. "Just how Fiske had managed to fly and land his plane in such atrocious pain it is impossible to say," squadron historian Tom Moulson would later write, "but the Legion knew why he did it, and within days his Hurricane was back in the sky over Hell's Corner." Source: Tom Moulson, *The Flying Sword: The Story of 601 Squadron* (London: MacDonald, 1964), p. 88.

22. "Sir Archibald Hope knew Fiske well," recalled Faulkner. "He was one of his buddies. It was known as the Millionaires' squadron. They were a lovely crowd. Max Aitken was a bit scary. He flew through the hangar once—fortunately, the doors were open at both ends—and then got grounded for a while. They were a bit of a wild bunch. There were quite a few Poles in the squadron and it was quite amusing: every time the [loud speaker] sounded, they thought it was a scramble and they went out tearing for their aircraft." Source: Jeffrey Faulkner, interview with author.

23. Jeffrey Faulkner, interview with author.

24. Ibid.

25. Norman Gelb, *Scramble: A Narrative History of the Battle of Britain* (London: Harcourt Brace Jovanovich, 1985), p. 172.

26. Faulkner received the Military Medal in March 1941 from King George VI. "I had joined up the day before the war broke out," recalled Faulkner. "I got called up on a Sunday and on the Monday I was in the Royal Air Force. Corporal Jones was a lot older than me. I was 20. He'd have been probably 40. Hope was full of beans. A happy-go-lucky sort of chap. Those men were very, very popular." Source: Jeffrey Faulkner, interview with author.

27. Dr. Courtney Willey, interview with author.

28. Jeffrey Faulkner, interview with author.

29. Ibid.

30. Richard Collier, *Eagle Day: The Battle of Britain* (New York: Avon Books, 1969), p. 92.

31. Martin Gilbert, *Churchill: A Life* (New York: Henry Holt, 1991), p. 671. Churchill would soon use the same words in his most oft-quoted speech about the Battle of Britain.

32. Battle of Britain Historical Society website diary, August 16–17, 1940. http://www.battleofbritain.net/0027.html.

33. Janet Aitken Kidd, *The Beaverbrook Girl* (London: Collins, 1987), p. 175.

34. *The Observer*, February 3, 2002.

35. Vera Brittain, *England's Hour* (New York: Macmillan, 1941), p. 141.

36. Adolf Galland, *The First and The Last* (New York: Ballantine Books, 1953), p. 26.

37. Karinhall was already legendary throughout the Luftwaffe. It was surrounded by the best hunting grounds in all of the Reich, stocked with wild boars as bloated as "Fatty Göring" and huge stags. Inside, guests could enjoy gold-plated baths the size of small swimming pools and marvel at a fast-growing collection of the great masters, culled from Paris and other conquered capitals. Even the attic boasted the most elaborate model railway in the world, complete with papier-mâché mountains six feet high and a switch that summoned toy bombers, suspended by thin wires, to drop bombs on a blue French train.

38. David Baker, *Adolf Galland* (London: Windrow and Greene, 1996), p. 118.

39. Adolf Galland, *The First and the Last* (New York: Ballantine Books, 1953), p. 28.

40. Ibid.

41. David Baker, *Adolf Galland* (London: Windrow and Greene, 1996), p. 120.

42. The ashes of Fiske's father and mother were interred with him at a later date. His epitaph reads: "He died for England."

43. "Pilot Officer W. L. M. Fiske" obituary by Lieutenant-Colonel J. T. C. Moore-Brabazon, MP, August 20, 1940, the *London Times*.

  "An American citizen, blessed with this world's goods, of a family beloved by all who knew them, with a personal charm that made all worship him, he elected to join our Royal Air Force and fight our battles," wrote Moore-Brabazon. "We thank America for sending us the perfect sportsman. Many of us would have given our lives for 'Billy,' instead he has given his for us."

44. Details on the funeral are drawn from contemporary accounts and the *London Times,* August 22, 1940.

45. Edward Bishop, *Their Finest Hour* (New York: Ballantine Books, 1968), p. 87.

Violet Asquith wrote to congratulate Churchill on his speech. His words "would live as long as words are spoken and remembered . . . Nothing so simple, so majestic and so true has been said in so great a moment of human history. You have beaten your old enemies the 'Classics' into a cocked hat!" Source: Martin Gilbert, *Churchill: A Life* (New York: Henry Holt, 1991), p. 671.

PART THREE

1. Gavin Lyall, editor, *The War in the Air, The Royal Air Force in World War II* (New York: Ballantine Books), p. 49.

Chapter Ten

1. Geoffrey Page, *Shot Down in Flames* (London: Grub Street, 1999).

2. Ibid., p. 69.

3. Quoted, Tony Holmes, *American Eagles: American Volunteers in the RAF 1937–43* (East Sussex: Classic Publications, 2001), p. 48.

4. Eugene Tobin, "Yankee Eagle over London," *Liberty* magazine, April 12, 1941.

5. Ibid.

6. Frank Ziegler, *The Story of 609 Squadron* (London: MacDonald, 1971), p. 114.

7. Tony Holmes, *American Eagles: American Volunteers in the RAF 1937–43* (East Sussex: Classic Publications, 2001), p. 48.

8. Tom Moulson, *The Flying Sword: The Story of 601 Squadron* (London: MacDonald, 1964), pp. 89–90.

9. David Crook, *Spitfire Pilot* (London: Faber and Faber, 1942), p. 65.

10. Ibid., p. 59.

11. Eugene Tobin, diary entry, August 23, 1940.

12. David Crook, *Spitfire Pilot* (London: Faber and Faber, 1942), p. 56.

13. Chris Goss, *Brothers in Arms* (Manchester: Crecy Publishing, 1994), p. 167.

14. Ibid., p. 15.

15. David Crook, *Spitfire Pilot* (London: Faber and Faber, 1942), p. 57.

16. Ibid.

17. Hector Bolitho, "Yanks over England," *Denver Post*, March 2, 1941.

18. Ibid.

19. Tony Holmes, *American Eagles: American Volunteers in the RAF 1937–43* (East Sussex: Classic Publications, 2001), p. 50.

20. David Crook, *Spitfire Pilot* (London: Faber and Faber, 1942), pp. 56–59.

21. Eugene Tobin, "Yankee Eagle over London," *Liberty* magazine, April 19, 1941. Before turning in that night, Tobin noted: "Andy's birthday— by all means don't give him a thing—don't forget Tobin . . . Today Andy got a cannon bullet from astern, shot at him, it went through his armor plating and thumped him in the back and that is all. He is without doubt the luckiest fellow I know of. We saw some DO17s but they were too far away to engage—that is all." Source: Eugene Tobin, diary entry, August 24, 1940.

Chapter Eleven

1. Arthur Ward, *A Nation Alone*, (London: Osprey, 1989), p. 125.

2. Frank Ziegler, *The Story of 609 Squadron, Under the White Rose*, MacDonald, London, 1971, p. 117.

3. Taking matters into his own hands, Darley had stalked into the kitchen and single-handedly prepared breakfast for his ravenous pilots. But the cooks had then complained bitterly to the station commander who reprimanded Darley for leaving dirty dishes in the kitchen— he was never to use it again! Darley had told him in no uncertain terms what he thought of the civilian cooks.

4. Ibid., p. 118.

5. Eugene Tobin, "Yankee Eagle over London," *Liberty* magazine, April 19, 1941.

6. Ibid.

7. Chris Goss, *Brothers in Arms* (Manchester: Crecy Publishing, 1994), p. 17.

8. Eugene Tobin, "Yankee Eagle over London," *Liberty* magazine, April 19, 1941.

9. Ibid.

10. David Crook and Osti ran into serious trouble. One of the Me-110s peppered one of Crook's wings with bullets and almost hit Crook in the leg. Osti managed to survive being caught in another German's crosshairs, but only just: one 20 mm cannon shell destroyed the top of the armor plating behind his cockpit, giving him a severe headache, another hit his engine, and yet another destroyed his brakes. Thankfully, he was as fortunate as Andy Mamedoff the day before and managed to get back to Middle Wallop. Without brakes, however, he could not avoid coming to rest in a perimeter hedge.

11. Chris Goss, *Brothers in Arms* (Manchester: Crecy Publishing, 1994), p. 19.

12. Eugene Tobin, "Yankee Eagle over London," *Liberty* magazine, April 19, 1941.

13. Ibid.

14. Hans-Karl Mayer, combat report, August 25, 1940, quoted, *Battle of Britain*, Len Deighton (London: Coward, McCann and Geoghegan, 1980), p. 140.

15. Eugene Tobin, "Yankee Eagle over London," *Liberty* magazine, April 19, 1941.

16. Richard Collier, *Eagle Day*, (New York: Avon Books, 1969), p. 138.

17. Frank Ziegler, *The Story of 609 Squadron, Under the White Rose* (London: MacDonald, 1971), p. 118.

18. Byron Kennerly, *The Eagles Roar* (New York: Harper and Brothers, 1942), p. 97.

19. Darley had both Poles promise never to use Polish while in the air because the other pilots could not understand what they were saying. They quickly learned rudimentary English.

20. The squadron's operations report recorded simply: "PO Tobin—after securing two 'probables' experienced G in a 18000" dive." 609 Squadron Ops, August 25 ,1940.

21. Eugene Tobin, diary entry, August 25.

22. 609 Squadron, August 30, 1940. National Archives (UK).

23. Frank Ziegler, *The Story of 609 Squadron* (London: MacDonald, 1971), p. 136.

24. August had been a brutal month with many airfields, including Tangmere, hit. What was worse was that so many pilots had been

lost: 224 since the battle started on July 10. And 205 others, including Art Donahue, were so badly wounded that they could not fly.

25. David Crook, *Spitfire Pilot* (London: Faber and Faber, 1942), p. 49.

26. Larry Forrester, *Fly for Your Life* (London: Panther Books, 1969), pp. 108–109.

27. On August 31, Fighter Command was 166 pilots below full strength.

28. Philip Kaplan and Richard Collier, *The Few: Summer 1940, The Battle of Britain* (London: Cassell & Co., 1989), p. 152.

29. Ibid., p. 154.

30. Patrick Bishop, *Fighter Boys* (New York: Viking, 2003), p. 331.

31. Ibid., p. 258.

32. Adolf Galland, *The First and the Last* (New York: Ballantine Books, 1953), pp. 24–25.

33. Jochen Prien, *Jagdgeschwader 53* (Atglen, Pennsylvania: Schiffer Military History, 1997), p. 142.

34. Richard Collier, *Eagle Day*, (New York: Avon Books, 1969), p. 197. The Me-109's greatest weakness during battle was its lack of range, allowing only a few minutes of fighting above London. Lingering too long over England was fatal: on one sortie alone, JG 26's II Group lost seven planes through ditching in the Channel and five more in belly landings after just managing to get back over the French coast.

35. Philip Kaplan and Richard Collier, *The Few: Summer 1940, The Battle of Britain* (London: Seven Dials, 1990), p. 8.

36. Ibid., p. 162.

37. Art Donahue, private correspondence to parents, September 21, 1940. Donahue family files.

38. Quoted, William Stevenson, *A Man Called Intrepid* (New York: Ballantine Books, 1977), p. 112.

39. Cajus Bekker, *The Luftwaffe Diaries* (New York: Ballantine Books, 1969), p. 240.

40. Peter Townsend, *Duel of Eagles* (London: Orion Publishing, 2000), p. 384.

41. Stephen Bungay, *The Most Dangerous Enemy* (London: Aurum Press, 2000), pp. 307–308.

42. Davis's Hurricane P3363, in which he had shot down his first German,

crashed in the back garden of Canterbury Cottage in the small village of Matfield around 9:30 that morning. Source: Tony Holmes, *American Eagles: American Volunteers in the RAF 1937–43* (East Sussex: Classic Publications, 2001), p. 55.

43. Sergeant Eric Hubbard, a Matfield policeman to the widow of Flight Lieutenant Carl Davis. Dated September 12, 1940. "I hope you will not mind receiving this letter from a stranger, one who saw the air battle in which your husband gave his life on Friday morning last, his plane falling in a cottage garden within a hundred yards of this house," wrote Sergeant Hubbard. "I am able to tell you that he died in the air instantaneously as a result of two bullets through the brain, his machine afterwards breaking in two and falling. I was the first to enter the cottage garden, and saw him sitting in his plane with his feet on the rudder bar and the belt still fastened round his waist, clearly showing that he had not moved again after being attacked. I placed a covering over him, and an ambulance was summoned and he was removed to the mortuary of our local hospital . . . In order to be certain of the facts, I visited the hospital two days later, where I found him lying with a bunch of roses on his breast, and, in company with the matron, I examined his head and she agreed with me that death had been instantaneous. As a fighter of the last war, I pay homage to a fighter of today, and while I know that nothing I may say can be of any real comfort to you, I do ask you to think of him as soaring into that glorious sunny morning, with a smile on his lips and a song in his heart, to do battle for this England of ours, and there making the supreme sacrifice. Please believe that there is no need for you to acknowledge this letter, if you would rather not. I shall be thinking of you and him at eight o'clock tomorrow morning." Source: Quoted, Tony Holmes, *American Eagles: American Volunteers in the RAF 1937–43* (East Sussex: Classic Publications, 2001), p. 57.

44. David Crook, *Spitfire Pilot* (London: Faber and Faber, 1942), p. 64.

45. Tom Moulson, *The Flying Sword: The Story of 601 Squadron* (London: MacDonald, 1964), p. 92.

46. Ibid., pp. 92–93.

47. Eugene Tobin, diary entry, August 27, 1940.

Chapter Twelve

1. Arthur Ward, *A Nation Alone* (London: Osprey, 1989), p. 175.
2. Derek Wood and Derek Dempster, *The Narrow Margin* (London: Hutchinson, 1961), p. 337.
3. Philip Kaplan and Richard Collier, *The Few: Summer 1940, The Battle of Britain* (London: Seven Dials, 1990), p. 194.

   "I was flying Red 3," recalled Ogilvie. "We climbed to 20,000 feet and attacked from the sun. Following Red 2, I delivered a beam attack on a trio of bombers. I gave them a couple of 3-second bursts and they started to break formation at a range of 200 yards closing to 75 yards. I gave one a solid burst of six or seven seconds, he turned over on his back and slid down. I kept going down, then climbed and returned to the attack. As I was diving close on the bombers again two 109s attacked me, one overshooting very close to me. At very close range I emptied my guns on him as we were diving. He turned on his back and, as I followed him down, started to burn. Out of ammunition, I returned to base." Source: http://members.lycos.co.uk/ErnieBurton/Pilots/Ogilvie_Alfred_Keith.

4. Eugene Tobin, diary entry, September 7, 1940.
5. Stefan Schimanski and Henry Treece, editors, *Leaves in the Storm: A Book of Diaries* (London: Lindsay Drummond, 1947), p. 82.
6. According to the notes of Nina Masel, a *Mass Observation* reporter: "Warning went at 5 p.m. Almost immediately afterwards terrific crashes, bombs falling all round. Women in shelters stood up, holding each other. Some screamed . . . All clear. Everyone groaned relief, went out and screamed with horror at sight of the damage. Every street was damaged, bombs everywhere. Smoke and flames streaming from the docks. Shouting, finding relatives, chaos. Unexploded bomb. Building fell on a group of men and women. Screams, groans, sudden rush back of people followed immediately by a rush forward. Women fainted, mass hysteria, man threw a fit. Men, women, and children crying and sobbing. Frantic parents searching for their young. Pub nearby full of casualties. Dead and dying on the pavements. Someone sick." Source: Masel notes, Blitz files, Mass Observation Archives, University of Sussex.

7. Philip Kaplan and Richard Collier, *The Few: Summer 1940, The Battle of Britain* (London: Cassell and Co., 1989), p. 198.

8. Ibid., p.199

9. Peter Townsend, *Duel of Eagles* (London: Orion Publishing, 2000), p. 393.

10. David Baker, *Adolf Galland* (London: Windrow and Greene, 1996), p. 133.

11. Peter Townsend, *Duel of Eagles* (London: Orion Publishing, 2000), p. 393.

12. Ibid., p. 392.

13. Philip Ziegler, *London at War* (New York: Alfred A. Knopf, 1995), p. 113.

14. Frank Ziegler, *The Story of 609 Squadron* (London: MacDonald, 1971), p. 140.

15. Eugene Tobin, diary entry, September 7, 1940.

16. 609 Squadron records and individual combat reports, September 7, 1940, National Archives (UK).

17. Martin Gilbert, *Churchill: A Life* (New York: Henry Holt and Company, 1992), p. 675.

18. Colin Perry, *A Boy in the Blitz: A 1940 Diary* (London: Corgi, 1974), p. 121.

19. Martin Gilbert, *Churchill: A Life* (New York: Henry Holt and Company, 1992), p. 675.

20. Norman Moss, *Nineteen Weeks* (New York: Houghton Mifflin, 2003), p. 310.

21. Fighter Command lost 515 pilots during the Battle of Britain.

22. Martin Gilbert, *Churchill: A Life* (New York: Henry Holt and Company, 1992), pp. 675–676.

23. Eugene Tobin, diary entry, September 11, 1940.

Chapter Thirteen

1. Eugene Tobin, "Yankee Eagle over London," *Liberty* magazine, April 12, 1941.

2. Eugene Tobin, "Yankee Eagle over London," *Liberty* magazine, April 26, 1941.

3. Vincent Orange, *Sir Keith Park* (London: Methuen, 1984), p. 109.

4. Alfred Price, *Battle of Britain Day* (London: Greenhill Books, 1990), p. 27.

5. Sometimes pilots would "do a Cap Griz Nez," which basically meant turning back once they reached the English Channel. It would have been totally unacceptable to turn back before the waters but once over the Channel many pilots finally lost their nerve and turned tail.

6. Richard Collier, *Eagle Day* (New York: Avon Books, 1969), p. 223.

7. www.Shoreham-aircraft-museum.co.uk/castlefarm.htm.

8. Stephen Bungay, *The Most Dangerous Enemy* (London: Aurum Press, 2000), p. 320.

9. Eugene Tobin, "Yankee Eagle over London," *Liberty* magazine, April 26, 1941.

10. Alfred Price, *Battle of Britain Day* (London: Greenhill Books, 1990), p. 53.

11. Eugene Tobin, "Yankee Eagle over London," *Liberty* magazine, April 26, 1941.

12. Robert J. Casey, "Yankee Ace in RAF Needs No Stopwatch," *Chicago Daily News*, December 11, 1940.

13. Ibid.

14. www.Shoreham-aircraft-museum.co.uk/castlefarm.htm.

15. Eugene Tobin, "Yankee Eagle over London," *Liberty* magazine, April 26, 1941.

16. Ibid.

17. Ibid.

18. Ibid.

19. www.Shoreham-aircraft-museum.co.uk/castlefarm.htm.

20. Richard Collier, *Eagle Day* (New York: Avon Books, 1969), p. 207.

21. David Baker, *Adolf Galland* (London: Windrow and Greene, 1996), p. 135.

22. Stephen Bungay, *The Most Dangerous Enemy* (London: Aurum Press, 2000), p. 327.

23. Ibid.

24. Donald L. Caldwell, *JG26* (New York: Ivy Books, 1991), p. 60.

25. Winston Churchill, *Their Finest Hour* (London: The Educational Book Company Ltd., 1949), pp. 257–258.

26. Frank Ziegler, *The Story of 609 Squadron* (London: MacDonald, 1971), p. 146.

27. 609 Squadron combat report by Vernon Keough, September 15, 1940, National Archives (UK).

28. Jim Goodson, *Over-Paid, Over-Sexed and Over Here* (Canterbury: Wingham Press, 1991), p. 14.

29. David Crook, *Spitfire Pilot* (London: Faber and Faber, 1942), p. 69.

30. Eugene Tobin, "Yankee Eagle over London," *Liberty* magazine, April 26, 1941.

31. 609 Squadron diary, September 15, 1940, National Archives (UK).

32. Keith Ogilvie, combat report, 609 Squadron records, September 15, 1940, National Archives (UK).

33. Frank Ziegler, *The Story of 609 Squadron* (London: MacDonald, 1971), p. 146.

34. Winston Churchill, *Their Finest Hour* (London: The Educational Book Company Ltd., 1949), p. 258.

35. Ibid.

36. The claim of 183 German losses was ludicrously exaggerated. Fighter Command had in fact destroyed 36 bombers and 23 fighters. Of the bombers, 22 had been Dorniers, 4 of which 609 had almost certainly destroyed. But the exact figures were not what really counted. Crucially, Fighter Command had proven that the Luftwaffe still could not control air space in preparation for an invasion—far from it.

37. Peter Townsend, *Duel of Eagles* (London: Orion Publishing, 2000), p. 409.

38. Egbert Kieser, *Hitler on the Doorstep* (London: Arms & Armour Press, 1997), p. 272.

39. Eugene Tobin, "Yankee Eagle over London," *Liberty* magazine, April 26, 1941. In fact hard evidence supports a claim for only four Dorniers.

40. It would soon be confirmed that Geoffrey Gaunt had been killed, either by a Dornier's machine gunner or an Me-110. "Geoff had been so popular," recalled Crook, "but we were now so consistently successful and strong in our confidence that we had the enemy 'just where we wanted him' that nobody was shaken in the least . . . But for me it was the biggest loss that I had ever

experienced." Source: David Crook, *Spitfire Pilot* (London: Faber and Faber, 1942), pp. 70–71.

41. Eugene Tobin, "Yankee Eagle over London," *Liberty* magazine, April 26, 1940.

42. Richard Collier, *Eagle Day* (New York: Avon Books, 1969), p. 245.

43. Ibid.

44. Denis Richards, *Royal Air Force*, Volume 1—The Fight at Odds. Quoted, *The Flying Sword*, p. 91.

PART FOUR

1. Peter Townsend, introduction to Jim Bailey's *The Sky Suspended* (London: Bloomsbury, 2005), pp. 3–4.

Chapter Fourteen

1. Norman Gelb, *Scramble: A Narrative Account of the Battle of Britain* (San Diego: Harcourt Brace Jovanovich, 1985), p. 288.

2. 609 Operations Book, September 19, 1940, National Archives (UK).

3. David Crook, *Spitfire Pilot* (London: Faber and Faber, 1942), p. 59.

4. Although the idea for an Eagle Squadron had met with Churchill's approval, most of the funding to get the unit up and running did not come from British sources. It came instead from the Sweeny family, who would eventually provide some $100,000 to ensure that the first Eagles got into the air. Sweeny's first choice to lead the proposed Eagle Squadron had been Billy Fiske, an old friend with whom he had played roulette in the late thirties in the south of France and with whom he had shared many an afternoon bobsledding while on vacation at St. Moritz.

5. 151 had lost all its prewar pilots over the summer.

6. Tony Holmes, *American Eagles* (East Sussex: Classic Publications, 2001), p. 60.

7. Frank Brinkerhoff, interview with author.

8. Atholl Forbes and Hubert Allen, editors, *Ten Fighter Boys* (London: Collins, 1942), p. 79.

9. Ibid.

10. Bobby Oxspring, *Spitfire Command* (London: William Kimber, 1984), p. 78.

11. Just four days ago, Mölders had riddled two Spitfires over Dungeness, marking his thirty-ninth and fortieth kills, and earning him the coveted Oak Leaves—he was the first Luftwaffe pilot to be awarded them. Galland had sent him a case of champagne, with a brief note stating that he was on his tail and his Revi gun sight was on.

12. Adolf Galland, *The First and The Last* (New York: Ballantine Books, 1978), pp. 35–38.

13. Jochen Prien, *Jagdgeschwader 53* (Atglen, Pennsylvania: Schiffer Military History, 1997), p. 163.

14. Ibid.

15. Adolf Galland, *The First and The Last* (New York: Ballantine Books, 1978), p. 38.

16. Bobby Oxspring, *Spitfire Command* (London: William Kimber, 1984), p. 76.

17. Jochen Prien, *Jagdgeschwader 53* (Atglen, Pennsylvania: Schiffer Military History, 1997), p. 178.

18. Bobby Oxspring, *Spitfire Command* (London: William Kimber, 1984), pp. 83–84.

Chapter Fifteen

1. James A. Goodson, *Over-Paid, Over-Sexed and Over Here* (Canterbury: Wingham Press, 1991), p. 22.

2. Donald McCormick, *One Man's Wars: The Story of Charles Sweeny, Soldier of Fortune* (London: Arthur Barker, 1972), p. 186.

3. Philip D. Caine, *American Pilots in the RAF* (Dulles, Virginia: Brassey's, 1998), p. 146.

4. One of the first Eagle pilots was Byron Kennerly, a congenital liar and wild man who was the only American volunteer to be sent back to America by the RAF after several warnings for antisocial behavior and drunkenness. He went on to pen a memoir that was mostly fictional. Kennerly eventually died in Los Angeles of lung cancer, a convicted bank robber.

5. Philip D. Caine, *American Pilots in the RAF* (Dulles, Virginia: Brassey's, 1998), p. 150.

6. Helen Maher's files, transcript of "Broadcast from Unnamed Eagle Pilot," December 14, 1940.

7. Charles Sweeny, introduction, p. xiii, *The Eagles Roar*, Byron Kennerly (New York: Harper and Brothers Publishers), 1942.

8. Art Donahue, private correspondence to his parents, November 14, 1940.

9. 71 Squadron Records, National Air Force Academy Archives, Colorado Springs. November 7, 1940 official diary entry.

10. Lupus is a chronic (long-lasting) autoimmune disease in which the immune system becomes hyperactive and attacks normal tissue. This attack results in inflammation and brings about symptoms such as swelling, exhaustion and, if untreated, chronic kidney failure.

11. Helen Maher, interview with author.

12. Michael Payne, "The Helmut Wick Story," *Aviation News*, 9–22 November 1990, pp. 584–588.

13. Also stationed at Kirton Lindsey was 616 Squadron's Pilot Officer "Johnnie" Johnson, who would eventually become the RAF's highest scoring WWII pilot with thirty-eight kills. "On the opposite side of the airfield," he recalled, "the pilots of the first Eagle Squadron were busy training on their Hurricanes, and we saw a great deal of these buccaneering young Americans. They were all tremendously keen to come to grips with the Luftwaffe and it was interesting to watch their widely different personalities combine to serve a common purpose. They were exhilarating company to live with and some of them could almost salute." Source: J. E. Johnson, *Wing Leader* (Manchester: Crecy Publishing, 2004), p. 65.

14. Undated press clipping, courtesy of Frank Brinkerhoff.

15. Eugene Tobin, diary entry, October 28, 1940.

16. Leckrone was a troubled man in the run-up to Christmas. He was no longer homesick, he explained in a letter to a sister, Nadine, back in Illinois, but he dearly missed his two young children, Donna, 8, and Dickie, 5. "Every once in a while," he confessed, "I get to thinking of Donna and Dickie—just how they talked and laughed and kissed me and I feel like I could break in two." Hopefully he would soon be too busy to be depressed—he wondered whether he would ever be truly happy again—and to think about his children and his mother. She was terribly worried,

he knew, about him flying with the Eagles, especially now after his near-death accident. "I am so tired of thinking," he also wrote his sister, before adding that he badly wanted to return to fighting the Germans. Source: Phillip Leckrone, private letter to Nadine Leckrone, November 14, 1940.

17. Eugene Tobin, diary entry, December 24, 1940.

18. Eugene Tobin, diary entry, January 7, 1941.

19. 71 Squadron Operations records, January 5, 1941, National Archives (UK).

20. Ibid.

21. Philip Caine, *American Pilots in the RAF* (Dulles, Virginia: Brassey's, 1998), p. 151.

22. Eugene Tobin, diary entry, February 9, 1941.

23. James A. Goodson, *Over-Paid, Over-Sexed and Over Here* (Canterbury: Wingham Press, 1991), p. 23

24. Vern Haugland, *The Eagle Squadrons* (New York: Ziff-Davis Flying Books, 1979), p. 35.

25. Ibid.

26. Hector Bolitho, "Yanks over England," *Denver Post*, March 2, 1941.

27. 71 Squadron Operations records, National Archives (UK).

28. Philip D. Caine, *American Pilots in the RAF* (Dulles, Virginia: Brassey's, 1998), p. 154.

29. Ibid.

30. J. E. Johnson, *Wing Leader* (Manchester: Crecy Publishing, 2004), p. 68.

31. Ronald Kessler, *The Sins of the Father* (New York: Warner Books, 1996), p. 206.

32. James Brough and Elliott Roosevelt, *An Untold Story: The Roosevelts of Hyde Park* (New York: Putnam, 1973), p. 298.

33. In fact, the first American airman to die in combat was Flight Lieutenant Jimmy Davis of 79 Squadron. He was shot down and killed on June 25, 1940, almost two months before Fiske. This came to light only after the war.

34. Memorial Service pamphlet, RAF Station Tangmere.

35. Eleanor Roosevelt would write on the first anniversary of Pearl Harbor to Fiske's mother: "My deepest sympathy goes to you but

I must express my pride in your son." Eleanor Roosevelt, private correspondence to Mrs. W. Fiske, December 7, 1942.

36. Bill Geiger, interview with author.

37. Ibid.

38. James A. Goodson and Norman Franks, *Over-Paid, Over-Sexed and Over Here* (Kent: Wingham Press, 1991), p. 33.

39. Ibid.

40. Bill Geiger, interview with author. On a subsequent sweep over France, just ten days later, Geiger would be shot down and become a prisoner of war.

41. Helen Maher, interview with author.

42. Ibid.

43. Cablegram, Quentin Reynolds to John McClain, September 9, 1941.

44. Philip D. Caine, *American Pilots in the RAF* (Dulles, Virginia: Brassey's, 1998), p. 163.

45. A. Mosier, International Red Cross Central Committee, letter to Helen Ann Haring, undated. Helen Maher's personal files.

46. Untitled, undated press cutting. Helen Maher's personal files.

47. George Sperry, unpublished memoirs, p. 15, Air Force Academy archives.

48. Ibid.

49. *Battle of Britain Remembered.* "Death of an Eagle." Undated clipping. Helen Maher's personal files. Steve Poole, interview with author. According to Philip D. Caine, the leading authority on the American Eagles: "Of the 260 members of the Eagle Squadrons, 109—more than 40 percent—were killed during the war." Philip D. Caine, *American Pilots in the RAF* (Dulles, Virginia: Brassey's, 1998), p. 162.

50. John J. Stephan, *The Russian Fascists* (New York: Harper and Row, 1978), p. 277.

Chapter Sixteen

1. Arthur Gerald Donahue, *Last Flight from Singapore* (New York: Macmillan, 1943), p. 133.

2. Art Donahue, letter to his parents, December 7, 1940.

3. In June, 1940, the State Department had notified London that

Americans joining the RAF would not be prosecuted as long as they had not sworn allegiance to the British sovereign, and if they had joined the RAF in Britain, not in America. Soon thereafter the RAF waived the regulation necessitating all recruits to swear allegiance to the British monarch, thereby removing the risk of prosecution for American volunteers. In November 1940, the State Department decided it would not take action against those Americans who had sworn allegiance. Nevertheless, several Eagle pilots were not officially reinstated as American citizens until many years after the war.

4. Arthur Gerald Donahue, *Tally-ho! Yankee in a Spitfire* (New York: Macmillan, 1943), p. 176.

5. Ibid., p. 177.

6. Ibid., p. 182.

7. Art Donahue, private correspondence to his family, October 28, 1941.

8. John "Red" Campbell, interview with author. Also see Vern Haugland, *The Eagle Squadrons* (New York: Ziff-Davis Flying Books, 1979), p. 114, for more details on Campbell and Donahue that winter.

9. Peter Townsend, introduction to Jim Bailey's *The Sky Suspended* (London: Bloomsbury, 2005), p. 5.

10. Vern Haugland, *The Eagle Squadrons* (New York: Ziff-Davis Flying Books, 1979), p. 114.

11. Art Donahue, private correspondence to his family, December 16, 1941.

12. Terrence Kelly, *Hurricane over the Jungle* (London: Arrow Books), 1990, p. 110.

13. Ibid.

14. Ibid., p. 111.

15. Arthur Gerald Donahue, *Last Flight from Singapore* (New York: Macmillan, 1943), p. 140. Kelly was also to recall that when he later became a POW "even the Japanese were to talk of it [the strafing] in awe. When we were [later] taken prisoner, we took off and destroyed our brevets [badges worn by qualified aircrew in the RAF] because we believed that had the Japanese in our camp known we were the pilots who had strafed them on the Moesi they would

have taken revenge." Source: Terrence Kelly, *Hurricane over the Jungle* (London: Arrow Books, 1990), p. 111.

16. Arthur Gerald Donahue, *Last Flight from Singapore* (New York: Macmillan, 1943), p. 141. According Kelly, Donahue was the only pilot to inflict significant damage.

17. Terrence Kelly, *Hurricane over the Jungle* (London: Arrow Books, 1990), p. 110.

18. Arthur Gerald Donahue, *Last Flight from Singapore* (New York: Macmillan, 1943), pp. 142–146.

19. Donahue's citation read: "This officer has carried out many low-level reconnaissance sorties and has successfully attacked enemy shipping and ground objectives. On one occasion, whilst carrying out an attack against enemy troops attempting a landing, Flying Officer Donahue silenced the enemy's fire, thus enabling the rest of the formation to press home their attacks with impunity. He has destroyed several aircraft." Source: John D. Lauher, Major USAF, Fort Leavenworth, Kansas, 1980, "American Pilots in the Battle of Britain," unpublished thesis, p. 58.

20. "I Fly Alone," unpublished memoir, Lieutenant A. C. Young, Donahue family files.

21. Ibid.

22. Donahue was officially credited with five kills and one shared, making him an ace.

23. *The Times*, November 16, 1943. Fagan had been the first officer to welcome Donahue to 64 Squadron in July 1940; Art had named him "No 1" in his book, *Tally-Ho! Yankee in a Spitfire*.

Epilogue

1. Vern Haugland, *The Eagle Squadrons* (New York: Ziff-Davis Flying Books, 1979), p. 3.

2. Ibid., p. 180.

3. Just seven Americans were listed in the RAF's official roster of the Battle of Britain, but one additional American, Hugh Reilley, would be included in the list of the American "few."

4. A scholarship foundation for aeronautics students has been established in his name at the University of Virginia.

5. Bill Edwards, interview with author.
6. Vern Haugland, *The Eagle Squadrons* (New York: Ziff-Davis Flying Books, 1979), p. 181.
7. Philip D. Caine, *American Pilots in the RAF* (Dulles, Virginia: Brassey's, 1998), p. 151.

Bibliography

Amery, L. S. *My Political Life,* vol. 3. London, Hutchinson, 1955.

Anderson, Verily. *Spam Tomorrow.* London, Rupert Hart-Davis, 1956.

Áster, Sidney. *1939: The Making of the Second World War.* London, André Deutsch, 1974.

Astley, Joan Bright. *The Inner Circle: A View of War at the Top.* London, Hutchinson, 1971.

Atkinson, Max. *Our Masters' Voices.* London, Methuen, 1984.

Arct, Bohdan. *Polish Wings in the West.* Warsaw, Interpress, 1971.

Austin, John (Gun Buster). *Return Via Dunkirk.* London, Hodder & Stoughton, 1940.

Bader, Group Captain Douglas. *Fight for the Sky.* New York, Doubleday, 1973.

Balke, Ulf. *Kampfgeschwader 100.* Stuttgart, Motorbuch, 1981.

Banner, Hubert. *Kentish Fire: Wartime Life in Kent and Sussex.* London, Hurst and Blackett, 1944.

Barclay, George. *Angels 22.* London, Arrow Books, 1971.

Barker, A. J. *Dunkirk (The Great Escape).* New York, David McKay Co., 1977.

Barnett, Corelli. *The Collapse of British Power.* London, Eyre Methuen, 1972.

———. *The Audit of War.* London, Papermac, 1987.

———. *The Lost Victory.* London, Macmillan, 1995.

Barrer, E. C. *The Fighter Aces of the R.A.F.* London, William Kimber, 1964.

Bekker, Cajus. *The Luftwaffe War Diaries.* London, Macdonald, 1964.

Bickers, Richard Townsend. *Ginger Lacey, Fighter Pilot.* London, Robert Hale, 1962.

Bishop, Edward. *Their Finest Hour.* New York, Ballantine, 1968.

Bishop, Edwin. *The Battle of Britain.* Allen and Unwin Ltd., 1960.

Bloch, Michael. *Ribbentrop.* London, Bantam Books, 1992.

Bolitho, Hector. *Combat Report.* London, B.T. Batsford Ltd., 1943.

Boorman, H. R. P. *Hell's Corner 1940*. Kent, Maidstone, 1943.

Bowyer, Chaz. *Fighter Command*. London, J. M. Dent Sons, 1980.

———. *Spitfire*. London, Bison Books, 1980.

Brickhill, Paul. *Reach for the Sky*. London, William Collins, 1954.

Brittan, Vera. *England's Hour*. London, Macmillan, 1941.

Brooks, Robin J. *Kent Airfields in the Second World War*. Countryside Books, 1998.

Bruetting, Georg. *Das waren die Deutschen Kampfflieger Asse 1939–1945*. Stuttgart, Motorbuch Verlag, 1975.

Bullock, Alan. *Hitler: A Study in Tyranny*. London, Odhams Press, 1952.

Burns, Michael G. *Bader—The Man and His Men*. Arms & Armour Press, 1990.

Butler, J. R. M. *Grand Strategy*. London, Her Majesty's Stationery Office, 1950.

———. *Lord Lothian (Philip Kerr)*. London, Macmillan, 1956.

Cadogan, Sir Alexander. *The Diaries of Sir Alexander Cadogan*. Ed. David Dilks. New York, Putnam, 1971.

Caine, Philip D. *American Pilots in the RAF*. Washington, Brassey's, 1998.

———. *The JG 26 War Diary*. London, Grub Street, 1996.

Calder, Angus. *The People's War: Britain 1939–1945*. London, Jonathan Cape, 1969.

———. *The Myth of the Blitz*. London, Jonathan Cape, 1991.

Caldwell, Donald. *JG 26—Top Guns of the Luftwaffe*. Airlife Publishing, 1991.

Calvacoressi, Peter, and Guy Wint. *Total War*. London, Allen Lane, Penguin Press, 1972.

Cannadine, David, ed. *Blood, Toil, Tears and Sweat—Winston Churchill's Famous Speeches,* London, Cassell 1989.

Carne, Daphne. *The Eyes of the Few*. London, Macmillian, 1970.

Carr, E. H. *The Twenty Years' Crisis 1919–1939*. London, Macmillan, 1942.

Churchill, Sir Winston. *The Gathering Storm*. Boston, Houghton Mifflin, 1949.

———. *Their Finest Hour*. Boston, Houghton Mifflin, 1949.

———. *The Second World War,* vols. 1 and 2. London, Cassell, 1949.

Cloud, Stanley, and Lynne Olsen. *The Murrow Boys*. Boston, Houghton Mifflin, 1996.

Collier, Basil. *The Defence of the United Kingdom.* London, HMSO, 1957.

———. *The Leader of the Few.* London, Jarrolds, 1957.

Collier, Richard. *The Sands of Dunkirk.* London, Collins, 1961.

———. *Eagle Day.* London, Hodder & Stoughton, 1972.

———. *1940: The World in Flames.* London, Hamish Hamilton, 1979.

Collyer, David G. *Battle of Britain Diary.* Kent Aviation Historical Society, 1980.

Colville, John. *The Fringes of Power: Downing Street Diaries,* vol. i. London, Hodder & Stoughton, 1985.

Constable, Trevor J., and Raymond F. Toliver. *Horrido! Fighter Aces of the Luftwaffe.* London, Macmillan, 1968.

Cooper, Alfred Duff. *Old Men Forget.* London, Rupert Hart-Davis, 1953.

Cooper, Matthew. *The German Air Force 1943–1945: An Anatomy of Failure.* London, Janes, 1972.

Corum, James S. *The Luftwaffe—Creating the Operational Air War 1918–1940.* University of Kansas Press, 1997.

Croall, Jonathan. *Don't You Know There's a War On?* London, Hutchinson, 1986.

Crook, D. M. *Spitfire Pilot.* London, Faber & Faber Ltd., 1941.

Crossland, John. "Britain's Air Defences and the Munich Crisis" in *History Today,* Vol. 38 (September 1988).

Cull, Jonathan. *Selling War: The British Propaganda Campaign Against American Neutrality in World War Two.* Oxford, Oxford University Press, 1996.

Dalton, Hugh. *The Fateful Years: Memoirs 1931–45.* London, Frederick Muller, 1953.

Davis, Kenneth S. *The Hero: Charles A. Lindbergh: The Man and the Legend.* New York, Doubleday, 1959.

Deere, Group Captain Alan C. *Nine Lives.* London, Hodder & Stoughton, 1959.

De Gaulle, Charles. *War Memoirs,* vol. 1: *The Call to Honour.* Trans. Jonathan Griffin. London, Collins, 1955.

Deighton, Len. *Fighter: The Story of the Battle of Britain.* London, Jonathan Cape, 1977.

Dickson, Lovat. *Richard Hillary.* London, Macmillan, 1951.

Dierich, Wolfgang. *Kampfgeschwader 55.* Stuttgart, Motorbuch Verlag, 1975.

Divine, David. *The Nine Days of Dunkirk*. London, Faber & Faber Ltd., 1959.

Ellis, John. *The Sharp End*. New York, Windrow & Creen, 1990.

Everett, Susanne. *London: The Glamour Years 1919–39*. London, Bison Books, 1985.

Faber, Harold., ed. *Luftwaffe—An Analysis by Former Generals*. London, Sidgwick & Jackson, 1979.

Farrar, David. *The Sky's the Limit*. London, Hutchinson, 1948.

———. *G Is for God Almighty*. London, Weidenfield & Nicolson, 1969.

Farson, Negley. *Bomber's Moon*. London, Victor Gollancz Ltd., 1941.

Fedden, Robin. *Churchill and Chartwell*. The National Trust, 1984.

Feiling, Keith. *Neville Chamberlain*. London, Macmillan, 1946.

Fiedler, Arkady. *Squadron 303*. New Cork, Roy Publishers, 1943.

FitzGibbon, Constantine. *The Blitz*. London, Allan Wingate, 1957.

Fleming, Peter. *Operation Sea Lion*. New York: Simon and Schuster, 1957.

Fleming, Thomas. *The New Dealers' War: F.D.R. and the War Within World War II*. New York, Basic Books, 2001.

Flemming, Peter. *Invasion 1940*. London, Rubert Hart-Davis, 1957.

Flint, Peter. *RAF Kenley*. London, Terence Dalton, 1985.

Flying Officer "X". *How Sleep the Brave*. London, Jonathan Cape, 1943.

Forbes, Wing Commander A., and Allen S/L II. *Ten Fighter Boys*. London, Collins, 1942.

Foreman, John. *Fighter Command War Diaries,* vol. I, September 1939 to September 1940. Airlife, 1996.

———. *Fighter Command War Diaries,* vol. II, September 1940 to December 1941. Airlife, 1998.

Forrester, Larry. *Fly for Your Life*. London, Bantam Books, 1956.

———. *Fly for Your Life*. London, Frederick Muller, 1962.

Foster, Reginald. *Dover Front*. London, Secker and Warburg, 1941.

Franks, Norman. *Battle of Britain*. London, Bison Books, 1981.

———. *The Greatest Air Battle*. London, Grub Street, 1992.

Galland, Adolf. *The First and the Last*. London, Methuen, 1955.

Gallico, Paul. *The Hurricane Sky*. New York, Doubleday, 1959.

Garnett, David. *War in the Air*. London, Chatto & Windus, 1941.

Gelb, Norman. *Scramble: A Narrative Account of the Battle of Britain*. San Diego, Harcourt Brace Jovanovich, 1985.

———. *Dunkirk—The Incredible Escape.* London, Michael Joseph, 1990.

Gilbert, Adrian. *Britain Invaded.* Random Century, 1990.

Gilbert, Martin. *Churchill's Political Philosophy: Three Lectures.* Oxford: Oxford University Press, 1981.

———. *The Second World War.* London, Weidenfeld & Nicolson, 1989.

———. *Churchill: A Life.* London, Heinemann, 1991.

Gleed, Wing Commander Ian. *Arise to Conquer.* London, Victor Gollancz Ltd., 1942.

Goodhart, Philip. *Fifty Ships That Saved the World.* London, Heinemann, 1965.

Grant, Ian, and Nicholas Madden. *The City at War.* London, Jupiter Books Ltd., 1975.

———. *The Countryside at War.* London, Jupiter Books Ltd., 1975.

Graves, Charles. *The Home Guard of Britain.* London, Hutchinson, 1943.

Green, William. *Aircraft of the Battle of Britain.* London, Janes, 1969.

Hart, Liddell. *The Defence of Britain.* London, Faber and Faber Ltd., 1939.

Haugland, Vern. *The Eagle Squadrons.* New York, Ziff-Davis Flying Books, 1979.

Henshaw, Alex. *Sigh for a Merlin.* London, John Murray Publishers Ltd., 1979.

Hering, S/L P.G. *Customs and Traditions of the RAF.* Aldershot, Gale and Polden Ltd., 1961.

Herzstein, Robert. *Roosevelt and Hitler.* New York, Paragon, 1989.

Hewes, J. V. *The High Courts of Heaven.* London, Peter Davies, 1942.

Hillary, Richard. *Falling Through Space.* London, Macmillan, 1942.

Hitler, Adolf. *Mein Kampf,* trans. James Murphy. London, Hurst & Blackett, 1939.

———. *Mein Kampf,* trans. Ralph Manheim. Pimlico, 1992.

Horne, Alastair. *To Lose a Battle: France 1940.* London, Macmillan, 1969.

Inglis, Ruth. *The Children's War: Evacuees 1939–1945.* London, William Collins Sons, 1989.

Ishoven, Armand van. *The Luftwaffe in the Battle of Britain.* London, Charles Scribner's Sons, 1980.

Ismay, Hastings. *The Memoirs of Lord Ismay.* London, Heinemann, 1960.

Jackson, Carlton. *Who Will Take Our Children?* London, Methuen, 1985.

James, John. *The Paladins.* London, Macdonald, 1990.

Jenkins, Paul. *Battle over Portsmouth*. London, Middleton Press, 1986.

Johnson, Air Vice-Marshal J. E. "Johnnie." *The Story of Air Fighting.* London, Arrow Books, 1987.

Johnson, B. S. *The Evacuees*. London, Victor Gollancz Ltd., 1968.

Johnson, David. *The City Ablaze*. London, William Kimber, 1980.

Johnson, Group Captain, J. E. *Full Circle*. New York, Ballantine Books, 1964.

———. *Wing Leader*. New York, Ballantine Books, 1964.

Jones, Ira "Taffy." *Tiger Squadron*. London, W. H. Allen, 1954.

Joseph, Shirley. *If Their Mothers Only Knew.* London, Faber & Faber Ltd., 1944.

Julian, Marcel. *The Battle of Britain*. New York, Orion Press, 1965.

Kaplan, Philip. *Fighter Pilot—A History and a Celebration,* London, Aurum, 1999.

Kaplan, Philip, and Rex Allen Smith. *One Last Look*. New York, Abbeville Press, 1983.

Kee, Robert. *The World We Left Behind: A Chronicle of the Year 1939*. London, Weidenfeld & Nicolson, 1984.

Keegan, John. *The Second World War*. London, Hutchinson, 1969.

———. *The Battle for History*. London, Hutchinson, 1995.

Kennedy, Joseph. *Hostages to Fortune: The Letters of Joseph P. Kennedy*. Ed. Amanda Smith. New York, Viking, 2000.

Kennington, Eric. *Drawing the RAF.* Oxford, Oxford University Press, 1942.

Kent, Group Captain J. A. *One of the Few*. London, William Kimber, 1971.

Ketchum, Richard M. *The Borrowed Years, 1938–1941*. New York, Random House, 1989.

Kiehl, Heinz. *Kampfgeschwader 53*. Stuttgart, Motorbuch Verlag, 1983.

Kieser, Egbert. *Hitler on the Doorstep*. London, Arms & Armour Press, 1997.

Killen, John. *The Luftwaffe*. London, Sphere Books, 1967.

Knight, Dennis. *Harvest of Messerschmitts*. London, Frederick Warne, 1981.

Knightley, Philip. *The First Casualty*. London, Pan Books, 1989.

Knoke, Heinz. *I Flew for the Führer*. London, Evans Brothers, 1953.

Kops, Bernard. *The World Is a Wedding*. London, MacGibbon & Kee, 1963.

Lamb, Richard. *Churchill as a War Leader*. London, Bloomsbury, 1991.

Lamberton, John. *American Visions of Europe*. Cambridge, Cambridge University Press, 1994.

Lampe, David. *The Last Ditch*. London, Cassell, 1968.

Langer, William L., and S. Everett Gleason. *The Challenge to Isolation 1937–1940.* New York, Harper & Row, 1952.

Lash, Joseph. *Roosevelt and Churchill 1939–1941: The Partnership That Saved the West.* New York, W. W. Norton, 1976.

Last, Nella. *Nella Last's War: A Mother's Diary.* Eds. Richard Broad and Suzie Fleming. London, Falling Walls Press, 1981.

Latham, Colin, and Anne Stobbs. *Radar—A Wartime Miracle.* Sutton Publishing, 1996.

Lee, Asher. *Goering: Air Leader.* New York, Hippocrene Books, 1972.

Lee, Raymond. *The London Journal of General Raymond E. Lee, 1940–1941.* London, Hutchinson, 1972.

Leske, Gottfried. *I Was a Nazi Flier.* New York, Dial Press, 1941.

Lewin, Ronald. *Ultra Goes to War.* London, Hutchinson, 1978.

Lewis, Peter. *A People's War.* London, Methuen, 1986.

Liddell Hart, Basil. *History of the Second World War.* London, Cassell, 1970.

Livesey, Anthony, ed. *Are We at War?—Letters to* The Times *1939–45.* The Times.

Longmate, Norman. *The Real Dad's Army: The Story of the Home Guard.* London, Hutchinson, 1974.

Longmire, Norman. *Air Raid: The Bombing of Coventry, 1940.* London, David McKay, 1976.

Lucas, Laddie. *Flying Colours.* London, Panther Granada Books, 1981.

Lukacs, John. *The Last European War, September 1939/December 1941.* London, Routledge & Kegan Paul, 1976.

———. *The Duel.* London, Bodley Head, 1990.

———. *Five Days in London, May 1940.* New Haven, Yale University Press, 2000.

Lynn, Vera. *Vocal Refrain.* London, Star Books, 1975.

Mack, Joanna, and Steve Humphries. *London at War.* London, Sidgwick & Jackson, 1985.

Mahl, Thomas. *A Desperate Deception: British Covert Operations in the United States 1939–44.* Washington, D.C., Brassey's, 1998.

Mann, Thomas. *The Coming Victory of Democracy.* New York, Alfred A. Knopf, 1938.

Marcus, Sheldon. *Father Coughlin: The Tumultuous Life of the Priest of the Little Flower.* Boston, Little, Brown, 1973.

Mason, Francis K. *Battle over Britain*. New York, Doubleday, 1969.

———. *The Hawker Hurricane*. London, Astor Publications, 1987.

Mathews, W. R. *St. Paul's Cathedral in Wartime 1939–1945*. London, Hutchinson and Co. Ltd., 1946.

Mayhew, Patrick, ed. *One Family's War*. London, Hutchinson, 1985.

McDonough, Frank. *Neville Chamberlain: Appeasement and the British Road to War*. Manchester, Manchester University Press, 1992.

McKee, Alexander. *Strike from the Sky*. New York, Lancer Books, 1960.

Michie, Allan A., and W. Graebner. *Their Finest Hour*. New York, Harcourt Brace, 1941.

Middleton, Drew. *The Sky Suspended*. Longman, Green and Co., 1960.

Mitchell, Alan W. *New Zealanders in the Air War*. London, Harrap and Co., 1945.

Mitchell, Cordon. *R. J. Mitchell—Schooldays to Spitfire*. London, Clifford Frost, 1997.

Mondey, David. *British Aircraft of World War II*. London, Hamlyn, 1994.

Monk, Noel. *Squadrons Up!* London, Victor Gollancz Ltd., 1943.

Moran, Lord. *Churchill Taken from the Diaries of Lord Moran*. Boston, Houghton Mifflin, 1966.

Morgan, Ted. *FDR: A Biography*. New York, Simon & Schuster, 1995.

Morgenthau, Henry Jr. *Years of Urgency, 1938–1941*. Ed. John Morlon Blum. Boston, Houghton Mifflin, 1965.

Morison, Samuel Eliot. *History of U.S. Naval Operations in World War II, vol. 1: The Battle of the Atlantic, September 1939–May 1943*. Washington, D.C., U.S. Navy.

Murray, Williamson. *Luftwaffe*. London, Allen & Unwin, 1985.

Murrow, Edward R. *This Is London*. New York, Simon & Schuster, 1941.

Neil, Wing Commander Tom. *From the Cockpit—Spitfire*. London, Ian Allan, 1990.

Nel, Elizabeth. *Mr. Churchill's Secretary*. London, Hodder & Stoughton, 1958.

Nicolson, Harold. *Diaries and Letters 1940–1945*. London, Weidenfeld & Nicolson, 1966.

Niven, David. *The Moon's a Ballon*. New York, Putnam, 1971.

Nixon, Barbara. *Raiders Overhead*. London, Lindsay Drummond, 1943.

Orange, Vincent. *Sir Keith Park*. London, Meutheun, 1984.

Page, Geoffrey. *Tale of a Guinea Pig*. London, Corgi Books, 1981.

Partridge, Eric. *A Dictionary of RAF Slang*. London, Michael Joseph Ltd., 1945.

Pelling, Henry. *Winston Churchill*. London, Macmillan, 1974.

Perry, Colin. *A Boy in the Blitz: A 1940 Diary*. London, Corgi, 1974.

Ponting, Clive. *1940—Myth and Reality*. London, Hamish Hamilton, 1990.

Price, Alfred. *Spitfire at War*. London, Ian Allan, 1974.

———. *Spitfire: A Documentary History*. London, Macdonald and Janes, 1977.

———. *The Hardest Day*. New York, Charles Scribner's Sons, 1979.

———. *The Spitfire Story*. London, Arms & Armour Press, 1982.

———. *The Battle of Britain, the Hardest Day*. London, Arms & Armour Press, 1988.

Priestley, J. B. *Britain Speaks*. New York, Harper and Brothers, 1940.

———. *Britain at War*. New York, Harper and Brothers, 1942.

Quill, Jeffrey. *Birth of a Legend of the Spitfire*. London, Quiller Press Ltd., 1986.

Ramsey, Winston, et al. *The Battle of Britain, Then and Now*. London, After the Battle, 1980.

Ray, John. *The Night Blitz 1940–41*. London, Arms & Armour Press, 1996.

Rendell, Ivan. *Reaching for the Skies*. London, Orion Books, 1988.

Reynolds, David. *The Creation of the Anglo-American Alliance, 1937–1941*. London, Europa, 1981.

Reynolds, Quentin. *A London Diary*. New York, Random House, 1941.

———. *By Quentin Reynolds: An Autobiography*. New York, McGraw-Hill, 1963.

Richards, Dennis. *The Fight at Odds (Royal Air Force 1939–1945)*. Crown copyright, 1953.

Richards, Denis, and Hilary Saunders. *The Royal Air Force 1939–1945*. London, HMSO, 1974.

Richardson, Maurice. *London's Burning*. London, Robert Hall, 1941.

Roberts, Andrew. *The Holy Fox: A Biography of Lord Halifax*. London, Weidenfeld & Nicolson, 1991.

———. *Eminent Churchillians*. London, Weidenfeld & Nicolson, 1994.

Robertson, Ben. *I Saw England*. New York, Alfred A. Knopf, 1941.

Robinson, Derek. *Piece of Cake*. New York, Alfred A. Knopf, 1983.

Roosevelt, Elliott, ed. *The Personal Letters of Franklin D. Roosevelt, vol. 3: 1928–1945.* New York, Duell, Sloan and Pearce, 1947.

Sackville-West, Vita. *Country Notes in Wartime.* London: Hogarth Press, 1940.

Sayers, W. C. Berwick. *Croydon in the Second World War.* Croydon, Surrey, Croydon Corporation, 1950.

Schimanski, Stefan, and Henry Treece, eds. *Leaves in the Storm: A Book of Diaries.* London, Lindsay Drummond, 1947.

Shachtman, Tom. *The Phoney War 1939–1940.* New York, Harper and Row, 1982.

Shirer, William. *The Rise and Fall of the Third Reich.* London, Secker & Warburg, 1960.

Shore, Christopher, and Clive Willim. *Aces High.* London, Neville Spearman, 1966.

Sims, Edward H. *The Fighter Pilots.* London, Cassell, 1967.

Stevenson, William. *A Man Called Intrepid: The Secret War.* London, Macmillan, 1976.

Sutton, Barry. *A Way of a Pilot.* London, Macmillan, 1942.

Taylor, A. J. P. *The Origins of the Second World War.* London, Hamish Hamilton, 1961.

———. *English History 1914–1945.* Oxford, Oxford University Press, 1965.

———. *Beaverbrook.* London, Hamish Hamilton, 1972.

Taylor, Telford. *The Breaking Wave.* New York, Simon & Schuster, 1970.

Terkel, Studs. *The Good War.* New York, Ballantine Books, 1984.

Terraine, John. *The Right of the Line: The Royal Air Force in the European War.* London, Hodder & Stoughton, 1985.

Thomas, Manfred. *Isolationism in America.* Ithaca, N.Y., Cornell University Press, 1965.

Thompson, Lawrence. *1940.* New York, William Morrow and Co., 1980.

Thompson, R. W. *Generalissimo Churchill.* London, Hodder & Stoughton, 1973.

Townsend, Peter. *Duel of Eagles.* New York, Simon & Schuster, 1970.

Trevor, Elleston. *Squadron Airborne.* New York, Ballantine Books, 1962.

Turner, E. S. *The Phony War on the Home Front.* London, Michael Joseph, 1961.

Turner, John Frayn. *The Bader Boys*. London, The Kensal Press, 1986.

Wallace, G. F. *The Guns of the RAF 1939–45*. London, William Kimber, 1972.

Wallace, Graham. *RAF Biggin Hill*. London, Putnam, 1969.

Watson, Mark Skinner. *The United States Army in World War Two: Chief of Staff: Prewar Plans and Preparations*. Washington, D.C., Department of the Army, 1949.

Watson-Watt, Sir Robert. *Three Steps to Victory*. London, Odhams, 1958.

Watt, Peter. *Hitler vs. Havering*. Aneley, Essex, Gariton Armitage Press, 1974.

Weal, John. *Bf 109D/E Aces 1939–45*. London, Osprey, 1996.

———. *Junkers Ju 87—Stukageschwader 1937–41*. London, Osprey, 1997.

———. *Messerschmitt Bf 110 Zerstorer Aces of World War Two*. London, Osprey, 1999.

Weld, Jim. *Flying Headgear of the World 1934–1945*. London, Jim Weld, 1980.

Wells, H. G. *War in the Air*. Odhams, 1908.

Wells, Mark K. *Courage and Air Warfare*. London, Frank Cass, 1995.

West, Nigel, ed. *British Security Coordination: The Secret History of British Intelligence in the Americas 1940–1945*. London, St. Ermin's Press, 1998.

Westall, Robert. *Children of the Blitz*. New York, Viking Penquin, 1985.

Whalen, Richard. *The Founding Father: The Story of Joseph P. Kennedy*. London, Hutchinson, 1965.

Wheeler-Bennett, John. *King George VI*. London, Macmillan, 1965.

———. *Special Relations: America in Peace and War*. London, Macmillan, 1975.

Wheeler-Bennett, John, ed. *Action This Day: Working with Churchill*. London, Macmillan, 1968.

Whiting, Charles. *Britain Under Fire / The Bombing of Britain's Cities, 1940–1945*. London, Century, 1986.

Whitnell, Lewis. *Engines over London*. London, Carroll and Nicolson, 1949.

Willis, John. *Churchill's Few: The Battle of Britain Remembered*. London, Michael Joseph, 1975.

Windrow, Martin C. *The Heinkel He-111*. London, Profile Publications.

———. *The Junkers Ju 88ᵃ*. Profile Publications.

———. *The Messerschmitt Bf 110*. Profile Publications.

Wilz, John E. *From Isolation to War 1931–41*. New York, Crowell, 1968.

Winterbotham, Frederick. *The Ultra Secret*. London, Weidenfeld & Nicolson, 1941.

Wood, Derek, and Derek Dempster. *The Narrow Margin*. New York and London, McGraw Hill, 1961.

Woon, Basil. *Hell Came to London*. London, Peter Davies, 1941.

Wright, Esther Terry. *Pilot's Wife's Tale*. London, John Lane, The Bodley Head, 1942.

Wright, Robert. *Dowding and the Battle of Britain*. London, Macdonald, 1969.

———. *The Man Who Won the Battle of Britain*. New York, Charles Scribner's Sons, 1969.

Wykeham, Peter. *Fighter Command*. London, Putman, 1960.

Zamoyski, Adam. *The Forgotten Few*. London, John Murray, 1995.

Ziegler, Philip. *London at War 1939–1945*. London, Sinclair-Stevenson, 1995.

NEWSPAPERS, MAGAZINES & PERIODICALS

Newspapers

Battle of Britain, Daily Telegraph Editorial Supplement, June 1990, *Guardian Weekly,* 26 August 1990.

Daily Express, 16 September 1940.

Stratford Express, 20 September 1940.

Sunday Times, 15 September 1940.

The Times, 16 September 1940.

Voelkische Beobachter, 15 and 17 September 1940.

Magazines

Aeroplane Monthly, IPC Magazines Ltd., August & September 1995.

Allward, Maurice, and Hooton, Ted, *"Battle of Britain Day, 15th September 1940," Air Pictorial,* September 1975.

Macmillan, Wing Commander Norman, *"Resolving the War's Great Controversy," Aeronautics,* October & November 1960.

Marrs, Eric, *"152 Squadron: A Personal Diary of the Battle of Britain," The Aeroplane,* 14 September 1945. *The War Illustrated,* 27 September 1940.

Periodicals

The Aeroplane (various issues 1937–40).
Flight (various issues 1937–40).
Air Pictorial (various issues 1950–60).
R.A.F. Flying Review (various issues 1953–60).
Wehr Wissenschaftliche Rundschau (various issues).
Luftwaffen Revue (various issues 1959–60).
Aircraft Recognition—The Inter Services Journal (various issues 1942–3).
The Journal of the Royal Observer Corps (various issues 1941–2).
Commander's Circular, Observer Corps (various issues 1939–40).
Scramble (various issues 2000–2006).

Documentaries

"American Warrior: Billy Fiske," History Channel, 2/18/05.
Olympic Preview Show Clip, ABC 2/18/80.

Index

64 Squadron, 79–80, 82–7, 89–98,
    103, 221–2
71 Eagle Squadron, 189–205, 211,
    222, 231–3
    creation, 189–91
    Church Fenton, 199–200
    discipline, 199
    inactivity, 199–200, 202, 205
    Kirton Lindsey, 205
85 Squadron, 101, 202
87 Squadron, 148
133 Eagle Squadron, 211, 215–16,
    231–3
151 Squadron and Americans, 190–1
152 Squadron, 148, 149
213 Squadron, 148, 182
601 Squadron (Millionaires'
    Squadron), 30–31
    combat, 65, 102–3, 106–8, 114,
    117–23, 136–7, 158–60
    County of London Auxiliary Air
    Force Squadron, 58–9
    escorts Churchill, 30–1
    Fiske joins, 58–60, 64–5
    Tangmere, 63, 107–9, 120–2
    withdrawn to Debden, 137
    withdrawn to Exeter, 160
    see also specific pilots
609 West Riding Squadron, 80–1,
    153–4, 156, 160
    airfield attacked, 111–14
    Americans join, 80–1
    Americans leave for Eagles, 189
    combat, 113–14, 135–6, 140–2,
    146–50, 162–5, 169–75,
    179–83, 201, 204
    cosmopolitan, 151–2
    Duke of Kent's visit, 137–8
    Dundas on, 151–2, 266n30
    at Dunkirk, 30, 31
    at Middle Wallop, 80, 136, 111–14
    Poles join, 80–1
    Tally Ho! motto, 80
    at Warmwell, 145–8, 150–1

Ace of Spades Squadron see JG 53
    Squadron
Adlerangriff [Eagle Attack], 78, 95,
    100, 102, 107–8, 112, 114, 118
Agazarian, Noel, 147
Air Force Academy, Colorado
    Springs, ix
aircraft summary/pictures, 237–9
Aitken, Sir John William Maxwell
    "Max" [2nd baronet], 58, 64,
    190, 269n22
Aitken, William Maxwell "Max"
    [1st baron], see Beaverbrook
Alfieri, Dino [Italian Ambassador to
    Germany], 16–17
Allen, Luke, ix
Anastase, Count, 216–17
Anderson, Dick, 112
anti-aircraft balloons, 62, 98, 118,
    157, 173, 265n20
Appleby, Michael, 136, 181
Aquitania [ship], 59
Ark Royal, HMS, 221

Armée de l'Air, 6, 8, 14, 35, 39–41,
    44–6, 55
Asia [Göring's train], 16, 161, 183

Baillon, Paul, 204
Balthasar, Wilhelm, 91
Baron Nairn [ship], 51
barrage balloons, 62, 98, 118, 157,
    173, 265*n*20
Bateman, Ed, 212
Bathurst, Ben, 59
Battle of Britain
    aircraft summary/pictures, 237–9
    Churchill and, 124–5, 131
    Eagle Day [Adlerangriff], 78, 95,
        100, 102, 107–8, 112, 114, 118
    Hell's Corner, 65, 99, 137
    memorial service 1976, 232
    Park and, 124–5, 164, 171–2,
        178–80, 182
    pilot nationalities (summary), 76
    war of attrition, 137–142, 152–7
    see also London Blitz; specific
        persons and squadrons
Battle of Britain Historical Society,
    ix
Baudouin, Paul, 42
Beaverbrook, Aitken, William
    Maxwell "Max" [1st baron],
    64, 124, 131, 153, 190
Becker, Siegfried, 147
Berlin/ London initial bombing,
    142–3, 151
Berliner Illustrierte, 203
Bf 109 aircraft *see* Messerschmitt
    Me-109/110
Bingham, Rose, *see* Fiske, Rose
Blanton, Alex, ix
Bloch 152 aircraft, 22
Bock, Fedor von, 45
Bodendiek, Erich, 155, 195

Bolsheviks, 8, 37
"Bombs on England" (song), 126
Bond, Bill, ix
Bracken, Brendan, 190
Brand, Lady Rosabelle, 130–1
Brief, Corporal, 146–8
Brinkerhoff, Frank, ix
British character, 62, 156–7, 189
British Expeditionary Force (BEF),
    28–32, 52
Brittain, Vera, 126
Broker, Josef, 139–40, 141, 146,
    148–51
Brown, George A., 215
Brown, Peter, 257*n*4
Bungay, Stephen, *The Most Dangerous
    Enemy*, 79
Bushell, Roger, 58, 65, 251*n*46

Caine, Philip, ix
Camm, Sydney, 64
Campbell, John A. "Red", x, 221,
    222, 285*n*8
Casey, Robert, 207
Chamberlain, Neville, 3
Channel patrols, 219, 220
Chequers [house], 125, 170, 182
Cherrill, Virginia, 57, 249*n*22
China Clipper [movie], 57
Church Fenton RAF Station, 199–
    200
Churchill, Randolph, 32
Churchill, Walter, 199, 205
Churchill, Winston Spencer
    and 601 (Millionaires) squadron,
        30–1
    and 71 squadron, 190
    and Battle of Britain, 124–5, 131
    becomes Prime Minister, 3–4, 9
    defies Germany, 28–9, 46
    and Dunkirk, 30–1

and fall of France, 14–16, 30, 41–3
at Fiske's funeral, 131
and London Blitz, 165–7, 170,
    171–3, 178, 180, 182–3
and London/ Berlin initial
    bombing, 142–3
and pilot shortage, 53
and USA, 12–15, 32–3, 42–3
circle of death [Luftwaffe tactic], 108
Cleaver, Gordon "Mouse", 58, 65,
    245n13
    on Churchill's visit, 31
    injured, 117–18
Cloves, "Tich", 141–2
Clyde, William, 58–59, 65, 122
    shot down, 117
Collier's magazine, *see* Reynolds,
    Quentin
Condor Legion, 22, 91, 139, 222
Conrad, Max, 61
County of London Auxiliary Air
    Force Squadron *see* 601
    Squadron
Coward, Noel, 210
Crame, Mark, x
Craven, Penny, 207–8, 212
Crook, David
    on Americans, 81, 114, 136,
        137–8, 142, 189
    combat, 112, 140, 149, 152, 181,
        184–5, 201
    on Polish pilots, 81
Czech pilots, attempted escape from
    France, 43–4

Dahmer, Hugo, 91
Darley, Horace "George", x
    609 leader, 81, 135, 152, 180–1,
        258n12, 273n19
    aircraft damaged by Tobin, 112
    and Warmwell attacks, 146–8, 150

and Warmwell conditions, 145–6,
    150, 272n3
Davis, Carl, 136, 159, 275n43
Davis, Jimmy, 283n33
Dawson, William, 88
De Gaulle, Charles, 43
Defiant [aircraft] 237
Demetriadi, R.S., 101
Dewoitine D.520 [aircraft], 23
Dickie, William, 66, 102
Dillon Read stockbrokers, 58, 59
Doenitz, Karl, 18
Donahue, Arthur Gerald, x, 61–62,
    78
    258 Squadron, 220–1, 223–8
    64 Squadron posting, 79–80
    91 Squadron, 228–9
    on American neutrality, 77
    arrival in England, 60–61, 62–63
    Channel patrols, 219, 220
    combat, 82–6, 87, 89–90, 92–5,
        98–9, 103–5, 225–8, 228–9
    on combat flying, 219
    death, 229, 235
    Eagle Squadron, 201–2
    Gibraltar, 223–4
    hatred of Nazism, 61, 98
    injuries, 105–6, 153, 156, 226–8
    Japanese invaders and, 224–8
    Kennard-Davis and, 76, 80, 86,
        95–7, 99, 106
    noncombat time, 96–7
    Pearl Harbor and neutrality,
        223–4
    Singapore, 224–8
    training, 74–5, 76, 78
    US visit, 219–20
    as writer, 221–2
Dornier Do-17 aircraft
    combat, 65, 66, 170–7, 181–2, 210
    description, 171, 239

Douglas, Sholto, 209, 210
Dowding, Sir Hugh "Stuffy", 16,
    114–15, 253n57
Dundas, Johnny "Dogs"
    609 squadron, 151–2, 266n30
    combat, 112, 174–5, 177, 182,
        201, 204
    death, 204–5
    and Warmwell, 146
Dunkirk evacuation, 28–32, 33, 81,
    89
Duxford RAF Station, 215

Eagle Day [Adlerangriff], 78, 95,
    100, 102, 107–8, 112, 114, 118
Eagle Squadrons, 189–217, 231–3
    total US pilots in, 231
    see also 71 Eagle Squadron; 133
        Eagle Squadron
Ebeling, Heinz, 103, 263n47
Edge, Alexander, 113
Edwards, Bill, ix, 231–2
Eglington RAF Station, 215–16
Elliot, William, 59
Emils, see Messerschmitt Me-109
Esquadrille Squadron, 6

Fagan, A.W., 229–30
Faulkner, Jeffrey, 123–4, 131,
    269n22–3, 269n26
Feary, Alan, 114, 165, 201
Fenlaw, Hilard, 213
Fighter Command (RAF)
    aircraft summary/pictures, 237–9
    Americans training for, 74–78
    Eagle Day and, 78, 95, 100, 102,
        107–8, 112, 114, 118
    operations control rooms, 88, 89,
        113, 119, 124–5, 170–2, 157,
        178, 180, 182, 260n7
    pilot nationalities, 76

pilot stress/ exhaustion, 109–10,
    118, 137–8, 152–4, 155–6, 187,
    192
radar stations, 88, 98, 100, 136,
    155, 157, 164, 172, 192, 195,
    204, 212
    total US pilots in, 231
    see also Battle of Britain; London
        Blitz; specific people and
        squadrons
Finland, US pilots and, 7
First American Squadron of the
    Home Guard, 53
Fiske, Rose, 64–65, 110–11
    and Billy's death, 124, 126, 130–1
Fiske, William Meade III [Billy], 51,
    56–59
    bobsled and, 51, 56–58, 60, 66–7
    combat, 99–102, 108–9, 118–19,
        122
    death/ funeral, 126, 130–1, 136,
        159
    injuries, 123–4, 125
    joins 601 Squadron, 58, 59–60,
        63–4
    memorials, 211, 233
    propaganda tour planned, 63, 67
    and Rose, 64–5, 110–11, 126
    training, 65–66, 76
    tributes to, 237, 266n42,43,
        276n35
Forrester, Larry, Fly for Your Life, 27
Fowlmere RAF Station, 216
France
    Armée de l'Air, 6, 8, 14, 35,
        39–41, 44–6, 55
    fall, 12, 14–19, 22–3, 41–7, 48, 53
    Tobin and, 7, 10, 13–15, 18–20,
        27, 33–5, 43–5, 51

Galland, Adolf, 90–1, 126–7, 261n13

combat, 25, 90–5, 96, 178,
      179–80, 203–5, 212–13
combat strategy, 25, 90, 102–3
and Göring, 126–30, 178, 184,
      193–4, 196
and Hitler, 193
Inspector of Fighters, 223
JG 26 leader, 90, 129–30
kills/ ambition, 25, 91, 130, 178,
      193–4, 196–7, 198, 203
and London Blitz, 163
and pilot stress, 126–7, 154–5
Gamelin, Maurice, 15
Gaunt, Geoffrey, 135, 147, 174,
      183–4, 279n40
Geiger, Bill, ix, 207, 211, 212, 213
Germany
   Britain invasion plans, 12, 52, 78,
      97, 151, 166, 184, 200
   France overrun, 12, 14–19, 22–3,
      41–7, 48, 53
   initial bombing by RAF, 142–3,
      151, 158
   see also Göring; Hitler; Luftwaffe;
      specific people and squadrons
Gibraltar, 223–4
Gillan, James, 66, 102
Goethe, Johann Wolfgang von, *Faust*, 21
Goodson, James A., 37, 199, 208,
      212, 214, 218
Göring, Emmy, 163
Göring, Hermann
   addiction, 128, 161, 183
   and Alfieri, 16–17
   Asia train HQ, 16, 161, 183
   and Channel airspace, 87–8
   "circle of death", 108
   and Dunkirk, 17–18, 28, 31
   and fall of France, 48
   and Galland, 126–30, 178, 184,
      193–4, 196

and Gestapo, 16
and Hitler, 17–18, 129, 194
hunting lodge, 193–4
Karinhall, 126, 127–8, 193–4
leadership style, 17–18, 128–9,
      178, 184, , 196
London/ Berlin initial bombing,
      142–3, 151
London Blitz, 157–8, 161–4
and Mölders, 21, 71, 73, 127–30,
      178, 193–4, 222
and RAF destruction
      [Adlerangriff], 95, 100, 102,
      107–8, 114, 118, 151, 157–8,
      177–8, 183–4
in WWI, 16–17, 129, 161
Gormanns, Christa, 161, 183
Gort, John Vereker, field marshal, 28
Goss, Chris, x, xi
Grant, Cary, 57
Gray, Trevor, x
Green, Charles Patrick, 57, 65
Green Hearts (JG54 1 Group), 84–5
Greenspan, Bud, on Fiske, 51
Grzymalla, Gerhard, 93–4, 103
Guderian, Hans von, 17–18

Halifax, Edward Frederick Lindley
      Wood, Earl, 42
Halifax, Nova Scotia, 12–13
Haring, Anne, 4, 18, 206, 214, 215
Harker, Gordon, 164
Haviland, John Kenneth, 190–1, 231,
      235
Hawk H-75A [aircraft], 22
Heinkel He-111 aircraft
   description, 17, 239
   Mölders killed in, 222
Heitsch, Rolf, 171–2, 173, 174–5,
      177
Higgs, William, 119, 121–2

Hillary, Richard, *The Last Enemy*, 133

Hitler, Adolf
Eagle attack directive, 78
and France, 22, 48
and Galland, 193
and Göring, 17–18, 129, 194
and London/ Berlin initial bombing, 142–3, 151, 158
on Soviet Union, 184
Vonsiatsky and, 36

Holmes, Tony, xi

Home Guard, 105, 177
American squadron, 53, 55

Hope, Sir Archibald, 66, 99, 120, 123, 267*n*6, 269*n*22, 269*n*26

Howell, Frank
combat, 141, 165, 174, 181–2
and Dunkirk, 30, 31
Flight Leader, 30, 135

Hubbard, Eric, 275*n*43

Hubbard, Tom, 118

Hurricane aircraft
description, 29, 53, 64, 74, 237, 253*n*57
Mölders on, 69–70
Park's, 89

Imperial War Museum, xi

Ingersoll, Ralph, 189

Ingle, J. J., 121

Isaac, Lewis, 85–6

Ismay, Hastings Lionel, Baron, 41, 124, 125, 165–6

Jaffe, Irving, 57

Japanese attacks, 223–4, 224–8

Jeschonnek, Hans, 17, 18, 260*n*3

JG 2 (Richthofen) Squadron, 91, 100, 102, 129, 154, 203, 244*n*7

JG 26 Squadron, 25, 103, 126, 154, 193
and 71 Squadron, 212–13
convoy attacks, 90–3, 94–5
and London Blitz, 163, 178–80

JG 27 Squadron, 88, 91, 97

JG 51 Squadron, 87, 95, 126–7, 154–5, 222

JG 53 Squadron, 21–6, 112, 138–40, 149–50, 172, 194–8
Mayer and, 25, 138–42, 150, 172, 194–5, 197–8
Mölders and, 21–5, 69–74
Portsmouth attack, 139–42
Warmwell base attacks, 146–8
see also specific pilots

JG 54 Squadron, 84–5, 178

Jodl, Alfred, 31

John M. [ship], 88

Johnson, J.E. "Johnnie", 117, 209–10, 282*n*13

Johnstone, Sandy, 125

Jones, George, 123–4

Jones, Len, 163

Jones, Richard, x, 90, 92, 261*n*11

Junkers Ju-88 bomber, 239
combat, 108, 113–14, 117–19, 146, 148, 194, 210, 229
pilot stress, 150

Junkers Ju-87B dive-bomber [Stuka]
combat, 28, 40–1, 65, 88, 112, 114, 118–22
description, 9, 17–18, 239

Karinhall [house], 126, 127–8, 193–4

Karl, Werner, 139

Kelly, Terrence, 224–5, 285–6*n*15–16

Kemal Atatürk, Mustafa, 37

Kennard-Davis, Peter, 76–7, 79, 97
Donahue and, 76, 80, 86, 95–7, 99, 106

Kennedy, Joseph
    character, 13, 29, 210
    on Churchill, 12–13
    and pilots, 52–3, 248n14
    reports on UK, 12–13, 28–9,
        200
    Roosevelt and, 13, 210
Kennerly, Byron, 281n4
Keough, Vernon Charles "Shorty",
        10–12, 55, 136
    609 squadron, 80–1, 95, 136, 172,
        189
    71 Eagle squadron, 189, 191, 205
    Armée de l'Air, 11, 35, 36
    combat, 161, 164, 172, 181–2,
        206, 208
    death, 208–9
    Duke of Kent's visit, 138
    Finland, 12
    France, 33–7, 38–41, 43–5, 46–7
    joins RAF, 54–56
    journey to England, 51, 53
    journey to France, 12, 14
    training, 74
Kent, Prince George, Duke of,
        137–8
Kesselring, Albert, 118, 157, 161, 170,
        177, 179, 183, 196
Kingcome, Brian, 69
Kircheis, Erich, 71–72, 73
Kirton, David I., 93
Kirton Lindsey RAF Station, 205,
        206–7, 209
Kolbe, Georg, 222

Lancastria [ship] attacked, 243n40
Layrargues, René Pommier, 23–4,
        25
Lee, Raymond, 78
Lillywhite, Simon, ix
Lindbergh, Charles, 200

Lindmayr, Alois, 170, 173, 177
London/ Berlin initial bombing,
        142–3, 151
London Blitz, 157–8, 161–7,
        169–85
    Churchill and, 165–7, 170, 171–2,
        178, 180, 182
    Göring and, 157–8, 161–4
    London/ Berlin initial bombing,
        142–3, 151, 158
    see also Battle of Britain
Lothian, Philip Henry Kerr, Lord,
        63, 67–68
Luce, Clare Boothe, 210
Ludwig, Paul, xi
Luftwaffe
    aircraft (summary/ pictures),
        238–9
    London's perimeter airfields and,
        129
    pilot stress, 126–7, 150, 154–5
    unit designations, 243n35
    see also Göring, Hermann; specific
        actions; aircraft; individuals;
        squadrons

MacArthur, James "Butch", 138, 162,
        165, 173
MacDonald, Alexander S., 122
MacDonell, Aeneas
    combat, 85, 94–5, 98–9, 262n26
    as leader, 79–80, 82–3, 85–6, 89,
        92, 95, 99, 202, 220
    prisoner of war, 220
MacFie, Colin, 191
Magee, John Gillespie, Jr. *High
        Flight*, xiii
Maher, Helen, x, xi, 11, 52, 213–14
Malan, Adolph "Sailor"
    dogfight with Mölders, 71–3
    on combat strategies, 71, 254n5

Mamedoff, Andrew, 4, 8–9,
    36–37, 195
  609 squadron, 80–1, 111, 138,
    164
  71 Eagle squadron, 189, 191, 205,
    211
  233 Eagle squadron, 215–16
  Armée de l'Air, 8, 38–41
  combat, 141–2, 151, 172–3, 179,
    181–2, 213
  death, 216–17
  Finland, 7
  in France, 33–7, 38–41, 43–5,
    46–7
  joins RAF, 54–56
  journey to England, 51, 53
  journey to Europe, 4, 6, 8, 9–11,
    12, 14
  and Keough's death, 209, 211
  and Penny Craven, 207–8, 211
  training, 74, 76
Mamedoff, Lev & Natasha, 8, 36–7,
    208, 216–17
Mann, Jackie, 94–5, 262n26
Marseille, Hans Joachim, 96–7
Martin, John, 170, 182–3
Martonmere, Lord *see* Robinson, J.
    Roland "Robbie"
Matthews, Rev. William, 163
Mayer, Karl-Hans
  character, 139
  combat, 146, 148–51
  and Condor Legion, 139
  death, 197–8
  JG 53 leader, 25, 138–42, 150,
    172, 194–5, 197–8
  kills/honors, 25, 91, 195, 196
McCall, Hugh, 215
Meares, Stanley, 212
Messerschmitt Me-109 [Bf 109;
    Emil]

  combat, 85, 21–2, 29, 84–5, 92,
    99–103, 135, 137–9, 159,
    172–6, 197
  description, 70, 80, 238
Messerschmitt Me-110 [Zerstorer]
  combat, 85–6, 100–2, 108, 117,
    119, 146–51, 159, 165, 182
  description, 238
Middle Wallop RAF Station, xi, 80,
    111–15, 136, 138, 140–1, 150
  bombed, 100, 111–14, 117–18
Miles Master [aircraft], 75
Millar, Hugh, 60, 250n30
Miller, Alice Duel, *The White Cliff*,
    111
Miller, Dusty, ix
Millionaires' Squadron *see* 601
    Squadron
Mines Airfield, Los Angeles, 7–8
Mitchell, Reginald, 5
Mölders, Werner, 21, 130
  combat, 70–4, 197–8
  death, 222–3
  dogfight with Malan, 71–3
  and Göring, 21, 71, 73, 127–30,
    178, 193–4, 222
  injured, 73–4, 91
  JG 51, 87, 95, 126–7, 154–5, 222
  JG 53, 21–5, 69–74
  kills/ honors, 21, 22, 72, 91, 154,
    178, 198, 203, 205, 220
  shot down/ POW, 23–5, 43, 69
  UK aircraft testing, 69–70
Montreal, pilot recruitment network,
    7–10
Müncheberg, Joachim, 93, 213
Murphy, Frank, 7
Murrow, Ed, 126, 156

National Air Force Academy [US],
    x, xi

National Archives [UK], xi
New York Public Library, xi
New York Times, 32–3, 183
New Yorker, 6, 37
New Zealand Air Force pilots,
    250n30
Nichols, Bill, 213
Nicolson, James, 119–20
Nieminen, Toni, 56
"Nightingale Sang in Berkeley
    Square" (song), 156
Nowierski, Tadeusz, 80–1, 111, 112,
    258n6, 265n22
Nutkins, Geoff, x

Oehm, Lieutenant,, 94–5
Ogilvie, Keith, 162, 181–2, 276n3
Ondarza, Dr., 161
Operation Sea Lion [invasion] plans,
    12, 52, 78, 97, 151, 166, 184, 200
operations control rooms, 88, 89,
    113, 119, 260n7
  attacks on, 157
  Park's bunker, 124–5, 170, 171–2,
    178, 180, 182
Orbison, Edwin "Bud", 206, 208
Ostaszewski, Piotr, 81, 111, 112,
    258n6, 265n20, 273n10
Osterkamp, Theo, 29
Oxspring, Bobby, 192–3, 195, 197,
    198

P.M. (newspaper), 156
Page, Geoffrey, 135
Paris
  bombed, 35
  Churchill and defence, 14–16, 30
  German capture, 39–40, 45, 259–
    60n3
  pilots journey to, 13–14, 27, 33–8,
    45

Park, Dol, 170
Park, Keith, 89, 114–15, 124
  Churchill visits to ops room,
    124–5, 170, 171–2, 178, 180,
    182
  his Hurricane, 89
  and London Blitz, 164, 171–2,
    178–80, 182
Pearl Harbor attacked, 126, 224–5
Peterson, Chesley, 208
Pfeiffer, Technical Sergeant, 177
Pflanz, Rudi, 204–5
Phillips, Norman T., 93
Pierre L.D. [ship], 14
pilots
  deaths of the "few" (summary),
    235
  Montreal, recruitment network,
    7–10
  nationalities, 76
  Paris, journeys to, 13–14, 27,
    33–8, 45
  popularity, 156, 183, 200, 207–8,
    219, 232–3
  reasons for joining RAF, 5,
    250n29, 255n14
  stress/ exhaustion, 109–10, 118,
    137–8, 152–4, 155–6, 187,
    192
  shortage, 53
  teenage, 153
  total US pilots in Eagles, 231
  US citizenship loss/ regain, 4,
    54–5, 63, 248n15, 284–5n3
  see also specific pilots; specific
    squadrons
Pisanos, Steve, ix
Polish pilots, *see* Nowierski;
    Ostaszewski
Portsmouth, JG 53 attack, 139–42
Potez 63 [aircraft], 22, 40, 41, 44

radar stations
  attacks on, 100, 136, 157
  role, 88, 98, 155, 164, 172, 192,
    195, 204, 212
Raeder, Erich, 184
RAF Museum Hendon, xi
Ream, Marion, 36–37
Reilley, Hugh William, 191–2
  combat, 192, 194, 195, 197
  death, 197, 198
Reston, Scotty, 55
Reynaud, Paul, 14, 15, 42–3
Reynolds, Quentin, 3, 55, 82, 156,
    207, 214
Rhodes-Moorehouse, Willie, 58,
    65–6, 99–102
  and Churchill's visit, 31
  death, 159
  and gas rationing, 102, 252–3n54
Ribbentrop, Joachim von, 48
Richey, Paul, 107
Richthofen, Manfred von [Red
    Baron], 16–17, 129–30, 171, 223
Richthofen Squadron (JG 2), 91,
    100, 102, 129, 154, 203, 244n7
Richthofen, Wolfram von, 88,
    266n29
Riddle, Hugh, 64, 122
Riddle, Jack, x, 64, 66, 100, 122
Robertson, Ben, 156
Robinson, J. Roland "Robbie" (Lord
    Martonmere), 54, 200, 209
Robinson, Michael, 204
Roger's Field, Los Angeles, 5
Rommel, Erwin, 17–18
Rook, Alan, 163
Roosevelt, Eleanor, 283–4n35
Roosevelt, Franklin Delano
  Churchill and, 12–15, 32–3, 42–3
  Kennedy and, 12–13, 28–9, 33,
    200, 210

Lake Placid Olympics (1932), 56
Lend Lease program of, 210
re-election, 210
Rosier, Frederick, 87
Rothenfelder, Rudolf, 100–1
Royal Air Force
  public respect for, 156, 183, 200
  see also Fighter Command; Battle
    of Britain; London Blitz;
    specific people and squadrons
Russian Civil War (1920s), 8, 37

Sanders, Hugh, 209
Saturday Evening Post, 221
Sauter, Technical Sergeant, 177
Schmid, Josef "Beppo", 17, 118
Schmidt, Stephan, 171, 173, 175, 177
Schonborn, Major Graf, 112
Sergison, Ed, ix
Ship pub, 66–67, 253n55
Sinclair, Sir Archibald, 63, 67, 210,
    211, 251n41
Singapore, 224–8
Smithers, J.L., 101
Snowdon, John, xi
Soviet Union, 7, 184
Spears, Sir Edward, 31
Sperrle, Hugo, 118, 157
Spitfire aircraft
  description, 5, 74–6, 80, 84, 237,
    253n57, 255n15, 255n19
  Mölders on, 69–70
"Sprogs", 109
Stalin, Joseph, 8
Stewart, Bert, 232
Stout, Roy, 215
Stuka dive-bombers [Junkers Ju-87B]
  combat, 28, 40–1, 65, 88, 112,
    114, 118–22
  Ju-87B, description, 9, 17–18,
    239

Sweeny, Charles (Colonel), 6
    Eagle Squadron, 199, 201–2, 209
    in Europe, 7–8, 38
    pilot payment, 162
    pilot recruitment, 6–8, 37–38
    threat from SS, 38
    US neutrality laws and, 6–7
Sweeny, Charles (nephew)
    Eagle Squadron, 190
    in Home Guard, 55

"Tally Ho!", 79, 98, 107, 179, 268n7
Tally-ho! Yankee in a Spitfire
        (Donahue), 221–2
Tangmere RAF Station, ix, 63–6,
        99–100, 107–10, 117–20, 136,
        158, 182
    attacked, 120–2, 125
Taylor, Norman, 122
Temme, Paul, 29, 244n7
Thompson, William, 4
Thomson, Jock, 220, 228
Times, The, 229–30
Tobin, Eugene Quimby "Red", 4–5,
        200–1
    609 squadron, x, 111–14, 160
    71 Eagle squadron, 189, 191,
        200–1, 205–9
    and Ann Haring, 4, 18, 206, 214,
        215
    Armée de l'Air, 7–8, 38–41
    arrival in England, 27, 51–3
    combat, 135, 138, 141, 146–50,
        151, 169–77, 184, 212–13
    death, 213–15
    and Finland, 7
    on flying, 49
    France, 7, 10, 13–15, 18–20, 27,
        33–41, 43–5, 51
    ill with lupus, 202–3
    joining RAF, 53–6

    journey to Europe, 4, 6, 8, 9–11,
        12–14, 18–19, 27–28
    and London Blitz, 161–4, 167
    Middle Wallop bombing, 113–14
    training, 74–7, 80–1
    Warmwell attacks, 146–8, 150
    Warmwell conditions, 145–6,
        150–1, 272n3
Townsend, Peter, 101, 157, 187, 202,
        221
Turley-George, Anne, 119, 121

U-boats, 8, 18–19, 52, 62, 184
Udet, Ernst, 69, 222, 254n2
Union Station [Los Angeles], 4–6
United States
    Churchill and, 12–15, 32–3, 42–3
    Citizenship Act (1907), and pilots,
        4, 54–5, 63, 248n15, 284–5n3
    and Dunkirk, 32–33, 33
    isolationists, 13, 15, 33, 43, 200,
        211
    neutrality laws, 4, 6–7, 14, 15, 34,
        52–3, 58–9, 63, 190, 207, 219,
        223–4
    RAF popularity in, 156, 183, 200

Versailles, Treaty of (1919), 58, 244n7
Vonsiatsky, Count Anastase, 36

WAAFs, *see* Women's Auxiliary Air
        Force
Warmwell RAF Station
    attacks on, 146–8, 150
    conditions, 145–6, 150–1, 272n3
Warwick, Earl of, 64–65
Waterloo, Battle of, 137, 247n8
Waterlow, Tom, 159
Watts, Harry, 45, 52, 54, 55
Wellington, Arthur Wellesley, Duke,
        137, 247n8

West, Rebecca, 157

Westphal, Lieutenant, 146, 148

Weygand, Maxime, 37, 46

White Cliff, The (Miller), 111

White Heat [movie], 57

White Russians, 4, 8, 36, 208

White, William, 215

White's Club, 58

Wick, Helmut, 91, 154, 178, 196, 203–5, 222

Wilkinson, Royce, 200

Willey, Courtney, x, 121, 124

Williams College, xi

Winant, John, 210, 211

Wolf-Dietrich [pilot], 69

Women's Auxiliary Air Force (WAAF), 265–6n23

    in operations control rooms, 88, 119, 121, 124, 162, 172, 178

    social life, 113, 119

Worthy Down RAF Station, 117

Wotzel, Walter, 147–8

Young, A.C., 228–9

Zerstorers, *see* Messerschmitt Me-110

He just wanted a decent book to read ...

Not too much to ask, is it? It was in 1935 when Allen Lane, Managing Director of Bodley Head Publishers, stood on a platform at Exeter railway station looking for something good to read on his journey back to London. His choice was limited to popular magazines and poor-quality paperbacks – the same choice faced every day by the vast majority of readers, few of whom could afford hardbacks. Lane's disappointment and subsequent anger at the range of books generally available led him to found a company – and change the world.

'We believed in the existence in this country of a vast reading public for intelligent books at a low price, and staked everything on it'
Sir Allen Lane, 1902–1970, founder of Penguin Books

The quality paperback had arrived – and not just in bookshops. Lane was adamant that his Penguins should appear in chain stores and tobacconists, and should cost no more than a packet of cigarettes.

Reading habits (and cigarette prices) have changed since 1935, but Penguin still believes in publishing the best books for everybody to enjoy. We still believe that good design costs no more than bad design, and we still believe that quality books published passionately and responsibly make the world a better place.

So wherever you see the little bird – whether it's on a piece of prize-winning literary fiction or a celebrity autobiography, political tour de force or historical masterpiece, a serial-killer thriller, reference book, world classic or a piece of pure escapism – you can bet that it represents the very best that the genre has to offer.

Whatever you like to read – trust Penguin.